W9-CEZ-722

ESSAYS IN CANADIAN WORKING CLASS HISTORY

Editors: Gregory S. Kealey
Peter Warrian

McClelland and Stewart Limited

Cover photo: Port Arthur Coal Handlers International Longshoremen's Association, c. 1912, used by permission of the Thunder Bay Historical Museum Society.

Coal dock district, Fort William, (p. 4), used by permission of the United Church Archives – Victoria University.

Orange parade, 1865, and Linotype operators, 1905, (p. 5), used by permission of the Metropolitan Toronto Library Board.

Lawren Harris, *Glace Bay*, 1921 (p. 184), used by permission of *The Canadian Forum*, July 1923, and Lawren P. Harris.

Contents

Coal dock district, Fort William, 1913.

THE JOURNALISTIC COWBOY.

Grip cartoon, *December 15, 1883.*

nge parade, Toronto, 1865.

otype operators, Toronto Telegram, c. 1905.

CONTRIBUTORS

Gregory S. Kealey teaches history at Dalhousie University. He is the editor of *Canada Investigates Industrialism* and co-editor of *Labour/Le Travailleur*.

Peter Warrian is a Ph.D. candidate in history at the University of Waterloo and is currently working in Toronto for the United Steelworkers of America.

Russell Hann is working on a Harvard doctorate in American Studies and living in Toronto. His previous publications include *The Agrarian Response to Industrial Capitalism*.

Harvey Graff teaches at the University of Texas in Dallas. He has published a number of articles on literacy.

Michael Doucet is completing a Toronto Ph.D. in geography, on housing in Hamilton.

Bryan Palmer is completing a Ph.D. for the State University of New York at Binghamton on the Hamilton working class in the late nineteenth century. He has published a number of articles in working class history.

Wayne Roberts, editor of *Forward*, is finishing a University of Toronto doctorate on the Toronto working class, 1896-1914.

Jean Morrison lives in Port Arthur and is now revising for publication her M.A. thesis on the working class in the Lakehead, 1903-1914.

David Frank is a Ph.D. candidate at Dalhousie University, preparing a thesis on the economic and social history of the coal industry in Cape Breton.

Introduction

Canadian historical writing has left little room for the inclusion of ordinary working people. Instead Canadian history has been painted as a sweeping heroic canvas where great men do battle against the insurmountable odds of a brutal climate and powerful rivals, in a triumphant struggle to create the Canadian nation. Ordinary Canadians rarely appear in this picture. We catch only brief glimpses of them paddling the fur traders' canoes, fighting imperial wars, or casting ballots for the political giants. Yet working people belong at the centre of the picture, not on the edges where they are now placed. The real 'makers of Canada' have been the ordinary men and women who shared the hardships and joys of daily life and work. Without them there would be no Canada and no heroic canvas. This book is an attempt to bring back ordinary working people from their long exile on the margins of Canadian history.[1]

In a limited way this has already begun. As a result of two distinct developments, more books have been published in the last five years dealing with Canadian workers than have appeared in the entire century previous: first, the general crisis of western capitalism and the resultant return of critical thinking; and second, the increasing familiarity of Canadian historians with recent historiographic developments in working class history in France, England, and the United States. To a large extent the historiographic breakthroughs both outside Canada and here at home have stemmed from the political debates of the 1960s and the re-emergence of Marxism.

What is this new social history? Although it encompasses fields other than working class history, our discussion will be limited to this area. The major contribution of the 'new' history has been to redefine 'labour history' as 'working class history.' Thus, labour history ceases to be simply a category of political economy, a problem of industrial relations, a canon of saintly working class leaders, a chronicle of union locals or a chronology of militant strike actions. Instead it becomes part of the history of society. Workers are no longer seen as isolated figures engaged only in trade unions, strikes, and radical politics; instead they are studied in a totality that includes their cultural backgrounds and social relations, as well as their institutional memberships and economic and political behaviour. In addition they must be seen neither as a class in complete social segregation nor as an undifferentiated mass. A class exists only in relation to another class and the new social history studies these relationships. Moreover, the working class is a variegated grouping. Class must be understood as both a 'vertical' or economic relationship and as a 'horizontal' or cultural relationship. In the vertical sense class involves the relationship of exploitation that exists between capitalist and wage labourer. In the horizontal sense class concerns the beliefs, values, ideas and traditions that people carry with them in their lives and work. These two categories are separated only in analysis; in reality they are dialectically intertwined. Class is a completely historical concept. It does not exist as a 'thing' as Edward Thompson has frequently pointed out.[2]

The new social history is not concerned with filling the interstices of the old Canadian historiographic tradition with odd facts and events that have escaped more conventional historians. Instead when completed it will constitute a new distinctive synthesis of Canadian history. This book is an attempt to begin this process. The essays that follow are connected not so much by methodology, which varies from quantitative to traditional, but rather by the new questions the authors ask of their material. The contributors received their post-graduate education in the late sixties and early seventies and were part of the political climate that led to the emergence of the new social history. Thus they are members of the first generation of Canadian historians trained in this approach.

The essays in this book study the period between 1850 and 1925. Canada experienced her industrial revolution during these years. The pre-industrial society of independent commodity producers, both farmers and artisans, was transformed into an industrial society. The authors describe the growth of industrial capitalism from the point of view of the workers. Changes in work process and the regional underdevelopment that accompanied industrial capitalism are viewed not as steps in the inexorable path of progress but rather as processes that changed people's lives in tangible ways. Here we are concerned not so much with the process but rather with its effects on the working class and their responses to it. These seventy-five years do not constitute a single period of Canadian working class history. The years from 1850 to the mid-90s represent a transitional period in which workers learned the new rules of industrial society and created their own defensive institutions. The militancy of this period often suggests a movement more advanced than one anticipates. This stems from the transitional nature of the period, for many of the devices that workers utilized to fight against the onslaught of industrial capitalism were adapted from the culture and experience of pre-industrial society. In effect the workers were not as yet totally incorporated into industrial society. Thus the high degree of control over work place practices in the printing and metal working trades, for example, drew directly on the craft traditions as well as on the skills of the workers. Or to cite another example, Knights of Labor and other pre-socialist labour reform ideologies rested upon notions of commonweal and justice that were based on mercantilist and pre-industrial assumptions about the nature of society. These residual cultural categories gave great strength to early working class movements.[3]

This transitional period ended in the mid-90s with the failure of the direct political challenge to industrial capitalist society by the Knights of Labor and the Patrons of Industry. The next period, from the mid-90s to the mid-20s, saw the maturation of working class institutions and the arrival of socialism as a political option. If the earlier years had been ones of learning new rules for both workers and bosses, then these next thirty years were a period of consolidation and entrenchment for industrial capitalism. This was the period in which capitalists decided that they must take minute control over the work process which they had previously left largely to the purview of the skilled workers. They named the new technique 'scientific management.' But this attempt engendered a working class response, the 'new unionism,' an overtly syndicalist and militant response that led in Canada to the events of 1919 in Winnipeg and later to the events in Cape Breton between 1922 and 1925.[4]

Struggles at the work place were only one part of the new consolidation, however. Mackenzie King, Minister of Labour under Laurier and later Prime Minister, promoted a new role for the state that augmented nicely the new management strategies of industry. Thus under a facade of concern for the workers came the Federal Department of Labour, the Industrial Disputes Investigation Act (IDIA), and, in general, a whole new theory of the role of the state in industrial relations. The state became the supposedly neutral arbiter ruling in the interests of the 'public.' The working class response to these innovations varied from initial grudging acceptance to overt hostility after they perceived that the 'public,' as interpreted by the courts and the government, seemed to have precisely the same interests as the capitalists.

If King represented the federal wing of Canadian 'Progressivism,' then one also needs to examine the provincial and local side of the movement. Reformers in these areas were, under the guise of good government and sometimes even public ownership, devising a system of undemocratic boards and agencies that would take power from public control and preempt the possibility of local political challenges. This was the meaning of much of the urban reform so often heralded as 'the search for order.' It was in reality a quest to maintain control over the working class who in the 1880s and 1890s had begun to mount a serious political challenge on the local government level. Articulate workers responded to the challenge of the urban reformers by trying to distinguish between those programs that had actual value to the working class and those that were only a more sophisticated method of social control. Their choices were not always ultimately in their best interests, but they never surrendered their critical faculties. They also imbued many of these programs with meanings unintended by the legislators which in periods when militancy declined could at least be used defensively.

This is also the period, however, in which some workers' resistance to industrial capitalism turned from the residual culture of producer ideology to newer emergent forms including socialism. Nevertheless the period is one of uneven development for, while some workers were turning to socialism, others were engaging in struggles over control of the work place that often combined residual and emergent forms, and still others were at times allowing the previously unincorporated notions of workers' control and producer ideology to be translated into job consciousness and business unionism à la Sam Gompers.[5] Thus an ideology that believed that workers knew far better than managers how to run industry and that labour was the source of all wealth could be transformed into either the radical syndicalism of the IWW and the OBU or into the conservative craft notions of the American Federation of Labor and its Canadian allies. These struggles make 1895-1925 one of the most interesting periods of Canadian working class history.

Four of the essays in this book are concerned with exploring the transitional period, 1850 – 1895. They range in subject from literacy to collective violence, from housing to popular culture. A second section, the papers by Bryan Palmer and Wayne Roberts, explores the strengths and weaknesses of the old artisan culture when it faced a later stage of industrial capitalist development. These essays connect the first section and the third, the articles by Jean Morrison and David Frank, which study early twentieth century labour struggles at the Lakehead and on Cape Breton.

The papers vary widely in subject matter and approach. A similarity they share, however, is that all deal with single cities, towns or regional communities. This immersion in local materials allows each author to capture the historical experience of these workers with real sensitivity to local variation. The very nature of the materials that social historians use makes this a necessity but the rewards should be apparent. This local approach is far closer to the realities of Canadian social and industrial development than the older national 'mythstory'. Industrial capitalism has contributed greatly to the regionalization of the country, creating a hinterland-metropolitan relationship that leaves the former woefully underdeveloped. Thus most of the struggles against industrial capitalism have played themselves out on a regional stage. Cape Breton coal miners or British Columbia lumber workers have been as aware of Central Canadian exploitation as have Western farmers. The deep regional variations in Canadian working class experience are to be forgotten only by those who seek myth rather than facts.

The essays in this book are mainly focused on Ontario. Although better balance would have been desirable, it is important that Ontario be seen as one *region* of Canada. All too often calls for local and regional history are taken to mean only studies of the Maritimes, Quebec or the West, leaving Ontario as the only region that is assumed to be synonymous with the nation. As the industrial heartland of the nation, it is especially important for the study of Canadian working class history. We hope that the approaches reflected in this book can be put to use by others studying other Canadian regions.

This is, of course, not to argue against longer and larger views. These are needed as well, but they unfortunately cannot come first. The richness of Edward Thompson's *Making of the English Working Class* or Eugene Genovese's *Roll Jordan Roll: The World the Slaves Made* are dependent on the hard work and local sensitivities of literally hundreds of previous scholars working in more limited settings. We are not ready for a great synthetic work yet in Canadian working class history.

Calls for more studies of the work place and for increased attention to the specificity of place are not meant to replace earlier injunctions to study the workers' non-work world. We need further studies of the material conditions of Canadian workers – of their diet, of their housing, of their wages, etc. We also need to know much more about the Canadian social structure, about mobility both geographic and social, about demographic patterns, about the role of women on the job and at home,[6] and a whole range of additional problems. Moreover we need far more study of Canadian workers' cultural beliefs. We know next to nothing about their religious sentiments, about the songs they sang, the pubs they drank in, the popular theatre they attended or the books that they read. In addition we also still need to know more about the pattern of trade unionism in the country, about the role of strikes and violence, and about working class politics both radical and conventional.

In spite of these limitations and unexplored areas of study, the field of working class history has made important strides in recent years in this country. Further thought needs to be given to developing more serviceable general conceptualizations in the field to ensure that it is not just absorbed like previous new approaches in historical study.[7] We hope that this book will lead to further discussion, debate, and writing about Canadian working class history. In a decade when Canadian and Québecois workers are becoming world famous for their militancy, far too much time is spent moaning about the 'labour problem.' We hope that this collection of essays will add to Canadians' understanding of working class traditions in this country and that this increased knowledge will be useful in critically assessing the struggles of the present. If nothing else, it should be clear that the 'problem' is not the worker but rather the continued existence of industrial capitalist society. Those of us who write working class history should, as E. J. Hobsbawm has recently reminded us, always remember that our history, like all social science, is concerned with changing the world as well as interpreting it.[8] Thus we need to constantly keep in mind that real people—Canadian working women and men—are the subjects of our study. This is not an injunction to romanticize the past, for that will not help working class people achieve their aim and ours—the ability to make their own lives and history.

The Orange Order in Toronto: Religious Riot and the Working Class

Gregory S. Kealey

Toronto the Good conjures up images of the quiet, conservative Hogtown known and disliked throughout Canada for most of the twentieth century. However, one nineteenth century appelation for the city carried quite different connotations. Toronto, *the Belfast of Canada*, witnessed over twenty riots between Orangemen and Irish Catholics in the quarter century following Confederation. One such riot on the occasion of Fenian leader O'Donavon Rossa's 1878 visit to Toronto received banner headlines:

> DEVILISH DEEDS!...LAWLESSNESS AND CRIME RAMPANT IN OUR MIDST...SCENES OF CARNAGE AND RIOTING NEVER EQUALLED IN TORONTO'S ANNALS...MURDEROUS INCIDENTS OF THE RIOTERS PROGRESS ALONG QUEEN STREET...

Unfortunately these outbreaks of collective violence in Victorian Toronto have received far more attention from yellow journalists than from Canadian historians. The latter, in their haste to deplore such illiberal behaviour, have failed to explore seriously the culture that generated these collective actions. Concern with the vagaries of Orange leadership in national politics has prevented discussion of the Order's social composition, its constellation of ideas, its roots in traditional Irish society, and its important local functions. More specifically historians of the Canadian working class experience have been satisfied with an easy dismissal of ethnic and religious associations as detrimental to the emergence of some ill-defined notion of class-consciousness.[1] Rather than dismissing Orangemen as bigots and class collaborationists, close study will demonstrate that Orangeism offered Toronto workers a profoundly ambiguous heritage; a set of traditions which, on the one hand, aided them in their struggle to exist in the industrializing city but which, on the other hand, led them on occasion into the streets in riots against their fellow workers.

The Orange Order in Canada provides us with a particularly successful example of the adaptation of an old world cultural form to the contingencies of a new society. This study suggests some reasons for the Order's Canadian achievements and demonstrates, not only its adaptation to the new world, but also its transition from a rural, pre-industrial movement to a society based in an urban industrial world. In both cases the internal tensions engendered by the changes were great. The ever-shifting resolution of these conflicts allowed Orangeism to remain an important factor in Toronto working class life throughout the nineteenth century despite the changing nature of the city and of the working classes.

An analysis of Canadian Orangeism must begin with the origins of the Orange Order in Ireland. The Irish countryside was permeated by agrarian secret societies as early as the mid-eighteenth century. The original groups – the Steelboys, Whiteboys, Rightboys, and Oakboys – were primarily economic in motivation and represented movements of agricultural labourers and small cottiers against farmers and landlords, without religious considerations. These movements existed in both the north and the south and were successful in achieving limited aims:

> Although the agrarian secret societies failed to achieve tithe reform in the years before the Union, they may have prevented the type of wholesale eviction which took place in Scotland in the last half of the eighteenth century . . . secret societies succeeded to some extent in enforcing tenant rights and other regulations which they believed necessary for their protection.

Nevertheless, the existence of deep hatred between Protestants and Catholics made it relatively easy for the landlords to transform these economic struggles into sectarian strife. In addition, the success of the American and French Revolutions transformed the nature of rebellion in Ireland as well as in the rest of the world. The ability of Jacobin agitators, such as Wolfe Tone, to unite the Defenders, a Catholic agrarian secret society, with his United Irishmen, an urban revolutionary grouping, led to a similar transition in the nature of Protestant peasant groupings. The Peep o'Day Boys evolved into the Orange Order and took on an avowedly sectarian, anti-Catholic and anti-revolutionary cast. The revolt of 1798 further reinforced these tendencies. Although agrarian secret societies re-emerged in pre-famine Ireland their potential for linking the Protestant and Catholic lower classes was gone. Sectarian warfare had gained primacy and ruling class interests now possessed societies such as the Orange Order which provided "an invaluable link between ascendancy power in terms of land on the one hand and the Protestant farming and working classes in Ulster on the other." Although serving this function in periods when the British connection was in question, the Orange Order continued to be quite troublesome to the established authorities at all other times. A movement of lower class forces which could never quite be trusted, Orangemen found their society outlawed on numerous occasions throughout the nineteenth century. Thus even in Ireland the Orange Order arose from a curious conjunction of peasant revolt and patriotic reaction. This legacy could only grow more ambiguous when transferred to a country where the economic underpinnings of sectarian strife were far less prominent.[2]

Orangeism came to Canada with the British army and with Irish Protestant immigrants in the first years of the nineteenth century. Initially the lodges were founded on the authority of the Irish Grand Lodge and the rituals, songs, degrees, and forms of organization were totally imitative of Irish practices. The formal history of Canadian Orangeism begins in 1830. In that year Ogle Gowan, an Irish immigrant with Orange leadership experience, called together representatives from central Canada's scattered pioneer lodges and knit them into a new Grand Lodge of British North America.[3]

In these early years Gowan did much to define Canadian Orangeism and move it away from pure Irish models. Gowan, after the proscription of the Orange Order in Ireland, had been a major force in creating the new Orange Patriotic and Benevolent Society. In this organization the militaristic and sectarian sides of Orangeism were de-emphasized. Instead, fraternal and benevolent functions were developed. Although unsuccessful in Ireland, this emphasis was well suited to Canadian conditions.

Partially due to his personal political aspirations, Gowan moved toward a broader definition of Orangeism as a type of immigrant aid society which might at times even ignore religious differences. This interest was evident in his alliance with Catholic Bishop Macdonnell before the Rebellion of 1837, at which time the threat of Republicanism united both Orange and Green. The early successes of the Order were largely due to Gowan's ability to implement these aims and thus adapt the old institution to its new home.[4]

This is not to deny the Order's militant Protestant Briton identification nor its sizeable representation in the Canadian militia. A Canadian tradition of patriotic struggle was being created to place alongside the Irish past. Thus for Canadian Orangemen the Rebellion of 1837 came to be almost as celebrated in song and verse as the Battle of the Boyne itself. Equally violent encounters with Irish Catholics such as the Slabtown affair of 1849 were laid beside famous Irish encounters such as The Diamond.[5]

What then constituted the curious amalgam that was Canadian Orange thought? The stated aims of the Order provide a convenient place to begin such an analysis. Although updated and revised throughout the century the basic tenets of Canadian Orangeism were formulated quite early. Certainly by the mid-forties the standard *Laws, Rules and Regulations* had been devised. The Orange declaration of principles committed members to four duties: to uphold the principles of the Christian religion; to maintain the laws and constitution of the country; to assist distressed members of the Order; and to promote other "laudable and benevolent purposes" consistent with Christianity and constitutional freedom. The latter two duties demonstrate how integral to the Order was the social welfare function.[6]

Ritual played a crucial role in Canadian Orangeism. All Orange candidates swore a sacred oath before entrance into the Order. This oath bound the prospective member to allegiance to the Monarch but qualified this loyalty with the proviso that the Queen must uphold the Protestant religion and constitutional rights. This curious qualification from a proudly loyal organization demonstrates how deep working class traditions of independence ran. The oath also committed the initiate to uphold the Empire, to fight for justice for all brother Orangemen, to hold sacred the name of William and celebrate in lodge his victory every July 12th, to refrain from becoming a Papist, never to disclose or reveal the secret work of the Order, and lastly to support and maintain the Loyal Orange Institution.[7]

The solemn oath formed part of the ritual of most nineteenth century secret societies. In societies involved in transgressions of the law these oaths represented a potent method of allying and binding the initiate to his new brothers. Even in Canada where much of the necessity for absolute secrecy was lacking, these oaths continued to be important. The oath was only the initiation part of an elaborate formal ritual inspired by Masonic forms. The Orange Order, for example, had five degrees which could be attained by faithful service: the Orange, the Purple, the Royal Blue, the Royal Arch Purple, and the Royal Scarlet. Initiation into each of these degrees demanded an unique ceremony involving a ritual introduction, a prayer by the chaplain, an obligation or oath on the part of the candidate, a ritual investiture, and finally a charge to the recipient by the Grand Master of the lodge or a higher official in the case of the highest degrees. The oaths and charges depict an interesting symbolic ascent as each degree accentuated different responsibilities and duties. The Orange only emphasized faithful personal performance. The Purple spoke of advance and called upon the member to scrutinize his brothers and proffer criticism and advice where necessary. The Blue reiterated that charge and called for yet greater diligence. The final two degrees were even more solemn. The ritual for the Royal Arch Purple cautioned that, the mysteries and solemnity of this degree require that the utmost respect, order and decorum be observed by all the brothers. No one shall be admitted into the lodge room in a slovenly or unbecoming dress, nor without a sash appertaining to the order . . . . No brother shall engage in any levity.

The charge of the degree demanded that the new holder take an increasing interest in the well-being of his brothers.

The final and most solemn degree was the Royal Scarlet. The ceremony of this degree was full of blood imagery drawing on Biblical accounts of the Passover. After being invested with a sword, spurs, a scarlet mantle, and a cord and tassel, the candidate was charged to use his sword "in defense of our glorious institution" and "to war against the enemies of destitute widows, helpless orphans, and the Protestant faith." The function of this hierarchy of degrees was undoubtedly to provide additional interest and to endow members with sufficient incentive to persevere and obey Orange strictures in order to attain the reward of a higher degree. An Orangeman's achievements were visible to the entire community each July 12th for each degree and office carried with it a distinctive attire.[8]

There were additional special rituals to accompany unusual events such as the dedication of a new Orange Hall. Funerals played a crucial role in traditional Irish society, and the Orangemen carried on this heritage. They had an elaborate funeral ritual, based on those of other secret societies. Attendance at the funeral of a lodge brother was mandatory and extremely important. A Harvard anthropologist reporting on the Irish countryside in the 1930s was so impressed with the vibrancy of funeral custom that he argued:

The most important secular ceremony of rural life is the wake and funeral . . . . Every man in death can command a multitude. To stay away, to make no recognition of the day, is to give deadly affront.

The Orange ceremony involved a eulogistic review of the deceased brother's achievements, a renewal of the solemn oaths of the remaining Orangemen on the grave of their late brother and finally the dropping into the open grave by each member of the rosette of his degree. There is a simplicity and reverence about many of these Orange rituals which still suggest how powerful they must have been for members of the lodges.[9]

Toronto, the Belfast of Canada, was the acknowledged centre of nineteenth century Canadian Orangeism. The tenacity of Orange traditions in rural areas of Ontario has misled some modern observers into assuming that the Order was weaker in the cities. A closer look at the Orange Order in Toronto should correct this error.[10]

Data on the early organization of the Orange Order in Toronto is quite limited.[11] Toronto lodges predated Gowan's reorganization of 1830 but for our purposes they will be regarded as prehistoric. Approximately twelve lodges were founded in Toronto in the thirties, seventeen in the forties, and fifteen in the fifties. However by 1860 only twenty of these still functioned. The sixties was a period of organizational quiescence in the Order and by 1871 attrition had reduced the number of active Toronto lodges to seventeen. These lodges contained 1494 members.[12] The next five years saw the Order grow quite rapidly and in 1876 there were twenty-six lodges with 2215 Orangemen.[13] By 1880 the number of lodges had grown to thirty but membership had fallen off to 1724[14] and by 1883 there was a further decline to 1632.[15] Membership continued to decline slightly until the late eighties. Those years saw the Order grow in Toronto at an unprecedented rate. From thirty-two lodges in 1884 the Order grew to thirty-six by 1886, thirty-nine by 1888, added seven lodges in 1889 and by the end of 1891 had grown to fifty-one lodges. Although statistics of individual membership are not available for the late eighties a conservative projection based on the lowest average number of members per lodge from the previous years would suggest that by 1892 Toronto Orangemen numbered over 2500. (See Table 1 and 2) Moreover, the influence of the lodges extended far beyond their official membership.

TABLE 1

Orange Lodges

Toronto: 1860-1890

Year	Number	Year	Number
1860	20	1879	31
1866	20	1884	32
1872	17	1886	36
1874	22	1888	39
1876	26	1890	45

Source: Saunders; Grand Lodge Annual Reports; *Globe*; City Directories

The pattern of the Order's growth in Toronto suggests an interesting conjunction of national and local causes. On the national level the periods of most rapid growth correspond both to economic downturns and to the Riel Rebellions. On the local level the exceptional incidents of violence like the Jubilee Riots of 1875, the Rossa riot of 1878 and the O'Brien riot of 1886 all seem to have fueled growth in the Order.

The Orange Order in Toronto was overwhelmingly working

TABLE 2
Orange Lodges Founded or Reorganized
Toronto: 1860-1890

Year	Number	Year	Number
1860-64	0	1880-84	2
1865-69	0	1885-89	14
1870-74	9	1890-91	7
1875-79	8		

Source: Saunders

class in composition. (See Table 3) Contrary to earlier impressions membership was not limited to successful artisans. The lodges were filled with labourers, street railway workers, grooms, teamsters, and others from the lower levels of Toronto working class life. No imaginative flights can transform Toronto Orangemen into a labour aristocracy.

An analysis of available manuscript lodge records reveals much about Orange membership patterns. Four lodges were studied: Armstrong Lodge 137 and Virgin Lodge 328 of Toronto Centre, both founded in the forties; Boyne Lodge 173, also of Toronto Centre, founded in 1878; and Enniskillen Purple Star Lodge 711 of Toronto East founded in 1872.[16] Each of these lodges had a distinctive social character and all but Virgin Lodge show a clear majority of working class members. The 'Virgins' are exceptional because of their unique emphasis on social control and their intent to cater to middle class sojourners in the city, which clearly made this lodge unattractive to workers:

> This lodge was originally opened, for the purpose of giving unmarried young men, students or mercantile men etc., a lodge where they could assemble together ... and also of improving on the working and discipline of the Order, as carried out at that time, which was very lax in many lodges.[17]

Its transformation in 1869 into a benevolent and temperance lodge did not augment its attractiveness for working class Orangemen. Armstrong Lodge, which also had a less clearly pronounced majority of working class members, possessed a number of socially prominent honorary members who played no role in lodge life. They attended no meetings and paid no dues.[18]

Boyne Lodge 173 contained a large number of street railway employees from its inception in 1878. It grew from nine drivers and a conductor in 1878 to six conductors, six drivers, and twelve grooms in 1885. The lodge also contained seven teams-

TABLE 3
Members, 1872-92

	Virgin Lodge 328 1872	Enniskillen Lodge 711 1872-74	Boyne Lodge 173 1878	Boyne Lodge 173 1885	Armstrong Lodge 137 1885-91	Enniskillen Lodge 711 1887	Enniskillen Lodge 711 1890-92 (new members only)
Professionals	2	0	0	1	2	1	1
Gov't Employees	2	0	0	0	0	1	0
Manufacturers	0	1	1	0	1	1	0
Merchants	4	3	1	9	5	3	4
Master Craftsmen	2	1	4	0	2	4	1
Clerks	5	1	4	5	8	4	2
Non-working Class Total	15	6	10	15	18	14	8
Artisans	8	7	17	21	9	35	16
Unskilled	6	15	32	56	19	33	12
Working Class Total	14	22	49	77	28	68	28
Number With Occupations	29	28	59	92	46	82	36
Total Number Listed	48	72	94	121	90	152	80
% With Occupations of Total Listed:	60%	39%	63%	76%	51%	54%	45%

Source: Manuscript Lodge Records, Toronto Public Library.

ters and three coachmen in the latter year to round out the picture of a concentration of workers in horse transport.

Toronto brewer Thomas Allen founded Enniskillen Purple Star in 1872. The lodge from its beginning held a large number of brewery labourers and teamsters. Fifteen years later the lodge contained five machinists from one shop, a number of teamsters and building trades workers employed by the same contractor, and several labourers from the Toronto Gas Works. Most of the members of this lodge lived in a neighbourhood bounded by Parliament St., Queen East, River St., and Spruce St.

Orange lodges, then, were not identical; each possessed its own history, and some articulated specific idiosyncratic aims. The splitting of the city into three Orange districts provided a further rationale for choice of lodge. The split, avowedly "to foster a friendly rivalry that will induce to the benefit of our order," reinforced the role of geographic propinquity in lodge selection. (No doubt the new districts, which conformed to Toronto's electoral divisions, were also intended to be politically more efficient.) A prospective lodge member chose a lodge (and was chosen) on the basis of an interaction of job-associated friendships and neighbourhood ties. The concentration of workers from single work places implies that the lodges could be used as forums for job-related controversies. No doubt Boyne Lodge, for example, was the scene of many heated discussions during the street railway strike of 1886 when all employees struck against the company's attempt to impose an ironclad contract against membership in the Knights of Labor. Equally, lodges in the new working class suburbs showed higher concentrations of working class members and probably provided ample time for issues of community concern. This lodge framework, where job, neighbourhood and leisure came together, contrasts sharply with modern patterns where the three are irreparably separated.[19]

If the membership of Toronto lodges was overwhelmingly working class, then what was the class background of Orange leaders? Did middle and upper class Orangemen exercise a pervasive control over lodge office? An analysis of the occupations of Orange leaders in Toronto suggests that they did not. A survey of Lodge masters from 1871-1888 indicates that, although middle class members held a majority of masterships in the seventies, this was reversed in the eighties. (See Table 4) Further, when one extends the analysis to include all lodge offices, the role of working class members increases strikingly. (See Table 5) Although middle class Orangemen supplied a disproportionate number of leaders their control was far less pervasive than has been previously claimed. Also the tables probably exaggerate the non-working class role for three of the categories are open to further investigation. The government employees and clerks categories include a number of patronage appointees who were working class in origin and earned these jobs as Orange leaders, not the reverse. Similarly, the merchants category includes many small publicans and grocers, both traditional working class entrepreneurial pursuits. Merchants at this level of local sales depended to a large extent on their Orange neighbours for their livelihood.[20]

TABLE 4
Lodge Masters

	1871	1876	1878	1880	1886	1888
Professionals	1	0	2	3	4	1
Gov't. Employees	1	1	0	3	1	2
Manufacturers	1	1	0	0	0	2
Merchants	1	4	7	4	5	5
Master Crafstmen	2	2	2	1	3	0
Clerks	1	1	2	2	1	2
Non-Working Class Total	7	9	13	13	14	12
Artisans	3	5	3	3	15	9
Labourers & Unskilled	0	4	1	4	5	7
Working Class Total	3	9	4	7	20	16
Number Identified	10	18	17	20	34	28
Total Number	17	27	29	30	35	39
Percentage Identified	59	66	58	66	97	71

Source: See Note 20.

Final conclusions concerning class and Orange leaders must await further study of the lives of individual Orange leaders. The Toronto Orange community contained not only working class lodge officers but also more eminent leaders. The editors of *The Orange Sentinel*, the Order's most influential organ, were prominent Toronto trade unionists. E. F. Clarke had been a leader in the Printer's Strike of 1872 and was one of those arrested at George Brown's behest. His co-editor, John Hewitt, had been international vice-president of the Coopers Union and perhaps the most important theorist of the Canadian Nine Hour Movement. Two other prominent Toronto Orange leaders who also played important trade union roles were J. S. Williams, a printer and editor of the *Ontario Workman* and Robert

TABLE 5
Orange Lodge Officers

	1871	1878	1886
Professionals	3	9	8
Gov't. Employees	4	8	9
Manufacturers	2	0	4
Merchants	9	21	14
Master Craftsmen	4	3	11
Clerks	8	11	23
Non-Working Class Total	30	52	69
Artisans	51	42	91
Labourers & Other Unskilled	19	10	47
Working Class Total	70	52	138
Number Identified	100	104	207
Total Number	190	197	315
Percentage Identified	53	52	66

Source: See Note 21.

Glockling of the Knights of Labor and the bookbinders union. Clearly the ties between organized labour and Orangemen suggest that easy assertions about the Order's preference for "leaders with social prestige" should be regarded with skepticism.[22]

The rapid growth of Orangeism in Toronto may have been precipitated by national issues of sectarian strife but what kept men in the Order when the tides of religious struggle retreated? What was the basis for the continued success of an institution which, as writers and pundits constantly asserted, had no reason for existence in a country with freedom of religion and no great land question? What motivated Toronto workers to maintain their Orange identities?

The answers to these questions lead one to an appreciation of the strength of Orangeism. The Order offered much to many quite different people. There was for some the obvious patriotic and Protestant defender appeal. For others there was the confidence that came from belonging to a society which would help carry you through the dangerous contingencies of working class life: if you were unemployed you could depend on your lodge brothers for aid; if you were sick the lodge would provide a doctor free and pay any additional medical expenses; or if you died the lodge would pay your funeral costs and pave your path into the next world with an impressive solemn ritual as well as providing financial aid to your widow and orphans. These benevolent functions tended to be informal until the eighties when, faced with the competition of a whole series of fraternal societies specializing in insurance and other types of aid, the Orange Order formalized their systems into the Orange Mutual Benefit Society.[23]

There was, in addition to these tangible advantages, the camaraderie and fraternity of the lodge. Here one found a male society away from women and the pervasive influence of the middle class inspired cult of domesticity. Faced with the increased size of their work places and their city, these men turned to institutions like the Orange lodges to create the old familiar intimacies of smaller communities. Others probably joined in the expectation of personal gain or at least increased security. It was clear that in Toronto at least there were a whole series of corporation jobs which were retainers for an Orangeman's faithful service. While never as formalized as Tammany, the Orange Order served similar uses in Toronto machine politics. Orange-controlled jobs included the post-office and the customs house on the federal level and the gasworks, water works, police department and fire department on the corporation level. *The Irish Canadian*, no friend of Toronto Orangemen, complained in 1876 that the city employed only two Catholics and that they had been recently fired. In the eighties *The Irish Canadian* ran a series of editorials exposing Orange jobbery in the civic corporation.[24]

For those who were more ambitious the possibility of making a larger mark and receiving the sinecures that came from higher political intrigue existed. And for the most ambitious there was the political route itself. For a generation of Conservative politicians the Order represented a method of breaking the stranglehold of Compact Tories on nominations. It should be noted that this route was open to few Orangemen and probably played a minor motivational role. On the local level the merchant, undertaker, or tavern keeper living in a working class neighbourhood found lodge membership a prerequisite for success. Each candidate for Orange membership probably mixed these motives in distinctive ways.[25]

The Orange Order's role in Upper Canadian political life was especially important in Toronto, where a series of politicians built or demolished their careers in relation to the lodges. The Order did not provide an easy path to prominence in public life for it immediately caught the politician between the Orangeman's continuing need and love for the traditional marches, songs, rituals and informal riots and the emerging industrial society's demand for order and control. Gowan's own political career demonstrates the snares upon the path to political success and respectability. His first electoral success was entirely contingent on Orange poll violence – a type of behaviour that he was instrumental in later attempting to suppress.

The conflict between Orange tradition and new societal demands continued throughout the fifties, sixties and seventies. The Order was considered an attractive organization partially because of its identification with old ways and happier days before the alienating onslaught of industrialism. The leaders, on the other hand, found themselves under ever-increasing social pressure to control their compatriots' excesses. Thus Gowan encouraged the inception of Temperance lodges in the fifties, which constituted a major break with Orange tradition that had placed a heavy emphasis on the social role of drink. Recognizing the importance of such a step he argued:

Our institution is not confined, wholly, or even chiefly, to uneducated classes of the community, but includes large masses of intelligent and educated men. Remove from them the mirth and hilarity of the festive bowl, and some other source of enjoyment must be provided.

As a solution he offered: "let every lodge have its own library and reading room." After 1859 Orange lodges were forbidden to meet in hotels, taverns, or saloons. Gowan, throughout the fifties, also proposed that lodges set up savings banks and that Orange bands be required to actually study music—until then an unheard of proposition.[26]

Virgin Lodge in Toronto was started avowedly as an attempt to stiffen Orange discipline and to socialize younger Orangemen to new models of Orange behaviour. Originally, the name Virgin, which they later adopted as their own, was hurled at them as an insult by their more senior and less 'controlled' brothers in the Order. The various attempts to assert social control over the membership were not totally successful in the fifties. They continued on into the seventies and eighties and heated lodge room discussions about to drink or not to drink became as much a part of July 12th as King Billy and his white horse.[27]

Another example of their increasing concern for respectability was the creation in 1875 of a Grand Lodge committee on regalia. This committee reported in favour of formalizing and regularizing the old traditional modes of dress:

The time has come when this Grand Lodge should adopt a uniform regalia; wanting this our processions fail to favourably impress the public, and the grotesque and ridiculous things often worn as regalia make a laughing stock not only of those who wear them, but of the Association.

They went on to describe in great detail the dimensions, colours, fringes, etc. for every degree and office in the order. The simplicity and cheapness of the old ceremonial attire was being replaced by specifications so detailed and strict that they laid the basis for the emergence of firms who specialized in manufacturing Orange regalia at exorbitant rates.[28]

The events of July 12th always created huge problems for Orange leaders in Canada. The day was deeply entrenched in the Orange calendar, which included in each member's Oath the duty of annually celebrating the Battle of the Boyne. In periods of great tension the civil authorities often exerted great pressure to prevent the Orangemen from marching. Orange leaders co-operated with such injunctions only in the most extreme cases and then were often unable to prevent their members from marching anyway. It was bad enough that the members should demand to march, but what was worse they usually insisted on fighting also. July 12th, March 17th, and November 5th were days in which riot had become ritual.

These riots, in Toronto at least, were controlled and not particularly violent. Only extraordinary happenings transformed them into serious outbreaks of collective violence in which severe damage or injury occurred. One historian of Orangeism has noted that:

> Even in Ireland the disorders caused by the July 12th processions were relatively minor irritations, the real evil being the nightly raids on Catholic dwellings and the reprisals which grew out of a land question that had no counterpart in Canada.

In Toronto the riots maintained a 'territorial' basis but they also took on an increasingly ritualistic aspect.[29]

Orangemen and Irish Catholics clashed twenty-two times in the twenty-five years between 1867 and 1892. On only two of these occasions did serious violence occur to fracture the pattern of restrained ritual riot. Before discussing the nature of those two events and analyzing what transformed them into bloodier occasions let us describe the calendar of sectarian conflict in Toronto.[30]

Twelve of the riots quite predictably took place around the events of July 12th and March 17th (eight and four respectively). One coincided with the Orange celebration of the discovery of the Gunpowder Plot in November and four others occurred around Orange and Green picnics in August. Thus seventeen of the twenty-two riots accompanied celebrations of import in the annual Orange and Green calendars. The pattern should not surprise us, for collective violence of this kind is neither random nor spontaneous and is most often "given some structure by the situation of worship or the procession that was the occasion for the disturbance."

Parades then were at the centre of violence in Toronto. This parallels precisely the Irish experience for "where you could 'walk' you were dominant and the other things followed." In Toronto, however, this testing of territory took on a ritualistic aspect and seldom progressed to the Belfast model of importing rural traditions of house wrecking to an urban environment. A more careful study of the events of July 12th and March 17th will clarify the ritualistic nature of this violence.[31]

The July riots were of three types: those prompted by Green aggression toward the Orange celebration; those prompted by Orange challenges to Green neighbourhoods; and finally Green aggression in revenge after the event. The first type was quite rare in Toronto because of the predominance of Orangemen, but in cities which were demographically more balanced or where Catholics were predominant, as in Montreal, it became more prominent. In Toronto this type occurred in 1870 when a foolhardy Green carter drove his cart, bedecked with green ribbons, through the July 12th procession. It should be noted that, although a risky business at best, he did attempt this disruption in the heart of a Catholic neighbourhood. An earlier example of Green interference occurred in 1833, when Irish Catholics imitated the Orangemen by marching with green flags and with one of their members astride a white horse, obscenely mimicking King Billy. Not surprisingly a riot ensued.[32]

Riots of the second type were the most frequent in Toronto. In 1870, 1876, 1877, and again in 1888 riots were caused by Irish Catholics attacking Orange fife and drum bands marching through the heart of the Green ghetto playing tunes such as 'Croppies lie Down,' 'Protestant Boys', and 'The Boyne Water'. For example, an Orange fife and drum band chose Cosgrove's Hotel, a centre of Irish Catholic activity, as a likely spot to serenade in 1877. When their lusty performance of 'Protestant Boys' was greeted with stones and jeers, they fought back. A crowd then gathered and proceeded to stone Cosgrove's Hotel, successfully smashing all the windows. This hotel was also attacked and wrecked in other riots in 1870, 1875, and 1878—the one importation into Toronto of the Irish model of wrecking in sectarian strife. Cosgrove was a prominent Green leader and on occasion served as Marshal in the St. Patrick's Day procession. His tavern was reputed to be a meeting place for Toronto Fenians. Nevertheless in the immediate events of 1877 there were no arrests and no reported injuries.[33]

The third type of riot, Green aggression after the 12th, was infrequent and occurred only in 1873 and 1874.[34]

Riots on March 17th occurred when Orangemen decided to challenge the Green marchers, as in 1871 when an Orange carter drove his horse through the Catholic procession, or when Orange bands availed themselves of the proceedings to choose to march in Catholic neighbourhoods playing their favourite party tunes, as they did in 1872 and 1889. The fourth incident of a March 17th riot will be discussed later, for O'Donavon Rossa's lecture on that occasion provided the fuel for one of the two exceptional riots.[35]

Most of these riots, then, were highly ritualized and delimited. They all revolved around territory and its defence. As in Belfast,"their parades constantly tested the area of that territorial domination....To tail ones coat is an Irish humour. Every riot followed an infringement of the right to walk." Thus they focused around the major fêtes of the Orange and Green calendar but unlike Belfast the violence was usually quite localized and slight. This had been true of an earlier period in Ireland also where:

> The marching around the countryside of large bands had about it something of the holiday spirit. Parties usually met by mutual agreement and exchanged shots and insults outside of effective range until the magistrates arrived.

Events in Belfast and in the Irish countryside had gone beyond that but they did not in Toronto. The Toronto events seldom involved shooting. Sometimes the parties came close enough to exchange blows, nevertheless the events always involved more bravado than blood.[36]

Many of the riots which did not conform to the strict calendar also fit the above description. A number of them involved the Orange Young Britons and the Young Irishmen, their Catholic counterparts, in altercations at dances and over female attentions. These adolescent wings of the Orange and Green resembled street gangs. They were certainly among the most militant on either side and when arrests occurred it usually involved these youthful sectarians. Certainly the events of September 1870 suggest the street gang analogy. A fight broke out between a number of Orange Young Britons who came to a 'low' (no doubt Irish Catholic) dancehall to avenge some slight that one of their more daring members had received there. The fight that followed set off a wave of OYB marching and riot. These events led one leading Orangeman, John Ross Robertson, to editorialize against these "Young Rowdies" who were motivated by nothing more than "a spirit of braggadocio and rowdyism." Orange leaders sprang to the defence of the OYBs. At a protest meeting held after the conviction of some of their colleagues for riotous and disorderly conduct, Orange leaders made motions condemning Robertson after denying that any of those arrested were in the OYBs:

> The Orange and the Green have at all times lived in this city in peace and harmony, each pursuing their own peculiar ten-

ets, religious and political, playing their own favoured music, religious and national, and celebrating their own peculiar anniversaries and fete days without offense, molestation or interruption and that this joyous and happy state of society it has now for the first time been attempted to be interrupted by the foul and atrocious articles which have recently been in certain newspapers in this city.

The same speaker went on to condemn the actions of the police in intervening in the altercation. This is the clue to Orange fury in this case, for the convictions following these events were among the first ever brought down against these ritual riots. Young Britons previously arrested had escaped with nothing more than a reprimand from the police magistrate. The Orange leadership rallied behind their members on this occasion for the last time. The willingness of civic authorities to suppress Orange riot and the support that Robertson lent them symbolizes the fact that Orange riot was on its way to becoming as much a memory as the Battle of the Boyne itself. This transformation, like other changes in the Orange Order, was bitterly resisted and was not accomplished overnight. Robertson's experience in attacking the OYB in 1870 was instructive:

The *Daily Telegraph* office was threatened with destruction: letters similar to those laid on the tables of obnoxious Irish landlords were received by the editor and reporters: and those taverns and shebeens in which the Young Britons concoct their fearful fights echoed with howls of vengeance against the *Daily Telegraph.*

If that was the case Robertson must have taken great satisfaction when Gowan moved in 1873 at the Provincial Grand Lodge that:

Whereas a number of societies or orders such as the Orange Young Britons . . . have been introduced into Canada, or have been organized in the last few years. And whereas such societies have been allowed in some places to walk in public processions and otherwise identify themselves with the Orange Institution, without being under the control, or owing any direct responsibility to the Grand Lodge of the Order for their acts, words or proceedings; and it has become highly desirable and necessary that if such bodies are to be continued, they should be placed under the direct control of proper officers, responsible to the Grand Lodge.

This was carried out in 1874 but the OYBs chafed under the authority of the Grand Lodge and a number of them led a split away from the Order in the early eighties. But even here the split between old Orange models and the new Orange design was present. One OYB leader argued for the new 'control':

> I would recommend the cultivation of the young mind... how much time do young men generally spend in frivolity or idleness; how much in what is worse—vicious indulgences: How frequently are hours passed in taverns, wasted away in smoking, gaming, riotous and ribald conversation, or indolent lounging, which ought to be devoted to the pursuit of knowledge and the attainment of business habits.... This is not as it ought to be. Every hour should be appropriated to some useful purpose. We should be as niggardly of time as is the miser of his hoarded treasure.

Following on that appropriate simile he went on to propose that they should become "valuable members of society, efficient businessmen, and active moral agents..." Things had moved a long way from the earlier 'festive bowl.'[37]

The conscious efforts of some Orange leaders to create tougher discipline and enforce a rigid social control over their membership came to fruition in the seventies. The slow disappearance of the social base for the older pre-industrial Orange behaviour like ritual religious riot played as large a part as the efforts of Orange leaders. But whatever the cause, of the twenty-two riots between 1867 and 1892 only four took place after 1878 and these all were clustered in 1887-1890. Perhaps even more persuasive was the changed nature of descriptions of July 12th events in the Toronto press in the eighties. A whole new tone of reminiscence was present as writers reflected on how July 12th used to be. It was even noted that some of the old ritual dress had been dropped. "The striking white trousers have practically become a thing of history", one journalist wrote with a tinge of regret. *The Irish Canadian*, a Green paper, noted gleefully throughout the mid-eighties that the numbers were falling off at Twelfth celebrations and that the celebrations were now 'quiet,' 'tame and flat.' They also described the decline of the "broils that in years gone by disgraced the Orange anniversary." They too emphasized the decline of the old:

> And then the traditional grey horse is not as prominent and ubiquitous as was his wont – a circumstance not without significance as indicative of that fatal indifference which preceded the final collapse.... We refer to these trifles merely to show that the discipline of the Twelfth is not as rigid as it used to be, and it looks as if a horse of any colour will now serve where formerly it was treason to hint at anything but the sleekest grey.

The two exceptional riots of the seventies provide further

clues about the changes in Orangeism in that period. The first, the Jubilee Riots of 1875, were undoubtedly the bloodiest sectarian struggles in Toronto's history. The second was the riot which greeted the Fenian leader, O'Donavon Rossa, when he lectured at a March 17th Hibernian celebration in 1878. In both cases the vehemence of the Orange crowds was aroused by the transgression of the informal limits set upon sectarian display by years of ritual riot. In both cases Toronto Catholics seemed to be extending their territory beyond previous definition. March 17th marches were acceptable, but the importation of an Irish revolutionary to speak in Toronto was an affront that could not go unchallenged. Equally, processions with green ribbons and Hibernian slogans were acceptable but a pilgrimage through quiet Toronto streets on the Sabbath carrying symbols of Popery and apparently on the direct bidding of the Vatican could not be allowed to pass unchallenged.[38]

The response of Toronto community leaders is instructive. They decided that they must defend the Catholics' right to religious procession. The entire police force and three companies of militia were utilized to assure Roman Catholics their right to march. In 1878 however they did little to protect Rossa. The police took a severe beating on both occasions but the copious arrests of 1875 contrast noticeably with the record of no arrests in 1878.

The use of Orange militia companies by an Orange mayor against an Orange crowd must have made it very clear to rioting Orangemen that their conduct no longer received tacit approval. It was of course partially this armed intervention that transformed the Jubilee Riots into a serious affray. An analysis of the twenty-nine arrested men shows eleven identifiable Orangemen. The occupations of the arrested men represents a cross-section of Toronto working class pursuits.[39]

The extraordinary nature of these Roman Catholic marches aroused Orange ire and, when combined with the aggressive attempt by the authorities to suppress the riot, changed the general form of Toronto ritual riot into a full-scale sectarian struggle. Why did the Orangemen feel called upon to try to prevent the procession even in the face of their leaders' disavowal of such actions? The answer lies again in a conjunction of national and local events. On the national level the Guibord Affair was still working its way to a macabre close and only weeks before the Toronto riots a crowd of Roman Catholics had prevented the burial of Guibord's body in a Montreal Catholic cemetery despite a court order to the contrary. Meanwhile in Toronto the Catholic community had only a month before hosted an unprecedented August O'Connell Centenary which saw Hibernians gather from all over the province.[40] This was probably the largest Catholic demonstration ever held in

Toronto. Local Orangemen thus had much on their minds when they were confronted with plans for a procession to be held for Catholic bishops visiting the city for a Provincial Council meeting. These plans were further complicated by additional Catholic plans to march on church visitations to gain indulgences connected with the Pope's declaration of 1875 as a Jubilee Year. All of this parading seemed like Catholics trailing coats and the Orangemen requested that Archbishop Lynch cancel these affairs. He refused and the processionists were met with a small riot on Sunday, September 26. After these events Orange leaders called a special public meeting. There, after speeches attacking Ultramontanism, they moved that both sides refrain from marching on the coming Sunday. Lynch again refused and instead demanded from the Mayor assurance that, if he forbade his laity to resist, they would be assured of police protection. This the Mayor reluctantly agreed to.

The riot that ensued reportedly involved as many as 6000 to 8000 people and the entire city core was out of control for a number of hours. Given the crowd's immense size one again is struck by its self-control. The pilgrims were attacked but there were few reported injuries and the only property damage was incurred by every Orangeman's favourite Toronto target, Owen Cosgrove's Hotel. One scene, reported in the press, vividly portrays the irony of the situation. A fervid anti-processionist appealed to the crowd to attack a Catholic church by reminding them of the old days "when they walked eight deep" on July 12th. The crowd did not sack any churches that day and indeed although they might continue to walk eight deep on the Twelfth, the years of ritualized riot were all but over.

The events of 1878 were limited to one night of riot. Insulted by the very attempt to bring Rossa to lecture, Toronto Orangemen gathered to prevent the lecture from taking place. In this they failed and when Rossa managed to elude them after the speech they proceeded to stone the hall and later to attack Cosgrove's. After 1878 Toronto was to enjoy relative quiet until the renewal of sectarian strife in the late eighties. Those years saw a few half-hearted attempts at religious riot but the times had changed. The re-emergence of anti-Catholic sentiments in various third party movements and the creation in the nineties of the Protestant Protective Association on the model of the nativist American Protective Association suggests both the breakdown of the old Orangeism and hints at one of its uses.[41]

The ritualized violence of Toronto Orangemen which seldom exceeded a set of informal limits was far less menacing than the nativist movements which arose to replace it in the nineties. Orangeism was never racist; its replacements were. The relative mildness of Canadian sectarian strife when compared with events in the U.S. suggest that the Orange Institution, which was never strong in the U.S., may have indeed played a major role in tempering sectarian strife by institutionalizing elements of it in affairs that more often resembled rugged games than vicious riot.

The Orange Order played an ambiguous role in the life of the Toronto working classes. Although clearly dividing the working class community in two, it nevertheless provided its members with a number of strengths that were usefully carried into the realm of trade unionism. The Orange lodges trained their members in parliamentary procedure and strengthened their commitment to the rights of free-born Englishmen. The Order also produced a number of men capable of providing leadership to the labour movement. Perhaps of more import however was the reinforcement that the Order gave to old themes of working class life. The virtues of mutuality, fraternity and benevolence had roots deep in the pre-modern community, and institutions such as the Orange Lodges transferred them to the increasingly fragmented world of the industrial city. Rowland Berthoff has argued that similar but less traditional societies in the U.S.:

... stood in reaction against the social, cultural, and spiritual inadequacies of the nineteenth century. Ineffectual or insubstantial though they might be, they had at least begun the evolution of new institutions and a new community capable of satisfying eternal human needs in forms suited to modern society.[42]

The other aspect of the Orange tradition with a positive heritage for working class achievement was its activism. The Orangemen carried with them an Irish dislike of constituted authority and a willingness to impose their own justice. As one scholar has argued of their Green brothers, but which applies equally well to the Orangemen:

Rioting to secure ... political recognition, or religious liberty as popularly construed can be explained by reference to Irish tradition and social organization. It was simply a continuation in Canada of all the devices, including oath-bound secret societies, developed extra-legally in response to legal, civil and religious deprivation.... The violence indicates not massive social disorganization but the persistence of a social order.

These traditions were carried on, he continues, in "early trade unionism and the political machine." The uses of violence then must always be carefully considered. Even in the extreme case of religious riot, the violence is explained not in terms of how crazy, hungry, or sexually frustrated the violent people are, but in terms of the goals of their actions and in terms of the roles and patterns of behaviour allowed by their culture.[43]

The divisive influence of the Orange Order in Toronto's working class community existed mainly in the realm of politics. D. J. O'Donoghue and Alf Jury, two working class leaders with Liberal party ties, often inveighed against the reactionary Orangemen, but one should treat the evidence of political losers with extreme caution. They were, of course, equally committed political partisans – all that differed was the party. Clarke and Hewitt's Toryism must be weighed on the same ideological scale, not on one that registers only Orangemen.

A distinction must also be made here between the sectarian strife of religious riot or of economic discrimination and that of partisan politics. Religious riot had all but disappeared by the eighties and riots to keep Catholics out of jobs had never occurred in Toronto. No examples of ethnic or religious riot at the work place have been found. Partisan political strife on the other hand was to continue. Nevertheless by the eighties common issues had emerged that united Irish Catholic Liberal trade unionists like O'Donoghue, Orangemen like Hewitt and Glockling, and even secularist Alf Jury and theosophist Phillips Thompson. In arriving at this point many rival and mutually exclusive cultural traditions played a role and Orangeism was by no means the least important.

Brainworkers and the Knights of Labor: E. E. Sheppard, Phillips Thompson, and the Toronto News, 1883-1887

Russell Hann

There have been few notions in the history of modern thought more persistent than that which views the world of the mind to be in fundamental opposition to the world of practical everyday reality. Some observers have viewed the intelligentsia as the protectors of all that is fine in the western tradition; to perform this function well, it must be well insulated from society. Others have claimed that the intelligentsia plays a crucial social role in the legitimation of the predominant system of social relations, even though it may proclaim its findings as eternal verities from what seem to be ethereal ivory towers. However antithetical these approaches seem, they both remove the intellectual from the sphere of everyday life, obscuring the fact that intellectuals of various kinds pervade almost every aspect of modern life. Indeed, they have grown far too diverse and unpredictable as a species to be viewed as the defenders of any particular ethos and far too numerous and visible to seem much removed from the common social life of modern industrial society, where the most esoteric theories regularly find mass applications and practical use. The transformations which have led to this situation constitute some of the major themes of modern cultural history: the steady expansion of the reading public, the growth of new kinds of periodical literature to meet wider demand, an altered relationship between the man of letters and his patrons (who gradually became his audience), and the development and exploitation of new kinds of media of communication. New styles of persuasion fostered by this new cultural context went hand in hand with the rise of new forms of opposition which dealt with the realm of social relations in industrial society. The intellectual estate came to share in the common life of most Western societies by enunciating its right to participate in the world of action through the medium of public opinion.[1]

A great deal of inquiry into labour history has been blind to these cultural developments. Most theoretical studies of the relationship of the intellectual to the world of labour stress a radical separation of interests and sympathies. Selig Perlman suggested that the "educated non-manualist who has established a contact with the labour movement" would find himself at odds with the kind of "prosaic matters" which constituted union activity. The "typical intellectual" was much more comfortable with "the clear-cut logic and symmetry of political platforms based on general principles" and "the opportunity for eloquent self-expression offered by parliamentary debates." Perlman felt that the intellectuals could make a contribution to the growth of the American labour movement better when safely confined in the public relations office of a national union. While Lenin was dedicated to an entirely different end for the labour movement, he described the role of the intellectual in similar terms. By its own effort the working class movement could not hope to advance beyond "trade union consciousness" toward revolutionary socialism: that step required the assistance of members of the bourgeois intelligentsia with their familiarity with social theories first "elaborated by the educated representatives of the propertied classes." The contribution of labour to revolutionary ideology increased as workingmen came to "acquire the knowledge of their age."[2]

Neither Perlman's nor Lenin's approach shows much understanding of the cultural reality of the late nineteenth century in most of the English-speaking world. While many intellectuals assiduously devoted their lives to escaping contact with working class life, few workers could escape the influence of intellectuals. When workers began to organize and to launch their own journals to advance their cause, they might find in their own ranks a handful of learned artisans and the odd self-taught journalist trained at the printers' case to staff their papers. More often, they relied heavily upon sympathetic journalists who became labour's intellectuals after observation and study, rather than in a Mechanics' Institute after a day's work at manual labour. Trained journalists rallied to labour's cause wherever radical workingmen set up labour papers. Moreover, the founding generations of North American labour organizations were not uncomfortable in the world of ideas and literature. They exhibited a deep respect for learning by voraciously reading books, essays, pamphlets, and novels. Cheap editions of the classics proliferated. They demanded and digested a steadily growing diet of periodical literature in the form of dailies, weeklies, and other journals. This activity formed a central feature of the response of the working class to the coming of industrialism. Intellectuals were always closely linked to this response. If they did not convince workingmen of the wisdom of a particular course of action, one cannot conclude that they made no contribution.[3]

In Canadian history most of the work on intellectuals and the working class movement has failed to transcend the kinds of separations found in theoretical appproaches to labour history. Martin Robin, whose *Radical Politics and Canadian Labour*·

1880-1930 deals with some of the subjects of this paper, saw the period as a kind of prehistory to labour's alliance with the "professional, university-based intelligentsia" through which Canadian social democracy was founded in the 1930s. Similarly, another predominant strain of Canadian writing on the subject suggests that, in Canada in particular, these early radicals should have found an eminently comfortable milieu in the "corporate-organic-collectivist ideas" of the prevalent tory ideology. These approaches display little appreciation of the historical processes by which cultural activity came to be assimilated into general social life. An intelligentsia did not fall from the sky at an appointed time to fill an instrumental role. Nor did the early socialists and radicals find a snug niche as the last piece in a jigsaw puzzle depicting a collectivist Canadian sunset. They found that the tory fragment had many sharp, grating edges. Bernard Ostry's depiction of the radical labour reform editor as a wishful thinker, "unrepresentative and peripheral" in the labour movement whose real leadership won practical gains by temporary alliances with old political parties does not do justice to the contribution of the radical intellectuals in the 1880s. However, it does suggest a tension not found in Robin or in the fragment theorists. Damned in their own time by Tory and Grit alike, these Labour Reformers seemed destined for an undeserved oblivion until Frank Watt described the contours of a late nineteenth century radical tradition in a pioneering 1959 essay. To explore the world of these early radicals and socialists (who were widely known and read in their own time) is to forego a simplistic, instrumental construction of the role of an intelligentsia, to dispel the myth of a tory environment salubrious to the collectivist impulse, and to narrow the gap between non-manualist and worker, between culture and society.[4]

On November 26, 1883, Edmund Ernest Sheppard became proprietor of the Toronto *News* and began a unique experiment in the annals of Toronto journalism. The *News* had been started by the owners of the *Mail*, John and Charles Riordan and C. W. Bunting in 1882 as Toronto's second evening daily. Sheppard caught the eye of the owners and was put in charge of the paper in early 1883. When the paper did not turn out to be as sure a money maker as had been predicted, Sheppard was offered control of the paper and its new building if he would assume a mortgage held by Charles Riordan. By the next year the paper was the largest evening daily in the city, having edged past the *Telegram* in circulation. Only the morning party organs, the *Mail* and the *Globe* boasted larger circulations, although much of that was outside Toronto. Determined to make his break from the *Mail*, the organ of the Conservative Party, as dramatic as possible. Sheppard announced that the paper would be devoted to Democracy which he defined as the extension of the elective principle into all areas of public life. Hostile to the "divine rights of kings" and a "titled or privileged class," the democratic *News* advocated on its first day the separation of church and state, the abolition of the office of Governor General and its replacement by an elected Chief Magistrate, and government issue of a national currency. He was cautious enough to add that this program of "simple democracy and common sense" was not to be associated with socialism, communism, nihilism, or annexationism. With its simple faith in elections and its disclaimer to anything more seditious than common sense, the *News* did not seem too radical a departure from a host of earlier ventures in journalism, which had then settled into comfortable roles as party organs. However, Sheppard's *News* came to the fore just as the Knights of Labor were entering a period of phenomenal growth. Workingmen formed the majority of the audience of the new evening dailies and the audience of the *News* invested democracy with more radical meaning than perhaps the proprietor intended. However, soon he would identify with the cause of his audience and the paper began to reflect many of the positions held by the Knights.[5]

Sheppard was an exciting figure in the Toronto newspaper world of the day. Born in Elgin County, he was the son of a clergyman in the Disciples Church who combined preaching with tending a small farm. Sheppard came to rebel against the stern domestic environment imposed by his father. His rebellion took the form of a lifelong hatred of pietists. However, he maintained an interest in rhetoric which he indulged by attending a different church in Toronto each week to judge the various sermon styles. Working at odd jobs, he saved enough money to enrol in a course in medicine at Bethany College in West Virginia where tuition was lower than in Ontario, but he lost interest and did not complete his course. Somehow he ended up in Texas near the Mexican border, where he claimed to have worked as a cowboy and stagecoach driver. Whether true or not, he adopted a style of dress and bearing which augmented what he thought was a striking personal resemblance to Buffalo Bill by wearing a large black slouch hat at all times, a black moustache and goatee, and riding boots of fine Spanish leather. He also chewed tobacco constantly and indulged in what one observer judged the most colourful barnyard language he had ever heard. One of his later employees said he resembled "one of Bret Harte's immaculate gamblers." Returning to Canada in 1878 with some American journalistic experience, he worked on papers in Western Ontario before coming to Toronto and the *Mail* in 1882.[6]

The editorial and reportorial staff that Sheppard assembled included a mixture of new blood and old employees from the *Mail*. During Sheppard's tenure as proprietor, the staff was never greater than eight (usually around six journalists and reporters), although it dropped to four in 1887 when Sheppard was strapped with law suits and was losing control of the paper. As his assistant editor and chief editorial writer he chose Phillips Thompson from the editorial board of the *Globe*. One of the ablest Toronto journalists of the time, Thompson had had a long association with independent journalistic ventures in Toronto since he had begun to work on John Ross Robertson's *Telegraph* as a police court reporter in 1867. Turning these reports into boisterous satire, he developed a wide following as a humorist under the *nom de plume*, Jimuel Briggs, D.B., of Coboconk U. (his degree was not a theological one, but that of Dead Beat from the esteemed, but mythical Coboconk U.). In the 1870s he had founded two papers of his own, the *Daily City Press* and the *National* before spending three years in Boston as the literary editor of the *Evening Traveller*. Returning to Toronto in 1879, he worked first for the *Mail* and then the *Globe* where he became a noted feature writer after he covered the Irish Land League agitation in 1881. He confessed to Henry George, whom he had met and interviewed in Ireland, that he felt that his well-paid position in a relatively plush editorial chair at the *Globe* provided him with little more than a comfortable vantage point at the "edge of the storm" of social unrest engulfing most of the Western world. After accepting Sheppard's invitation (and a cut in pay), he was able to fire off more than the "occasional shot" permitted him by the *Globe*. His fellow employees included: Louis Kribs, a popular columnist who used the pseudonym Pica in his humorous columns; T. A. Gregg, a former *Mail* staffer known as "the fat Mephistopheles;" Watson Griffin; C. W. Pirie, the perennial Bohemian, police reporter, and practical joker; and Charles Ryan who became city editor of the *News* after Sheppard's departure. It was a small and familiar group. All had known each other before they moved into the *News* building. Kribs and Griffin were avowed Tories and the staff as a whole had a Tory tone to it, since most of them had come from the *Mail*. However, Sheppard's arrangement with the Riordans gave the paper a real independence from partisan influences.[7]

The physical appearance of the *News* was not radically different from that of most of the established Toronto journals. In format it was a four page daily and an eight page weekly which sold for two cents a copy. It offered a mélange of news similar to that of most dailies of the time. Perhaps it did correspond, with other new urban dailies, to what Paul Rutherford has termed "people's journalism." The *News* did offer a more lively, sensational fare with a greater emphasis on local reporting and labour news than did the regular party press. However, it would be misleading to suggest that the *News* pioneered a new kind of sensationalism, designed to capture a wider market of less discriminating readers. The use of cartoon illustrations in the weekly editions, Sheppard's dialect humour column by the Farmin' Editor, and feature stories on the social condition of the poor were innovations that had been tried by the regular party press earlier. What differentiated the *News* from its partisan contemporaries was its ideological perspective, rather than its style and format. After the publicity gimmicks died away, the *News* was radically different from the *Mail* and *Globe* mainly for its enunciation of a political course that was clearly independent of Grittism and Toryism. Its politics were concerned not with the practical achievement of power, but rather with the fostering of a new kind of opposition to the basic political, social, and cultural assumptions of late nineteenth century Canadian society. J. W. Bengough hailed the arrival of Sheppard, "The Journalistic Cowboy," with a full page cartoon in *Grip*. Mounted on the untamed mustang of Democracy, Sheppard galloped into town disrupting the stolid world of the Toronto press. The *News* offered an alternative to the "snob rule" and "toadyism" of the *Mail*, the "fogyism" and "retrogression" of the *Globe*, the "nothingism" of the independent *World* and *Telegram*, and even the "*Week*-kneed independence" of Goldwin Smith's *Week*.[8]

Nevertheless, there were obvious tensions among the staff, some of whom had open partisan connections. Phillips Thompson was Sheppard's strongest ally in guiding the *News* along a course of independent democracy. Often he would come into conflict with Sheppard, whose later career as a Tory politician, a society editor, and a jingoistic editor of the Toronto *Star* suggests the mercurial nature of Sheppard's personality. When Thompson came to the *News*, he was already an active member of the Knights of Labor. In September, 1883, he had most likely begun his contribution to the Hamilton *Palladium of Labor* which was devoted to the cause of the Knights. Thompson was probably the author of "Our Social Club," a series which ran until late November, 1883, when Thompson joined the *News*. This fictitious symposium of self-taught workingmen, a free thinker, a middle class social reformer, a Tory, and a Grit met weekly in the pages of the *Palladium* to discuss Henry George's *Progress and Poverty*, the foibles of classical political economy, female suffrage, currency reform, partyism, and other topics relating to the labour question. They abandon their preconceived positions as the debate goes on, forming a labour

political association at its conclusion. Many of the themes from
"Our Social Club" were echoed in Thompson's weekly *Palladium* column secretly written under the pseudonym Enjolras
which began immediately after "Our Social Club" stopped.
These columns continued until the demise of the *Palladium* in
1887, forming the basis of Thompson's book *The Politics of Labor* published that year.[9]

This simultaneous work on the *News* and the *Palladium* constituted a period of phenomenal productivity by Thompson
who also worked as a public speaker for the Knights on many
occasions. While the pace must have been frenetic, it was also
fraught with certain tensions. Sheppard was not as familiar or
comfortable with advanced reform theories as Thompson; the
editorials of the *News* were never as explicit in their espousal of
a clearly radical course as were Thompson's for the *Palladium*
and often pandered to what Thompson felt were unwholesome
working class prejudices. Thompson worked under this pressure
because he recognized the educational value of a popular daily
like the *News* in promoting the Knights. He balked on only one
occasion; when asked to write editorials supporting the execution of Louis Riel, a project that Sheppard was vigorously
promoting at the time, Thompson refused and took on a special
assignment for the *Globe* for a time. More often he gave in,
probably after long argument. Though Thompson was perceived as "peculiar in many ways" and "radical" by Daniel J.
O'Donoghue, a fellow member in Thompson's Toronto Local
Assembly of the Knights, he was nevertheless "one of those
who realizes the great difficulties of harmonizing the almost
warring elements composing the working classes." The fruits of
compromise were evident not only in a certain vagueness at the
News on the nature of future society (which Enjolras could outline specifically as "what might be"), but also in a broad critique of cultural institutions and the role of "brainworkers"
who laboured in them that Thompson developed in his *Palladium* columns.[10]

As the anonymous Enjolras, Thompson could step beyond
the narrower strategies of the *News* to make more pointed and
specific arguments about an ultimate strategy for labour. This
dual activity brought Thompson to a clear understanding of the
relation of cultural activity to the working class movement. In
an editorial which appeared in the *Palladium* on December 5,
1883, the feelings of ambivalence that Thompson must have
shared were expressed:

> The ranks of progressive journalism have recently had an
> important accession in the Toronto *News* which has cut
> loose from the *Mail*. It is brimful of radical ideas and advo-

cates Canadian independence on a thoroughly democratic basis of government, manhood suffrage, the election of national and provincial governors, and the extension of the electoral principle. . . . Such a paper is a marked advance upon anything we have yet had in the way of daily journalism. . . . We are thorough believers in democracy. . . . But what we wish to point out is that mere democracy will never of itself redress social injustice or remedy the evils of the industrial system. . . . Nevertheless, democracy is a most essential step towards a better state of things – but its attainment will mark the beginning and not the end of the journey.

By the late summer of 1884 Sheppard and Thompson had both appeared as speakers at Knights meetings and the *News* had endorsed the Knights and their program. In a labour procession in 1886, the entire *News* staff – management, clerical labour, printers, compositors, mailers, and journalists – marched in a single group, all wearing white plug hats which Sheppard had ordered for the occasion.[11]

The *News* appealed to a wider audience than did the *Palladium*. Through an analysis of the present leadership of Canadian society, it sought to demonstrate the necessity for democracy based on the electoral principle. Only by radically extending it to a whole range of offices and positions which were then appointive would it be possible to break the power of certain "feudal remnants" in Canadian society. While these were not as obvious as the "massive walls of ancient castles," the "standing army of officials" from the perennial "first families" monopolized most of the important positions in the government bureaucracy and served as a check to popular control. Only when election determined the composition of this bureaucracy would the power of the "official caste" be abrogated.[12]

The *News* opened its campaign on this front with a series of "Open Letters to Prominent Men" written by John Charles Dent, under the pseudonym Ranger. Appearing weekly, these letters were written as evaluations of the personal histories of the leaders of church and state. The second published letter, addressed to Charles Tupper, set off a storm of criticism throughout the Ontario press. Tupper's career was held up to critical scrutiny and found lacking. Opponents of the *News* did not challenge Dent's depiction of Tupper's lacklustre career. However, an old charge that Tupper had seduced a female patient while in medical practice was referred to obliquely in the letter. The *World* passed over the substantive charges, fastening on the obscure reference to seduction and charged that the "newspaper blackguards" and "sewer rats" in the editorial chairs at the *News* had overstepped the bounds of the permissible, hoping to redeem financial losses with an appeal to pru-

rient interest. Sheppard defended the Ranger letters and continued the series. He claimed that the foibles of public men were a
legitimate field for inquiry for a newspaper concerned with
"purifying public morals." He suggested that newspapers often
stooped to personal vituperation in the heat of a political campaign. However, at that time, few people ever took such charges
seriously, he concluded.[13]

Goldwin Smith followed the lead of W. F. McLean of the
World, publishing an attack in *The Week* on the *News* and the
Ranger letters soon after the letter on Tupper appeared. The
unrestricted wrath of Canada's leading man of letters in Canada's leading journal of literary opinion was vented on the "gang
of libellers" on the staff of the *News*. For Smith, they were a
mixture of "mendacious" journalists, "malignant" secularists,
and socialists intent on fomenting "class hatred." A greedy capitalist, "who would be equally ready to make money by the
ownership of a brothel," was the culprit whom Smith deemed
to have brought together these "purveyors of slander." The
Ranger letters attempted to provide a critical picture of the
backgrounds of Canadian public men and such public men
viewed these attacks with considerable alarm. The unanimous
denunciation by their literary defenders suggested that from the
beginning the *News* was perceived as a threat by established
Toronto journalism.[14]

Both Sheppard and Thompson viewed the vice-regal system
in Canada as the basis for false teachings on the superiority of a
gentility which preferred the "ragged edge of professional 'respectability'" to the life of the manual labourer. This form of
snobbery gave rise to a peculiar form of class consciousness:

> We see instances of it every day in Toronto in the ridiculous
> airs and pretensions of those who assume to constitute our
> upper tenth. Obsequious and grovelling before a lord or
> "sir," and consequently fooled . . . by any shrewd Englishman
> who travels on a bogus title, they are pompous, insolent in
> their demeanour to those whom they consider beneath them.
> They are apt to [stay] shy of the York pioneers, for the old
> residents often smile knowingly at their ostentatious display
> recalling with inconvenient precision of detail their early car-
> eer in a shop or tavern or kitchen. Many of our "first fami-
> lies," now notorious for their high-handed arrogance . . .
> spring from the very lowest rung of the society ladder. . . . In
> America, where we are all plebians together and wealth is the
> only test, [distinctions of rank] are not only odious, but ab-
> surd.

The focus for many similar "displays of snobbery" in Toronto
was the occasion of a vice-regal visit. The *News* condemned the

"tuft-hunting" and "hanging on to skirts" that occurred during Lord Landsdowne's visit in early 1884 as an affront to the "true nobility" of "moral worth or intellectual eminence." The *News* reporter covering the visit was ejected from a ball for the Governor-General held at the Royal Canadian Yacht Club because of the virulence of the *News'* attack on such proceedings. Thompson explained his denunciations of the relics of class distinction in the *Palladium* arguing that anything which suggested the permanent inferiority of one section of the community to another would serve as a "bulwark of capitalistic injustice." The English honours and awards that had been hastily invented to satisfy the vanity of colonial politicians helped to shore up such false values. They also tended to create rulers whose concerns for their fellow men took a back seat to their own quest for the badges of counterfeit respectability.[15]

The cruelty that the *News* felt was an inevitable by-product of a vice-regal system valuing obsequiousness was also reinforced by the role that militarism played in the dominant cultural ethos of English Canada in the 1880s. The military caste which grew up around such institutions as the Royal Military College at Kingston possessed a low opinion of the nobility of labour. A *News* editorial made this clear:

> Of all the curses with which a nation in the position of Canada could be afflicted, next to whiskey, the worst is the so-called military spirit. In this case, we shall not have the genuine article, bad as it is, but a shoddy imitation. The young swells who are attracted to this service know very well that there is one chance in a hundred of their ever being called upon to smell powder on the battlefield. It is the charms of an idle, lounging existence, rather than the "pride, pomp and circumstance of glorious war" which appeal to their feelings. "If there is anything," wrote James Russell Lowell, "more foolish than military glory, it is militia glory." And militia glory is the only kind that the warriors of the Royal Military Academy have any hankering after. It is outrageous that the hardworking people of Canada should be taxed to build up a caste of scarlet-coated and epauletted loaferism to eat the bread of idleness at their expense, and hold honest industry in contempt.

However, when one surveyed many of the local appointive institutions, it was found that those with military training found positions which further extended the influence of militarism. In law enforcement Chief of Police Draper brought with him to this office "inherited snobbishness . . . further developed by military training." "Shoulder strapped lounger" that he was, as Chief of Police he demanded from his inferiors "unquestioning obedience to the most arrogant orders and a grovelling servility of demeanour, such as the Old Country peasant observes in the presence of his landlord." Another pseudo-soldier Colonel Denison, found a position for himself as Police Magistrate. When those with military training found law enforcement positions in civilian life, strikers, drunks and other offenders felt their heavy hand helping to reinforce the authoritarianism which vice-regal offices could only suggest by example.[16]

The *News* also condemned all of the schemes to give the military caste a whiff of real gunpowder on overseas battlefields that were then being proposed by the nascent Imperial Federation movement. As well as reinforcing reactionary patterns of authority in Canadian society, Canadian contributions to British Imperial endeavours could only involve Canada in the oppression of other nationalities. The use of experienced Canadian raftsmen in Wolseley's 1884 expedition up the Nile encouraged the Canadian exponents of imperial federation (a "spaniel-like attachment to distant rule") in their attempts to get Canada involved in the British campaign against the Mahdi. That war which "cost the unfortunate masses of Britain so much blood and treasure" seemed designed for no other purpose than to secure "titles and pensions to so many blue-blooded aristocratic scions".[17]

Sheppard, however, made distinctions between such foreign adventures and the one domestic opportunity for unleashing the Canadian military during his ownership of the *News*. He pitched in enthusiastically to support the defeat of the North West Rebellion and the subsequent execution of Riel, even violating the Toronto sabbath by printing Sunday bulletins of news from the front. While the *News* probably gained much popularity from this support, Thompson felt only a profound sense of embarrassment at the jingoism of the paper. The bitterness and antagonism never surfaced in the pages of the *News* although Thompson, writing as Enjolras in the *Palladium*, did denounce the "Bloody Assize" at Regina which condemned Riel, saying that it would lower Canadians in the estimation of all civilized people.[18]

This society, in which martial virtues flourished, was supported in many ways by the world of high culture. As Claude Bissell has correctly pointed out, *The Week* served as a focus of "cultivated literary taste" in English Canada. It enshrined some of the attitudes of Matthew Arnold on the social necessity for a clerisy – that small group of learned men and women separated from the philistinism of everyday life, who were capable of creating enlightened opinion and social leadership. The *News* held *The Week* to its own high standards. How could such a journal, dedicated to enlightenment, sit in silence over the "nauseating sycophancy" of the Ottawa court circle where the Governor-General was a "third-rate Anglo-Irish lordling" whose devotion to culture was so slight that he refused to inaugurate the new Free Library on a visit to Toronto? Such protectors of culture could not be taken seriously. When they participated in political life they gathered about a Canadian "Mugwump" like Edward Blake who met the criterion of having the "supercilious standoffishness of the political aristocrat," although his actual abilities amounted to "trimming, shuffling evasion." For Thompson their kind of political activity always resolved itself into the narrow impotence of the Canada First Movement of the 1870s:

> It was never a popular movement. It was altogether confined to a little clique centred around Goldwin Smith – a fact in itself sufficient to secure its early demise. The aim of its leaders – and everyone connected with it was a "leader" – was to keep the organization "select." Instead of holding discussions in public halls they started a club on exclusive principles. It was a very nice party – as a dinner party. Any man who ate fish or peas with a knife was read out of it. Its adherents in Toronto never numbered more than a baker's dozen, but they all knew how to use their napkins and what finger bowls were for.... They complained that the old parties were run by cliques and as a remedy, they organized a clique to run a new party. They got the clique all right, but the party did not come forward and ask them to please be so kind as to run it.... In fact some humorists said during the days when it existed, the Canada First Party is "Goldwin's Myth."

To the *News*, the Canadian clerisy never applied its standards rigorously enough to Canadian politicians and public life. As a result, it was not surprising that the partisan rascality it decried so loudly always emerged triumphant over the finest efforts of its "best men."[19]

Little of positive value emerged from the exclusive debates of the elevated guardians of culture. Moreover, much of their work not only reinforced the cruelty and power of Canada's "leading" citizens, but also fostered harmful notions about the political and social potential of the "masses." On many occasions the *News* confronted Goldwin Smith's arguments against the strategy of general combination of the Knights of Labor, gasping in mock disbelief at the way he tortured and twisted the time worn canons of classical political economy to fit his purpose. In early 1884, the *News* examined the theories of Matthew Arnold, who had been making a lecture tour of Canada. The points at issue between democracy and clerisy were clearly elucidated in an editorial:

The most perceptible flaw in the lecturer's reasoning is the non-recognition of the fact that the great majority are neither "bad," as he puts it, nor yet good in the highest acceptation of the term. Human nature is a compound and strangely mixed article. Men are subject to conflicting passions. They act from mixed motives.... It is unscientific and unphilosophical to speak of men in the mass as "bad" or "good".... In estimating the worth and weight of the average mass of humanity, and the effect of their influence upon social order and national life, why in the name of fairness and justice are their virtues ignored?... There is an immense reserve fund of latent courage, endurance and heroism in the masses of the people which is only to be called out by the stress and strain of extraordinary crisis. We hold that the good sense and natural instincts of the masses are a safer guide than the learning and the reason of the cultivated few.

Sheppard and Thompson went on to attempt to direct the "good sense and natural instincts" towards a political economy not bound by the dead hand of the past and a theory of culture which did not rely upon an aristocracy of superior men. Many of the logical conclusions Thompson would have liked to make in the *News*, he was forced to make in the *Palladium*. Both sources give a sense of a carefully developed political economy worked out with an eye to popular acceptance and an effort to correct prejudices. Although they may have been "self-appointed tribunes of the people," the opposition that they strove to create would come to nothing without broad popular support.[20]

The *News* began its effort at constructing a new political economy with a highly empirical examination of the effects of industrialization. Many of the local news features were far more than examples of sensationalist yellow journalism, indeed they brilliantly documented the ravages of industrial capitalism. The series of articles, "Toronto by Gaslight" (May 19 – June 7, 1884), dealt with most of the seamier aspects of Toronto night life of the time. While this might have appealed to some readers as vicarious entertainment, it probably struck most readers as evidence of social degeneration. Similar articles on the misfortunes of the Toronto poor were a continuing feature of the *News*. Articles appeared from time to time describing the Police Court, the House of Industry, the Gaol and other institutions which dealt with the unfortunate. The *News* also kept a sharp eye on such schemes as the one by which Toronto capitalists had applied for a provincial charter that would enable them to expropriate humble residences for the construction of tenements. The former homeowner was destined to become "the inmate of a huge human hive." Editorially the *News* was very specific about the reasons for the development of an urban *lumpenproletariat*:

> With the growth of great cities in the United States, as well as in other countries there has come into existence a large and increasing class – the failures of our social system – who have nothing to hope for and nothing to lose. The pressure of competition in every department of industry has driven them to the wall. For them anarchy has no terrors—nay it may even be welcome as a relief from the monotony of arduous and ill-requited toil, or enforced idleness. Such a class, which has always existed in the cities of Europe and is only kept in subjection by police and military establishments on a great scale, has now been developed under the changed conditions of American life and industry resulting from the tremendous influx of immigration, the increase of city populations, and the exhaustion of the supply of land.

Proceeding from an empirical survey of the development of urban poverty, the *News* exposed "the delusions which had obtained that the masses of the people have been largely benefited by the enormous industrial expansion of the age."[21]

The monopolization of resources and land had turned most of the themes of classical political economy into empty platitudes. On the "so-called free continent of America" where most workers were now dependent on large scale industry for their livelihood, the freedom of contract had come to mean very little. Exploitation could not be avoided by going elsewhere. In an Enjolras column Thompson castigated Goldwin Smith for urging this as a solution to the labour question:

> It is a wearisome task to thresh over again such chaff and to repeat the very A,B,C of the discussions.... [Smith] repeats the old platitude about workingmen being free to leave their employers if they choose.... Suppose Prof. Goldwin Smith, on his recent voyage back from England, had been deprived of comfortable accomodation and made to sleep on the deck; that he had been robbed of needful food and kept on bread and water; and then on remonstrating with the captain, had been told: "Well, my dear sir, there's no need for you to stay on this ship for a moment longer than you wish. You are at perfect liberty to get out and walk!" Wouldn't he have thought that this was adding insult to injury?

The realities faced by labour in the industrial workplace rendered the free market an unsatisfactory method of solving the impoverishment of labour. In fact, the mechanism of the market and the operation of supply and demand contributed to this continuing impoverishment of the workingman. As a reaction to the changed conditions of industry the outline of a new strategy began to appear. Connected with the Knights of Labor, it was broadly international in character and sought humane control over the means of production rather than simple amelioration of particular conditions through the "old trade union method of isolated action on the part of each individual class of worker."[22]

A new political economy was needed that did not simply analyse and describe the chaos of industrial capitalism. Those trained in classical political economy could wax eloquent on the problem of "overproduction," but would blanch at the thought of any general limitation of the hours of work by which cyclical inflation and stagnation might be replaced with equilibrium. In the "universal democracy" which Enjolras pictured, the state would play a leading role in the "superintendance and direction" of all industrial functions. The captain of industry had played a creative role in taming the absolute chaos of earlier eras. The logic of his work should continue and the enterprises he founded brought under public control. Thompson chided Herbert Spencer for his analysis in *Man versus the State* of the reforms of the preceding quarter century as an encroaching "new Toryism." Whatever control or restriction that these reforms had imposed was to be praised. In place of the uncertainty that strikes posed to working men in their individual unions through competition and scabbing, a general combination of labour would be able to force a favourable system of arbitration by which industrial disputes could be worked out diplomatically. Thompson had been deeply influenced by Spencer's notion of gradual social evolution and it formed a crucial aspect of his thought. The new kind of opposition suggested required patience with the evolutionary workings of history. The idea that the struggle for labour reform would have its outcome in some distant epoch was an important contribution to the creation of a new political and cultural strategy.[23]

The city of the future would be so altered in form and intent that it would scarcely be recognizable to one steeped in the present. The permanent opposition that would bring about this millennium was sustained by the belief that humanity had been slowly transforming itself from epoch to epoch, and that the improvements in the life of earlier times, visible from the perspective of the nineteenth century, had been wrought by the persistence of the long line of opponents of fraudulent monopoly who first voiced their arguments in "homely Saxon speech." The seed planted by the nineteenth century journalist would bear fruit in the next epoch.[24]

Roadblocks in the path to the millennium were everywhere. It seemed futile to hope that labour conflict or violent activity by revolutionaries would lead to anything but unequivocal defeat in North American society. The *News* had supported the locked-out employees of the Toronto Street Railway in a dispute with management that lasted on and off over four months. Despite an alternative transportation service provided by a strikers' cooperative, the support of the reform mayor, William Howland, and widespread public sympathy for the strikers and hostility to management, the strike was broken. The disruption of the lives of these men and their families and of those who participated in other strikes during the years of the Knights of Labor upsurge brought home to the journalists on the *News* that strikes were always uncertain of success and that lost strikes retarded the growth of a working class movement. The full force of the police and the courts reinforced the rights of management and were brought to bear hardest in any strike where there was the slightest hint of violence. In the case of violence explicitly designed to foment revolution, it seemed clear after 1886 that such activity was counter-productive. Thompson differentiated between serious philosophic anarchists like Kropotkin and the random violence which was widely condemned in the press as the "anarchistic tendencies of the age." He explained the occurrence of such violence which he deplored as the natural reaction of people beset by frustration and deprivation:

> There is not a day passes in London in which there are not ten times as many poor victims who go down to death in the terrible struggle for existence [as do by anarchist bombing]. ... Custom has so blinded men to the consequences of the fearful state of social anarchy in which we live at all these daily and hourly tragedies are passed by as ordinary incidents, while the infinitely smaller amount of suffering resulting from the dynamite explosions is the signal for a howl of vengeance and an outburst of flaming indignation.[25]

Sheppard took an easier route than Enjolras did on the question. He added to the general denunciation of the anarchists by suggesting that the Chicago anarchists should be hanged and that support for them could only damage the Knights of Labor. The *News* earned a slap on the wrist from Enjolras for disseminating such "capitalistic flapdoodle." In an editorial responding to Enjolras' attack (which Thompson probably helped write) the *News* demanded an apology from Enjolras for his "mistaken sympathy." Any violence, no matter how trivial or minor, seemed to bring down upon the labour movement a wholesale condemnation which attributed such actions to the efforts of anti-social agitators and demogogues. Thompson noted that words like *socalist* could no longer be carelessly or even scientifically used. The primitive red-baiting that appeared in the press after every bomb exploded convinced Thompson that the long revolution by which labour might regenerate the world should be an eminently peaceful one.

In the sphere of practical politics many ingenious methods were inaugurated to prevent the defection of workingmen from the traditional parties. In the federal election of 1887, E. E. Sheppard ran as an independent labour candidate in West Toronto and he encountered the concerted and unified opposition of both *The Week* and the traditional parties. The Liberals, however, conceding that they had no chance in a Tory stronghold, ran no candidate, thus making it a two-way race. *The Week* accused Sheppard of attempting to foment class hatred and working class domination of the community and of serving as one of the "liegemen" of a vast organization with its headquarters in a foreign country (that is, the Knights of Labor). It also noted that Sheppard and his ilk were "not really representative of labour at all, but professional incendiaries trading on the labour agitation, who, instead of having the 'scars of labour' have nothing to show but the inkstains of malignity and libel." After a long and relatively successful campaign in which Thompson spoke often for Sheppard, Sheppard lost to the Tory candidate by 547 votes (3891-3344) despite the unfailing support of Toronto's third largest daily paper.[27]

The *News* recognized the continuing attraction of traditional parties for members of the working class community. Enjolras understood how the "enthusiasm of numbers, the social pressure of old friendships, the excitements of the campaigns" worked their magic. The traditional political campaign with its torchlight parades, stump oratory which was skillfully prepared, and a large number of solicitous ward heelers made it possible for men like John A. Macdonald, the creator of the C.P.R., Edward Blake, the Chancery lawyer, and Alexander Mackenzie, the one-time master mason turned insurance company executive to masquerade as the "workingman's friend." Evocations of a vague sense of national duty usually succeeded in blinding workingmen to their own best interests. Patronage enabled the party in power to set up pseudo-working class organizations like the Workingmen's Liberal Conservative Association of Canada which, in return for patronage for its members, provided a "workingmen's forum" for John A. Macdonald in the late 1870s and throughout the 1880s. Most of the appointees to the Royal Commission on the Relations of Labor and Capital of 1886 were given their positions in return for service to the party on the labour front. As "wishful thinkers," the *News* men possessed keen insights into the cultural and social basis of Canadian politics and the attractions it had for working people. They did not propose the millennium through rose-coloured glasses.[28]

The *News* did not hold the workingman solely responsible for the failure of independent political activity. If the political party was skilled in seducing working class voters, the realm of popular culture also worked effectively to dissuade the workingman from an independent course. Thompson suggested that the all-pervading influence of "copy book morality" deceived the worker with the false promise that by harder work, sobriety, diligence and the avoidance of unsavoury radicals he could escape the fate of his fellow workers:

> Writers such as Samuel Smiles and the whole tribe of cheap moralists are never tired of peddling out their platitudinous sermons about the rewards that are sure to attend industry and the certain punishment that awaits idleness and improvidence.

The just and fulsome reward of the exemplary conduct of self-made men was recounted every day in the press and on Sunday in the sermon. The eventual success through perseverance of the mythical "penniless Yankee boy, pacing the streets of New York or Chicago with the determination to make his fortune" obscured the multitude of failures who "struggled in vain, and live on in poverty, or fill unknown graves."[29]

The omnipresent Horatio Alger myth showed the way to a fuller understanding of "education" in the emerging culture:

> The whole tendency of modern education – not merely in the restricted sense of book-learning, but in the broader significance which includes every influence which shapes men's thoughts and contributes to their intellectual and moral development – is to make rascals. The teaching of the fireside and the school, the newspaper and the platform, by inference if not by precept, encourage the spirit of acquisitiveness. The boy from his earliest years is exhorted to "be somebody"–to aspire to rise in the world. . . . Even in church and the Sunday school, religious precepts are intermingled with worldly-wise counsel.

The informal teaching of everyday life merged with formal instructions to inculcate atomistic, competitive attitudes. The obvious strategy presented itself to a journalist:

> We have to create a revolution in public opinion before we can hope to revolutionize the system. We have to change not only men's formally expressed beliefs, but their aspirations and desires – to eradicate the deep-rooted selfishness begotten of competition and to instill in its place a love for humanity and a strong sense of justice.

Thompson placed a great deal of responsibility for the failure of independent action on the shoulders of the "'colonels' of the garrison of capitalism," the intelligentsia, who created and maintained the prevailing cultural institutions.[30]

Thompson proposed that a major effort at undoing "centuries of false education" should be directed towards "brainworkers," the heretofore "sycophantic, abject creatures" who staffed the various enterprises of the literary world. Disabused of the false notions of superiority to the manualist who was often better paid, this "intellectual proletariat" could form the spearhead of an independent movement once it had realized its lot was no better than that of any other worker. The Knights of Labor organized the Toronto L.A. 7814, Victor Hugo Assembly for non-manual workers; Thompson and a group of other journalists and white collar workers formed the membership. In confronting the newspaper Thompson thought it was similar to every other form of business enterprise:

> The modern daily newspaper is a big capitalistic machine. It represents hundreds of thousands of dollars and to earn dividends for its stockholders it must stand in with all forms of monopoly and legalized thievery. If it told the truth and stood up for right and justice its advertising patrons would leave it. So it lies. It hires editors to pervert the truth and present the public with distorted views of history and philosophy and political economy. Some of these men are honest because they have not brains enough to think for themselves and accept current opinions on these subjects. Others know better but cannot afford to be true to their convictions. If they were they could not get employment. The monopolist organs would have no use for them.

The brainworker and manual worker had common interests. Once the journalist and literary hack stopped complaining that "the miserable, underpaid position of intellectual labor" was the result of an "unappreciative public," he would naturally come to confront the capitalist who exploited his labour as he would that of any other worker. Once this occurred, the brain-worker might begin to transform the role that culture played in maintaining the iniquities of the social system.[31]

A body of active intellectual workers would also cease to support the present system by which mediocre literature was promoted by second-rate "charlatans." Thompson regretted the passing from vogue of the old masters and saw little to praise in the work of what Claude Bissell has termed the "multitude of clever aspirants" who sought to don their mantles through shameless self-promotion. The News mourned the "great chasm in the ranks of European literature" left at the passing of Victor Hugo who was described as a "true, tried, and steadfast friend of the people – the ideal democrat – the believer in the progress and freedom of humanity." The average contemporary writer was a man of "bourgeois education" which stifled "every generous feeling" and who felt his best interests lay in the flattery of "the prejudices of society." A wide gulf separated him from the likes of Gibbon, Macaulay, Parkman, Carlyle, Burns, Emerson, Lowell, Whittier, Whitman, Longfellow, and Wendell Phillips who formed the pantheon of Enjolras' heroes. No matter how much vice-regal patronage the newly formed Royal Society of Canada spread over the seed bed of Canadian literature, no great literature would arise until fundamental changes had taken place to rid the world of culture of the astringent effects of bourgeois education.[32]

Despite the difficulties, the contours of a vigorous new intellectual life seemed to be forming. Along with the cruelty and hardship associated with the rise of the mass market in industrial society, a valuable democratization of culture had occurred:

A man writes a book. What is to determine whether it is to become a classic and a textbook or to cumber the shelves of a second hand bookstore for awhile and then be forgotten? Why the favour of the class for which it is written! Only within the last generation or so have books been written for the masses. What chance would a book like *Progress and Poverty* have of obtaining the endorsement of the very class at whose unjust privileges it is aimed? Fifty years ago such a book would have fallen dead. It could not have obtained a constituency. The rich and well-to-do classes, then almost the only book buyers – no cheap editions in those days – would have scouted it as a seditious, dangerous publication, and the poor in their ignorance would never have heard of it. It is only the cheap press and popular education that have made its success possible. To how many obscure, unheard of men, the same idea may have occurred we have no means of knowing. Had a thousand men entertained it at a time when education was the monopoly of the rich and literature the slave and creature of Mammon, it could never have been popularized.

The growth of the reading public was seen as a positive, energizing feature in cultural life, giving birth to new perspectives on social problems. The *News* also applauded the participation of English men of education like William Morris and H. M. Hyndman who had thrown aside the traditions of social caste to make a common cause with the people. The "regenerating" influence of a great cause – the cause of Labour Reform – would make its influence felt throughout politics, literature and society. The cynicism and snobbery which prevailed would be swept away. However, the democratization of culture intensified the need for intellectual and moral leadership. For a democratic culture offered new opportunities for capitalist enterprise and control as well as for the creation of a more humane social order. Phillips Thompson held up the anti-slavery crusade as an example for labour reformers:

> [The men who worked up the American anti-slavery movement] were men of sterling principle and intense convictions, bound to stick to a cause which in their inmost souls they believed to be righteous and all important, through good report and evil report, in adversity as well as in prosperity, even unto death. They weren't afraid of adverse majorities, nor the sneers of time servers and trimmers. Nor the laughter of fools and toadies. They had the courage of their opinions and they struggled bravely on though deserted by false friends and popularity hunters. They were enlisted for the war and they didn't expect it was going to be a summer day's picnic – or that it was going to be settled in one year or a dozen years.[33]

· The *News* served the cause of Labor Reform in Toronto for slightly less than four years. On November 23, 1887, having fallen behind in his mortgage payments, Sheppard was forced to turn the *News* back over to the Riordans who promised to maintain an editorial policy as "thoroughly independent" as that of Sheppard. His funds had been depleted in a libel suit brought by a Montreal regiment that Kribs had suggested was lax in fighting the North-West Rebellion in 1885. Sheppard and Thompson both left the *News* and the older group of Riordan employees stayed on, with Thomas Gregg assuming the editorship. Three years later Sheppard quarrelled bitterly with Thompson, sneering that Thompson had a "nature as gentle as a girl's" and that he would spend the whole day trying to figure out how to get to work without stepping on a potato bug. In an 1893 address to the Canadian Press Association, Sheppard cynically suggested that to conduct a journal as a moulder of public opinion was a good way to go bankrupt. For the most part Thompson recalled his days on the *News* fondly, claiming in 1891 that it had been under Sheppard's editorship, "a genuine Labor Reform paper, going further in this respect than any Toronto daily had ever done before...." Nostalgia did not modulate the acidity of the satire when Thompson used a candid letter from a society columnist, which Sheppard had become, to expose the vapidity and uncertain manliness of such a profession. The society editor explained his job to *Grip*:

> ...I can always arrange my materials in print so as to mean anything or nothing. It always seems tolerably safe, however, to scorn the Female movement. Last week I had a fling at women as druggists, and I certainly should never call in a

lady physician, if one can imagine such a very *bizarre* sort of person!...And yet the ladies chiefly admire my inanities about this, that and t'other. Many of my correspondents actually inquire whether I am really a lady or a gentleman, and it seems difficult to convince them. Occasionally I am in doubt myself.[34]

While they worked at the *News* the tension that later degenerated into name-calling was profoundly creative. For four years at the height of the Knights' agitation, Toronto's largest evening daily was a source of radical ideas, a great organizational and educational aid to the Knights, and a journal of uncommon intellectual vitality. Phillips Thompson's book, *The Politics of Labor*, has recently been described as a "constructive minor critique of the American political-economic system"; in fact, it was in many ways the culmination of these years of frenetic activity, reflecting the high hopes and bitter disappointments of an endeavour that was meant to be neither "minor" nor "constructive." The *News* contributed imaginatively to the growth of a working class movement during Sheppard's tenure. Without it, the Toronto Knights of Labor would have been immeasurably poorer. The relationship between the radical intellectual and the trade unionist was not one of automatic compatability in the 1880s. The Knights served as an opportunity for brainworkers to help to create new forms of opposition as well as to critically explore the world of their own work. The attempts of these early radicals to push labour to an independent course did not meet with automatic success. However, it is incorrect to argue from the failure to put across a specific course of action that they had no effect whatever. While these "wishful thinkers" may seem less ostensibly successful than the practical thinkers of social democracy, or even the non-utopian thinkers of a series of sectarian movements, they helped forge a response to the ravages of industrial capitalism when there were few blueprints to follow. If Canadian workers in the twentieth century were truly less hostile to collectivist ideology, it probably had more to do with the real experience these pioneers helped shape during the upsurge of the Knights than with the mysterious workings of a fragment culture.[35]

Finally, a study of the *News* under Sheppard demonstrates how shallow it is to analyze cultural activity by the objects it produces. Such analysis has often suggested that the growth of the reading public resulted in a degeneration of the "ideal of literary excellence." In this vein, Stephen Leacock complained that the "everlasting man with the dinner pail" had become the arbiter of cultural standards, demanding that newspapers be "written down to his level." To judge the *News* superficially by its purported proclivities to yellow journalism is to ignore both the major themes that it succeeded in publicizing and to ignore the process by which it was produced. When these latter elements are analyzed dispassionately, the lowered cultural standards of the newspaper written for the masses are less evident. If anything, the *News* men raised the level of debate in Toronto to heights where the journals of elevated literary opinion felt less than comfortable. Furthermore, their analysis of the world of literature and journalism integrated culture and society in a way which broke through the classical separation of the world of action from the world of the mind. Industrialization did not automatically decree that cultural activity would resolve itself into various ranks, roughly corresponding to the various levels of the social order. The divisions between popular culture and high culture were not as compelling to many late nineteenth century figures who, in retrospect, only appear to have laboured all their days in inferior cultural enterprises. The education and elevation of public opinion through a popular daily seemed to be the natural work of intellectuals in the late nineteenth century. While they may have satisfied certain popular needs uncritically, their larger perspective involved a more humane social order. The difficulty that we experience in understanding a world where vital minds could be fulfilled by working on a popular daily like the *News* is a measure of the magnitude of their failure.[36]

Respected and Profitable Labour
Literacy, Jobs and the
Working Class in the Nineteenth Century

Harvey J. Graff

In 1848, Egerton Ryerson, The Chief Superintendent of Education for Canada West, addressed himself to, "The Importance of Education to a Manufacturing, and a Free People." Commencing from the premise that a system of mass education was prerequisite to a system of manufacturing – the symbol of the incoming social order – he proclaimed that "education is designed to prepare us for the duties of life." While moral principles and values of social order dominated among these duties, the importance of proper preparation for work was not lost to Ryerson. Moreover, he asked, "how is the uneducated and unskilled man to succeed in these times of sharp and skilful competition and sleepless activity?" Education he must have; it was a natural right of each child "to receive such an education as will fit him for the duties of life."[1]

One year later, Ryerson enlarged upon his view, bringing the role of literacy more specifically into play. Discussing "Canadian Mechanics and Manufactures," he claimed that the mechanic

> will be a member of society; and, as such, he should know how to read and write the language spoken by such society .... This supposes instruction in the grammar or structure of his native tongue.

Social order and society were the supreme beneficiaries of all education in Ryerson's archetypical Anglo-American world-view. To his eyes and mind, "educated labour is more productive than uneducated labour." Workers with a common school grounding were thus thought to be less disruptive, superior workmen, orderly, punctual, and of good conduct. In all, the "proper education of the mechanic is important to the interests of society as well as to his own welfare and enjoyment."[2]

Yet, the key question was more complex than Ryerson's statements would allow. Just how important have literacy and education been to occupational and economic success? Traditional wisdom, modern sociology, the canons of modernity and nineteenth century school promoters all sang out the praises of education and the skills of literacy in the determination of success. Yet, not all the evidence, past or present, lends credence to this view. Consider this:

58

Wanted immediately FORTY ABLE BODIED MEN, to serve as JUSTICES OF THE PEACE, for the COUNTY OF HURON. A plain English Education is desirable but not indispensable – each candidate however must be able to make his mark, unless he has learned to write his name, and will be expected to produce a character signed by the Deputy Commissioner of the Board of Works and the Collector of Customs Goderich.

and

[For all children,] except the 10 per cent who will earn a living by the use of their verbal ability there is a case for substituting practical for academic education.[3]

The relationship of education in general, and the skills of literacy in particular, to work and occupation remains an imprecise one, complex and often contradictory. This study is devoted to an explication of the relationship, examining both the real and perceived connections surrounding the economic value of education. The views of middle class school promoters and reformers and those of the working class will be examined. The literacy levels and differentials of the urban Ontario working class will be explored, as well as the intellectual context of the discussion of the economic importance of education. Finally, a case study based on the employment contract ledgers of an Ontario lumbering firm will be offered: an attempt to isolate the importance of literacy to working men in a specific social situation. The thrust of the essay is to illuminate the contradictions in the perceived connections between education, as measured by literacy, and employment level, to show that literacy was not always so central to jobs and earnings in the nineteenth century.

The terms *education* and *literacy* thus far have been employed interchangeably. This has been done purposefully. However, they do not have the same meaning. Education implies the broader process of socialization and acculturation in addition to mere schooling, while literacy applies much more specifically to the cognitive skills of reading and writing. It is essential that this difference in meaning be understood. However, measures of education, necessary to test the opinions of the value of schooling to a workingman, are scarce at best. Literacy has the advantage, although it correlates indirectly with years of schooling and regularity of attendance, of providing a simple index of the presence or absence of some education in the individual case. In this way it serves as a proxy for education, and will be employed as that symbol as well as in its more specific connotation.

Industry, skill, and wealth could be individually obtained without education, yet education itself was viewed as central to the development and the maintenance of the economic system, as it was to the social order. This was the claim of the nineteenth century schoolman: educated and literate labour was more productive and of more benefit to both society and the individual. As Egerton Ryerson claimed, "every man, unless he wishes to starve outright, must read and write, and cast accounts, and speak his native tongue well enough to attend to his own particular business."[4]

Ryerson long felt that education underlay any of the main branches of career pursuits. In his first report, of 1846, he laid the foundation,

> the establishment of a thorough system of primary and industrial education, commensurate with the population of the country, as contemplated by the Government, and is here proposed, is justified by considerations of economy as well as of patriotism and humanity.

He further argued, employing evidence from Switzerland, that uneducated workers have neither logic, power of systematic arrangement, capacity for making sound deductions, nor collecting observations. Furthermore, "this want of capacity of mental arrangements is shown in their manual operations." Quite simply, it was the well-informed, well-educated workers who were thought to produce the most and the best, to possess superior moral habits, and to save. Uneducated, illiterate workers did not.[5]

There was little doubt or hesitation in proclaiming the benefits of education to the individual worker or the economic system. Yet, it is important to note as does Alison Prentice that "statements relating specific occupational groups to social status tended to be vague and contradictory." To Ryerson there were but two kinds of labour. Workers were either "rude, simple or uneducated" or they were educated. These were the classes of society, as status increasingly included demeanour and gentility as well as the skills obtained. "And by skills, few school promoters meant manual dexterity." Literacy was just one such skill, an important one but not the only one. The benefits of education were not to be simple or direct, following from the advantages of literary training. They involved the inculcation of the proper code of behaviour, which included morality and savings. Literacy revealed that process had begun.[6]

More than upward mobility through education, Ryerson emphasized the loss of status and downward mobility which he claimed would accompany the lack of schooling. Educated men might advance; the uneducated would surely fall. The burden he placed on the shoulders of the fathers:

Does a man wish his sons to swell the dregs of society – to proscribe them from all situations of trust and duty in the locality of their abode – to make them mere slaves in the land of freedom? Then let him leave them without education, and their underfoot position in society will be decided upon.

Additionally, Ryerson taught that all men were not to be educated to despise their occupations. Not all should aspire to the highest statuses of work. Practical men were needed too, and the supply of farmers and mechanics must not diminish. Education therefore could not alienate labour; it should not, for labour, he claimed, did not deaden the mind. The ideal mechanic then would combine "in his own person, the qualifications and skills" of both the manufacturing superintendent and the operative.[7] In sum, all members of the working class required that which "is essential to the successful pursuit of any one of the several departments of human activity and enterprise." This was "what is rudimental, or elementary in education." In addition to this – reading, writing, arithmetic, and grammar, – "each must learn that which will give him skill in his own particular employments,"[8] all the while making for more productive and more easily managed labour, advancing the nation's development. The individual came not first, in the benefits of education.

Ryerson of course was not an isolated spokeman for the economic benefits of education, for he was joined by many others throughout Anglo-America.[9] To a certain extent the spokesmen of the labour movement in Canada (and the United States) tended to agree with the voices of the middle-class school promoters when the benefits of education were discussed. Yet, to an important degree, labour's views were marked by a tension between a hunger for public schooling and doubts about the value of that form of education. As well, education represented to them something more than the making of better workmen.

That workmen desired educational provisions cannot be doubted. Their case was put forth in the first issue of the *Ontario Workman* in 1872: "a thorough and general system of education we consider to be one of the first duties of the state; to see that in all its branches it is placed as near as possible within the reach of every son and daughter of the land." The whole body of workmen should be raised by education and mental training to a higher intellectual level, not merely to permit isolated cases of social advancement. As the Hamilton *Palladium of Labor* claimed, "an education is the practical side of American industrial success. In the industries where your working people have the best common school education, there you will find them earning the best wages." This situation, however, was related to the absence of child labour and therefore to the absence of cheap competition. Education cut two ways in its benefits for working men: education was valuable in raising and maintaining wages and standards of labour, all the while it restricted the supply of workers. Yet, simultaneously, "educated workmen, skilled workmen, and moral workmen ... [made] labor respected as well as profitable." Can we doubt that respect was less important than profit.

To make better workers was not the sole emphasis of the labour press, and their educational program was not quite that which Ryerson *et al.* had urged. Education ought to be mechanical, scientific, and technical: for the hand and body as well as the mind. They recommended a combination of work and study, four hours of each per day, certainly not the common school education of Ryerson. Literacy was at best a part of this process.[10]

Yet education was not primarily viewed as job preparation; it represented a higher ideal. A boy "should be regarded, rather as the man that will be, than as the future doctor, lawyer, tradesman, farmer or mechanic." Would such education intersect with economic productivity? The *Workman* suggests that workers were not to be educated to increase the value of capital through their labours. They were not simply *to be* educated: "they must educate themselves to think; they must also learn to think for themselves." To a large degree, education was to instil a direction, a goal, and the correct set of personal qualities – all more important than either skills or a mere hunger for gold. Education was, in one sense, character-building: it enabled workers to see their calling as useful and dignified. Morals, wisdom, and honourable careers ranked above the skills of the job. Were such men to be the loyal, punctual, non-disruptive workers the mill-owners desired, and Egerton Ryerson had promised if allowed to fashion a system of common schools? Education could lead to a rather different direction as the *Palladium* saw it:

> Educate first, agitate afterwards. Ignorance, superstition and timerity are the weapons which our oppressors have used most effectively against us in the past. Secure an education at any cost, put the ballot to its proper use, and then the fall of the venerable structure of legal robbery, alias monopoly, will shake to its centre. ... [11]

Furthermore, the working class was more than a bit ambivalent about education and its value; this tension brought contradiction to their apparent endorsement of mass education:

'A self-made man' awakens in most all a glow of appreciation and regard which we do not feel for the man, equally distinguished for ability and learning he has got, who has been regularly taught in the schools. The one has had the countersign, and has been invited into the fort, the other has scaled the ramparts and conquered his place.

Success without the benefit of education was admired above that "aided" by the schools, sharply contrasting with Ryerson's view. A curious tale related in the *Workman* indicates a further lack of regard for education-related skills. A man in England, the story went, had been jailed. To obtain bail, he was advised that he must sign his name. Overnight he taught himself to do so. The implications drawn were important; there was no *a priori* reason for illiterates or poor workers to be barred from the ballot. Inability to read or write need not disqualify a man from exercising his rights nor did it signify an inability to carry them out. A final point is implied. When needed, one could quickly and easily gain the skills of literacy.[12]

Ambivalence went even further. For example, *Fincher's Trades Review* reprinted "Proverbs of the Billings Family," which included "if you kan't git clothes and education too, git the clothes." A more interesting notice came from the Lawrence, Massachusetts, Mutual Benefit Society. The society began its operations with a system of bookkeeping for accounts, but:

We are now doing it with checks. Our checks are printed on cardboard, of the following denominations ... fifty cents, white; one dollar, blue; two dollar, pink; three dollar, yellow; five dollar, orange; ten dollar, salmon color. We find that this system is much easier than booking....

Storemen and members need not even know the decimal system or how to read numbers; the colours differentiated for them. Literacy or schooling need not figure in workers' everyday transactions.

More important, perhaps, was the view that the present system of education was beset with certain evils. The *Palladium* urged its readers to learn a trade, not to be seduced by class education, with its examples in school of millionaires, for "schools love to dwell too much on the achievements of professional men." The school curriculum itself was found to be class-biased and the ideas of classical literature antiworkingmen; "it is generally felt that our educational methods are one-sided." Or, as Phillips Thompson expressed it, education "if perverted by the inculcation of the untruths and half-truths of bourgeois political economy, is a hindrance rather than a help." This he called "wrong education," tempting the worker with self-aggrandizement and wealth. And, the system of state education, compulsory by the 1870s, taught reading and "then gives them dime novels for perusal, having previously given them a taste for such reading." Such an education was not desirable; it would not benefit the workingman.[13]

The greatest evil of all rested at the pinnacle of the educational system – the university, which all working-men supported by taxation, but whose expense was prohibitive to most:

> It is an injustice that all the farmers, mechanics, and laborers should be taxed to teach the sons of the wealthy merchants and professional men Greek and Latin, and to support a lot of imported professors at high salaries to inculcate false and undemocratic notions of social caste, and teach an obsolete system of political economy. As a training for practical life and usefulness the ordinary university education is well-nigh valueless.

The educational system, from the top down, was biased against the workingman and his children. Lest the working class be falsely accused of anti-intellectualism, we must note that the *Palladium* urged that as good an education could be secured by well-directed reading.[14]

Reading, moreover, was often discussed (particularly in the pages of The *Ontario Workman*) in terms of amusement, enchantment, comfort, consolation, and leisure. "Let the torch of intelligence be lit in every household." The family hearth was the place for reading to begin, for the taste for reading ("one of the true blessings of life") to be found, and where parents were to guard against the taint of bad books, magazines, or newspapers. Relief from toil came through literature, making "study the more refreshing," and the delights of reading and contemplation brought wisdom "in common with all mankind." Here lay one real value of literacy to the workman. Knowledge is "always power," but this sense was not economic or material.[15]

Similarly, there were reasons more important than book-learning in the establishment of mechanics' institutes, working men's reading rooms and ancillary public institutions. Workmen needed a place to become better acquainted with one another, where their various interests could "harmonize," where committees could meet. Two hours of leisure each day spent in mental and physical culture "would result in the shame and discomfiture of our opponents. ... " Knowledge was power, in the purely political sense, much as Phillips Thompson would have it. Yet mass literacy need not be a requirement for the development of a shared consciousness, political culture, or the exchange of ideas or information. Merely a few readers could enlighten a greater number given the chance of congregation. As E. P. Thompson argued, "Illiteracy by no means excluded men from political discourse." They could listen and discuss. Activities such as those of "Captain Swing" give validity to the argument, for it was the areas lowest in literacy that experienced the greatest amount of action. Moreover, it can not be obscured that "the ability to read was only the elementary technique. The ability to handle abstract and consecutive argument was by no means inborn; it had to be discovered amid almost overwhelming difficulties...." Much more than literacy or education is related to cohesion, consciousness, and activity; factors of social structure, economics, psychology, leadership and organization, numbers, and opportunity are equally if not more important. Easier communications, which literacy may advance, may aid the process, but literacy is hardly the key variable.[16]

Labour, in spite of an apparent clamour for equal educational opportunity, deviated from the premises of leading schoolmen who sought more education of the workforce for greater productivity. Ambivalent about the proper role, form, and content of education, and often placing its benefits and applications quite aside from their jobs, they sought to be free and independent, powerful in ways which would not please the men who desired to have the masses educated. More fundamentally, they did not always equate education with the skills required to gain a good job. Their notions of education and the uses of literacy were hardly the same as those of the schoolmen.

In the face of these discussions and arguments about the needs, uses, and benefits of education and literacy, what was the social distribution of literacy and what rewards did it bring? The question will be approached on two levels: first, the urban Ontario workforce at large, as revealed in routinely-generated census records, and second, the worker in a specific setting, the lumber industry.

Ontario in the 1860s and 1870s was an overwhelmingly literate society. Adult (twenty years and older) literacy ranged over ninety per cent as measured by the censuses of those years. In terms of wealth and occupation, there was a significant amount of stratification relating to illiteracy, for the majority of illiterates were employed as semi- and unskilled workmen. Yet, large numbers of men, lacking education, assumed positions of skill. These positions, moreover, were maintained over the course of the decade 1861 and 1871.[17]

One hundred and thirty-five illiterates in Hamilton, Kingston, and London, Ontario, held skilled labouring and artisanal occupations in 1861; forty-four held higher ranking jobs. Open to at least some illiterates were the occupations of blacksmith, builder, cabinetmaker, carpenter, clergyman, clothier, constable, customs collector, engineer, grocer, bailiff, innkeeper, joiner, mason, merchant, manufacturer, moulder, plasterer, printer, stonecutter, tailor, farmer, tavernkeeper, tinsmith, wheelwright, shoemaker, and watchmaker. (See Tables 1 & 2).

TABLE 1

Occupational Structure of Literacy

		Hamilton Literates	Hamilton Illiterates	Kingston Illiterates	London Illiterates	Hamilton Illiterates as a % of Adult Workforce
Professional/	N	306	3	1		
Proprietor	%	7.4	0.8	0.4	–	.9
White Collar	N	768	21	13	6	
	%	18.6	5.4	5.4	3.9	2.7
Skilled	N	1467	72	34	29	
	%	35.4	18.6	14.2	19.2	4.7
Semi-skilled	N	959	75	85	32	
	%	23.2	19.4	35.4	21.2	7.3
Unskilled	N	638	216	107	84	
	%	15.4	55.8	44.6	55.6	25.3
Total Number		1138	387	240	151	

Source:Census, 1861.

In fact, no single occupation in Hamilton was comprised of a majority of illiterates; only one-fourth of the adult common labourers, fifteen per cent of seamstresses, and five per cent of female servants could not read or write. The remainder of those occupying these positions – low on the social order – were literate. Seventy-five per cent of the unskilled and ninety-three per cent of the semi-skilled possessed the skills of literacy, yet they had climbed no higher in occupational class. Their literacy was no advantage; to some illiteracy was a disadvantage – but not to all illiterates.

The distribution of wealth held by illiterates strikingly parallels that of occupation. The majority of illiterates whose wealth (as measured by total annual value on the 1861 city assessment rolls) could be determined were poor: below a poverty-line struck at the fortieth percentile of the assessed population. (See Table 3) Nevertheless, sizeable numbers of illiterate workers achieved middle-class or higher economic ranking. Illiteracy did not consign all men to poverty. Similarly, many literate workers remained poor.

More important, though, than either the occupational or economic ranking of illiterate workmen was the relationship of literacy to the economic rewards of occupation. Among the

TABLE 2
Illiterates: Selected Occupations

	Hamilton	– as % of Hamilton adult workforce	Kingston	London
Barber	2	10.5	3	1
Blacksmith	8	10.3	–	2
Builder	2	7.2	–	1
Cabinet Maker	1	1.9	–	–
Carpenter	14	4.7	4	4
Clergymen	1	3.2	–	–
Clothier	2	13.3	–	–
Constable	1	11.1	–	–
Customs Collector	1	33.3	1	–
Dealer	1	9.1	1	–
Dressmaker	1	1.4	2	–
Engineer	1	2.1	1	1
Farmer	3	10.0	3	2
Grocer	1	1.1	1	1
High Baillif	1	50.0	–	–
Innkeeper	1	6.7	3	–
Joiner	1	5.9	–	–
Labourer	205	25.2	105	83
Mail conductor	2	50.0	–	–
Mariner	1	2.0	10	–
Merchant	1	0.9	–	–
Mason	2	3.9	3	1
Moulder	2	3.6	–	–
Painter	2	3.2	–	–
Pedlar	2	6.1	1	1
Printer	1	2.5	1	–
Seamstress	8	15.1	2	–
Servant (f)	33	6.1	34	–
Tailor	8	6.2	8	–
Tavernkeeper	7	9.3	1	–
Tinsmith	2	5.1	–	–
Wagonmaker	2	18.2	–	–
Wheelwright	1	50.0	–	–
Gentleman	1	1.5	1	–
Watchmaker	1	7.2	1	–
Porter	3	4.8	1	2
Teamster	4	13.3	–	–
Plasterer	3	6.9	–	2
Clerk	–	–	1	–

unskilled and the semi-skilled, little economic advantage accrued to the more literate. (See Table 4) However, stratification appears at the artisanal or skilled level of work, a line at which literacy's perceived advantages bespoke of reality. Yet, some illiterates fared well, especially those in white collar or small proprietor positions.

TABLE 3

Economic Structure of Literacy

Total Annual Value—Linked Heads of Household

$		Hamilton Literates	Hamilton Illiterates	Kingston Illiterates	Hamilton Illiterates as % of Hamilton assessed heads	%-ile
0-23	N	329	76	16		0-19
	%	12.9	40.6	22.2	18.8	
24-42	N	609	62	36		20-39
	%	23.9	33.2	50.0	9.2	
43-71	N	477	22	11		40-59
	%	18.7	11.8	15.3	4.1	
72-168	N	593	15	8		60-79
	%	23.2	8.0	11.1	2.5	
169-375	N	230	10	1		80-89
	%	9.0	5.3	1.4	4.2	
376-700	N	141	1	—		90-94
	%	5.5	0.5	—	0.7	
701-2367	N	117	1	—		95-98
	%	4.6	0.5	—	—	
2368-9999	N	55	—	—		99-100
	%	2.2	—	—	0.9	
Total		2551	187	72		
Mean		$98.8	53.6	38.9		

Source: Census and Assessment, 1861

TABLE 4

Illiterates: Occupation and Wealth Percentiles of Total Annual Value
(Linked heads of household)

Unskilled Labour

		0-19	20-39	40-59	60-79	80-89	90-94	95-98	99-100
Hamilton	N	150	143	44	24	10	3	—	—
Literates	%	40.1	38.2	11.8	6.4	2.7	0.8	—	—
Hamilton	N	47	35	8	5	1	—	—	—
Illiterates	%	49.0	36.5	8.3	5.2	1.0	—	—	—
Kingston	N	9	20	5	1	—	—	—	—
Illiterates	%	25.7	57.1	14.3	2.9	—	—	—	—

Semi-Skilled Labour

		0-19	20-39	40-59	60-79	80-89	90-94	95-98	99-100
Hamilton	N	25	56	43	33	8	4	1	—
Literates	%	14.7	32.9	25.3	19.4	4.7	2.4	0.6	—
Hamilton	N	1	4	5	1	—	—	—	—
Illiterates	%	9.1	36.4	45.5	9.1	—	—	—	—
Kingston	N	2	7	1	2	—	—	—	—
Illiterates	%	16.7	58.3	8.3	16.7	—	—	—	—

Skilled Labour

		0-19	20-39	40-59	60-79	80-89	90-94	95-98	99-100
Hamilton	N	68	257	222	198	56	33	28	8
Literates	%	7.8	29.5	25.5	22.8	6.4	3.8	3.2	0.9
Hamilton	N	13	14	7	2	2	—	1	—
Illiterates	%	33.3	35.9	17.9	5.1	5.1	—	2.6	—
Kingston	N	—	5	4	2	1	—	—	—
Illiterates	%	—	41.7	33.3	16.7	8.3	—	—	—

White Collar

		0-19	20-39	40-59	60-79	80-89	90-94	95-98	99-100
Hamilton	N	17	52	54	154	58	29	23	8
Literates	%	4.3	13.2	13.7	39.0	14.7	7.3	5.8	2.0
Hamilton	N	—	2	1	1	6	—	—	—
Illiterates	%	—	20.0	10.0	10.0	60.0	—	—	—
Kingston	N	2	2	—	1	—	—	—	—
Illiterates	%	40.0	40.0	—	20.0	—	—	—	—

Possession of literacy did have its rewards, though its benefits were not clear or unambiguous ones. The relationship of basic education to work and earnings was very complex, complicated moreover by other social structural determinants, such as age and ethnicity. Illiterate workers were far from a homogeneous lot; indeed, they possessed a social ordering within their own ranks, one which duplicated that of the larger society. As such, Irish Catholics, illiterate or not, (though the largest group of illiterates) and the aged (again, most often illiterate) are generally found in the lowest classes, occupational or economic. Much more than mere literacy operated in the establishment and maintenance of the stratification system of the nineteenth century. Education alone would not often dramatically affect class or social status.[18]

Lack of education similarly would not reduce status or class as the society modernized and industrialized. The social mobility of persistent illiterates (1861 to 1871) directly contradicts any such notions. Occupationally, stability was the normative experience as skilled workers held their positions, not slipping to lower class ranks. Economically, improvement and acquisition of wealth was the dominant experience, exclusive of occupation or ethnicity.[19]

Lack of education and absence of the tools of literacy did not remove all opportunity for higher-ranking occupations, wealth, or social mobility. Ethnicity favoured some illiterates, hindered others; often it required more years for their success. Factors such as chance and personality figured too, undoubtedly countering some of the disadvantages that illiteracy could bring. An illiterate could then achieve some success in the working world of the nineteenth century. These conclusions form a crucial baseline against which to assess the rhetorical economic claims of middle-class school promoters and against which to test the publicly-enunciated educational aspirations and criticisms of the working class. Far more than the skills of literacy were fundamentally at issue; other matters were thought to be as central to the curriculum for the future worker.

The schoolmen's emphasis on the advantages of schooling, as illustrated by literacy, did not hold true for many workers. Literacy did not benefit all who possessed it nor handicap many who did not. Class, status, and discrimination functioned to prevent the direct rewards of education for some individuals, if not for the larger society. Perhaps the workers had a better vantage point from which to view the social order and realized that education did not guarantee a better position and its commensurate reward. Perhaps they saw the possible economic limits of literacy as well. Education, no doubt, could aid in economic life to a not insignificant degree—this they recognized—

but it was not the morally dominant middle-class education. Moreover, to them literacy did have other important uses.

The paradoxes of literacy's relationship to work may be further explored, this time in a specific work setting focusing on one large lumbering concern, the Hawkesbury Lumber Company, located in the rich timberland of the Ottawa River Valley.[20] Hawkesbury was in important ways a common large-scale nineteenth century firm. Lumbering was firstly a primary extractive industry, yet had a large component of secondary processing (or more properly industrial) functions. Lumbering, certainly capitalist-based, may be viewed as a transitional operation, between traditional and seasonal rhythms of work, and the discipline and internal control of the factory which milling would represent.[21] It was a mixture of two historical developments of economic organization, preindustrial and industrial structures. Yet, it represents the large work setting, as 795 men were employed, or rehired, during the years, 1887-1903. The number hired varied from year to year from a maximum of 208 in 1880 to a low of six in 1906. Rather than indicating the introduction of new technology or mechanization, or a drastic response to the business cycle, this fluctuation illustrates the stability of the workforce, as most hands retained their positions.

The Hawkesbury Lumber Company is of special interest, as its detailed records of employment contracts have survived. Ledgers of annual contracts were maintained, for 1887-1888 (Hamilton Brothers) and 1889-1903 (Hawkesbury). Exceptional records, they provide for each employee, contract date, occupation, name, wage rates, and a signature or mark – a measure of literacy.[22] From these records, the occupational hierarchy, wage structure, and the distribution of literate and illiterate workers may be reconstructed.

The functional structure of occupations is readily discernible from these records. (See Table 5). The largest group of workers were the semi-skilled, although the group "millmen" may well have included some skilled workmen. Skilled workers comprised the second largest group, twice the number of white collar, three times the unskilled. The diverse processes of work are easily seen from the list, including the extractive and the processing. The larger number of factory occupations (millman, ironworker, mechanic, millwright, etc.) – perhaps a third of the total – reveals the industrial side of operations.

Large variation existed in monthly rates of earnings, from $1.00 (a day's work) to $87.00. The mean wage was $24.00, the median $22.50, certainly not atypical for the area or the period.[23] (See Table 6).

How did literacy intersect with the structure of earnings and occupations, our key concern? Fifty-two per cent of employees were literate and forty-eight per cent were not, though the measure underestimates the level of reading ability. (Table 7). This was a high rate of illiteracy for Ontario, Canada, and North America for the last quarter of the century, but it reflects the traditionally high rates of Eastern Ontario and Quebec, and the French Canadian origins of the great mass of the workers.

TABLE 5
Occupational Classification and Literacy: Hawkesbury Lumber
Company
(N = 672)

White Collar (8.5%)	N	% Literate
Foreman	17	88.2
Clerk	27	100.0
Timekeeper	6	83.3
Jobber	5	40.0
Lumber Inspector	1	100.0
Contractor	1	100.0
Total	57	89.5
Skilled Labour (17.7%)		
Blacksmith	11	81.8
Carpenter	19	52.6
Cutter	28	64.3
Millwright	14	57.1
Watchman	5	100.0
Mechanic	11	90.9
Gardener	2	100.0
Painter	1	0.0
Saddler	6	100.0
Sawyer	4	50.0
Trimmer	1	100.0
Wheelwright	1	100.0
Miller	1	0.0
Plasterer	1	0.0
Filer	1	100.0
Edger	6	50.0
Ironworker	7	0.0
Total	119	63.9
Semi-Skilled Labour (68.8%)		
Handyman	21	47.6
Teamster	149	36.9
Courier	1	100.0
Lumberman	2	0.0
Cook	1	0.0
Blockmaker	1	100.0
Fuller	1	100.0

Housekeeper	1	100.0
Stableman	3	66.7
Chainer/Raker	9	66.7
Picket	8	50.0
Spareman	3	0.0
Barkman	5	40.0
Pileman/Piler	69	40.6
Stabber	7	71.4
Slideman	16	31.3
Chopper	21	28.6
Loader/Striker	6	0.0
Boorman	8	50.0
Butter	3	0.0
Millman	99	32.3
Road Cutter	13	23.1
Logmaker	14	21.4
Total	462	36.8
Unskilled Labour (5.1%)		
Labourer	28	35.7
Choreman/Boy	6	16.7
Total	34	32.4

TABLE 6
Rates of Wage and Literacy
(N = 752)

Rate Month	N	%	% Literate
$ 1 - 10	12	1.6	25.0
11 - 20	298	39.6	43.3
21 - 30	341	45.4	49.0
31 - 40	48	6.4	89.6
41 - 50	40	5.3	72.5
51 - 60	2	0.3	50.0
61 - 70	7	0.9	100.0
70 +	4	0.5	50.0
mean	$24.12		
median	22.53		

TABLE 7
Literacy
(N = 795)

	N	%
Literate	413	51.9
Illiterate	382	48.1

Importantly, literacy did not always represent higher earnings, supporting the general outline presented above. Among the lowest-paid, ten or fewer dollars per month, illiterates dominated. The succeeding levels represented near parity, however. These ranges, $21-30, which encompassed a plurality of the workforce, and $11-20 together comprised over eighty per cent of employees and herein illiterates were hardly disadvantaged. With the exception of the lowest paid (probably casual or part-time), literate workmen fared little better than did their illiterate colleagues. Yet, there was a limitation on the level of earnings to which the majority of illiterates could achieve, much as the tabulations for assessed wealth revealed earlier. Here, however, it was the top twelve per cent from which illiterates were largely excluded, as they comprised just one-fifth of those earning $31 or more each month. Yet, some illiterates did make it to these higher levels (See Table 6). What such men lacked in education or booklearning, they no doubt compensated for with skill, experience, or common sense.[24] Presumably their employers did not find that their illiteracy made them less productive, and their skills were rewarded.

TABLE 8
Wage Differentials and Literacy
(N = 794)

Change in Wages	N	%	% Literate
− $1	2	0.3	50.0
0	605	76.1	57.6
1-5	125	15.7	31.5
6-10	42	5.3	30.9
11-30	20	2.6	50.0

The rewards of illiterate workers were also illustrated by the benefits of rising wages. The contracts in some cases (24 per cent of all) provide two rates of remuneration for a workman: the initial wage used above and a subsequent higher rate. (See Table 8). These men often were employed to hold more than one occupation, often a seasonal variation, showing a versatility of skill if not necessarily a high initial wage or occupational status. Illiterates dominated among men exhibiting this flexibility. One-and-a-half times as many illiterates increased their earnings than did literate employees, encompassing 70 per cent of all increases $1-10, 50 per cent of those above that line. These wage differentials strikingly demonstrate the ability of the uneducated to both perform a variety of skills and to benefit directly in the rewards.

Skills mean occupation, a matter of less interest than economic rewards in the determination of literacy's roles and an inadequate measure of skill or status.[25] As in the larger society, literacy related directly to occupational status in the Hawkesbury operation. Literacy increased directly with occupational class, with large differences separating the white collar from the skilled, and the skilled from the rest. However, these sharp divisions did not carry over into wages, certainly contradicting analyses of social or class structure based solely on occupation, a quite common sociological procedure. In fact, skilled workers were more highly paid than white collar and several semi-skilled workers attained high salaries. Important, as well, the obvious factory occupations were not all marked by high levels of literacy.

Moreover, some illiterates were able to achieve higher ranking occupations: 11 per cent of white collar and 36 per cent of skilled labour were unable to sign their names. Blacksmiths, carpenters, cutters, millwrights, mechanics, millers, and iron-workers could be illiterate. Though largely disadvantaged in occupation, illiterates held a great variety of jobs, only slightly handicapped in earnings. Lack of schooling did not significantly restrict them in the pay envelope or pocket.

Ninety-six men, longer-term employees, signed more than one contract. The influence of literacy on both this form of persistence within the firm and on the changing wage rates, advances the argument. Illiterates outnumbered literate workers in this category, and they dominated among those who increased earnings. Illiteracy, it would seem, was not the salient factor; more probably it was factors involving skills and performance about which the ledgers are silent. Illiterates' greater persistence is important; their greater volatility is intriguing. (See Table 9A). Literacy's importance is seen more in the magnitude of the changes, as literate workmen gained a greater proportion of larger increases and larger decreases. Illiteracy may have placed restraints once more on mobility, but the restraints operated in both directions. Such limitations regulated that frequency of changes. (See Table 9B)

Analysis of literacy's role in a specific occupational situation, the Hawkesbury Lumber Company, reveals the limits of illiteracy. These operated largely in the occupational sphere, but not in wages, flexibility, or salary increments. Literacy related to occupation strongly, but not completely, and very little to remuneration.[26] The Hawkesbury experience contradicts the expectations and perceptions of Ryerson and other middle-class school reformers and some working class opinion. Yet, it provides support for working class claims that education figured not always or necessarily in work, but could relate more directly to other aspects of life.

TABLE 9

Changing Wage Rates: Employees with Two or More Contracts
$(N = 96)$

			Literate		Illiterate	
A.	Same Rate		9	20.9%	7	13.2%
	Increasing Rate		27	62.8%	34	64.2%
	Decreasing Rate		7	16.8%	12	22.6%
			43		53	
B.	Increase	$1-5	15	55.6%	23	66.7%
		6-10	7	25.9%	10	29.4%
		11-18	5	18.5%	1	2.9%
	Decrease	$1-5	4	57.2%	9	75.0%
		6-8	3	42.8%	3	25.0%

Horace Mann, Secretary of the Massachussetts State Board of Education, was a middle-class reformer and a correspondent of Ryerson. In his *Fifth Report* (1842), he argued that education brought labour economic rewards. From a survey of manufacturers, he estimated that literate labour received 50 per cent more in pay than illiterate workers. Mann's estimate of a 50 per cent greater return from educated labour cannot be accepted, and a 10-20 per cent differential puts the question into a radically different light. Such a difference need not seem significant to the average working man, and key questions surround the reasons why he chose—and the majority did—to acquire some education and to send his children to school. An answer must lie with the contradictions inherent in the working class attitudes as well as the perceived non-economic benefits of education. Equally important questions pertain to how much schooling made a significant difference in wages.

We must ask, moreover, why discussions of the productivity of education so rarely spoke to specific job skills, those beyond abstract thought processes. Certainly a partial answer derives from an awareness of the moral virtues and behavioural traits which Egerton Ryerson, Mann, and his manufacturers all found central in the making of a contented and productive working class. In this, they were undoubtedly correct; as Gintis has found and Dreeben has argued, it is precisely the non-cognitive functions of schooling which most directly relate to the creation of a workforce acceptable to modern industrial capitalism. Toward this end their schools were designed to control, to prepare the masses.[27] And the schools were attended. Yet this does not sufficiently answer the basic query of how education related to the skills of individual occupations. Neither schoolmen nor labour spokesmen addressed this question to any meaningful degree. So we do not yet know, beyond educated guesses or modern analogies, how much education a carpenter, shoemaker, mechanic, painter, storekeeper, or hotelkeeper would need to do his job. They might need arithmetic, but, this could be gained without schooling.[28] Examples of the self-taught, to read or to write, are almost legendary. Yet, to what extent these skills, the tools of literacy, were required remains questionable for those not employed in professional clerical endeavours.

Moreover, it is very possible that reading was not often required in the search for employment. Advertisements for jobs are rarely found amidst the plethora of announcements and solicitations in nineteenth century newspapers. Work was most often gained informally. Gareth Stedman Jones reported on the labour market of London, England, in the second-half of the century. Workers circulated among the trades, from one to another in a seasonal pattern:

> Skilled workers could gain information about the availability of work either from press announcements or from local trade union branches. But neither of these channels was really open to the casual worker. The only way he could find out about work was either by chance conversations in pubs or else by tramping around the yards and workshops in his districts ... being known at local centres of casual work was more important than degree of skill and where character references were not required.[29]

Reading and writing were to such men – a sizeable proportion of the workforce in nineteenth century cities – relatively inconsequential to their quests for work, perhaps relatively unimportant in doing a good job. Jones' conclusions may hold for many skilled workers, journeymen, and artisans as well. The benefits of literacy lay elsewhere.

In the partly industrial setting of Hawkesbury, literacy did not significantly relate to individual rewards and presumably it did not relate to productivity. In this section, the more general question of the connection between education, literacy, and industrialization will be discussed. Recent research in economic history and development has begun to contradict the received wisdom that primary education is central to the process of industrialization and that it must logically precede "take-off into sustained growth." However, education and economic development need not be collateral or sequential processes. Productivity and wealth do not necessarily follow from mass literacy, as the history of Sweden and Scotland demonstrate. Both achieved mass literacy before the nineteenth century, yet remained desperately poor.

The larger issue is taken up by Roger Schofield who remarks, "today literacy is considered to be a necessary precondition for economic development (and this one may question); but the historian might well ask himself whether this was so in England at the end of the eighteenth century" or in North America in the nineteenth. Schofield continues:

The necessity of literacy as a precondition for economic growth is a persistent theme running through many UNESCO publications. Correlations between measures of industrialization and literacy both in the past and in the present are established in UNESCO *World Illiteracy at Mid-Century* (Paris, 1957), pp. 177-89. These measures are very general and throw no light on the question of why literacy should be considered essential to economic growth.[30]

In various studies, C. Arnold Anderson and Mary Jean Bowman have attempted to demonstrate the ways in which literacy should be considered essential to economic development.[31] Operating from the premise that education is one of the few sure roads to economic growth, they find increasingly a tendency to "justify" education in economic terms.[32] In 1965, Anderson claimed that "about 40 per cent of adult literacy or of primary enrolment is a threshold for economic development."[33] Of course, he added that a level of education alone is an insufficient condition in a society lacking other prerequisites. Throughout their writings, Bowman and Anderson have stressed the necessity, if not the sufficiency, of a literacy threshold for sustained growth, a stage to be maintained until a level of 70-80 per cent is attained. Yet, they have not shown with any precision that these thresholds have meaning with historical evidence.

David McClelland, on the other hand, finds in his data that investment in education at the elementary or literacy level is inadequate; investment in education does not correlate positively with growth rates. He concludes:

Primary school attendance has a doubtful relationship to significant improvements, in the labor force or even to literacy itself. That is, the marginal product of a primary school education would seem likely to be low, because skilled artisans may function as well without being literate. Furthermore, primary school attendance is not enough by itself to lift a person to the level of being able to perform jobs characteristic of the middle class.

A strong relationship, however, derives from post-primary education, if the lag-time between training and effect on the economy is considered. "Education is a long-term investment from the economic point of view." This approach seems more sound, in historical context, though problems do remain, especially within the industrial revolution.[34]

What about the past, and the transition to the factory itself as the work-setting for industrial capitalism? In the most general sense, John Talbott has remarked, "in the first decades of industrialization, the factory system put no premium on even low-level intellectual skills. Whatever relationships existed between widespread literacy and early industrial development must have been quite roundabout."[35]

Ironically for those who perceived the productive value of educated and literate labour, the relationship, at least in England, was less than direct. Early industrialization was, first of all, disruptive to education, and adult literacy levels fell as a result. The demand for child labour, in England and in North America, greatly reduced the chances for a lower-class child to attend school.[36] Factory schools were, on the whole, rare, ineffectual, and irregularly attended. Secondary education was unheard of for the children of the working class.

The logical result, Roger Schofield and Michael Sanderson have concluded, was reflected directly in the literacy rates of late eighteenth and early nineteenth century England. Sanderson discovered that "the English Industrial Revolution cannot be seen as one nourished by rising educational standards at least at the elementary level.... "[37] The decline in literacy did not impede the upsurge of economic growth because the nature of industrialization was such to make very low literacy demands on the educational system. Or, as Schofield expands:

> Thus, insofar as economic growth in this period entailed the acquisition of a large number of practical skills by a growing proportion of the population, developments in literacy and education were probably largely irrelevant to it. And, insofar as economic growth resulted from the increased productivity of labor brought about by the shift from domestic to factory production, literacy and education were also probably largely irrelevant for many of the new industrial occupations recruited a mainly illiterate work force ....[38]

Knack, as Sanderson calls it, was of greater importance than booklearning in the process of industrialization.

In the historical case, then, of English industrialization, there is good evidence to part from the company of those who must relate mass education directly to economic development. England had reached the 40 per cent "threshold" level of literacy by 1750 (at least for males); it remains for researchers to isolate an exceptional case to that rule of thumb. The threshold level may well be so general as to be meaningless. The relationship of higher levels of education to development continues to be obscure, though post-primary education played no role at this early stage. As Roger Schofield ably expressed it, "for England, at least, the usual causal relationships between literacy and economic growth might probably be reversed. In this alternative perspective the reduction in illiteracy in nineteenth century England would appear more as a cultural change brought about by economic growth than as the cause of growth."[39]

If not education as preparation for productive labour, what then? Sidney Pollard and Edward Thompson, in pathbreaking analyses, have revealed that the labouring population had to be trained to the workings of the factory, broken to industrial spirit, rhythm, and pace in ways to which literacy was far from central. As Pollard demonstrates, it was not necessarily the better worker, but the stable one who was worth more to manufacturers; "often, indeed, the skilled apprenticed man was at a discount because of the working habits acquired before entering a factory."[40] The problem was of course one of discipline, and factory-owners suffered great difficulties in training men to "renounce their desultory habits of work, and identify themselves with the unvarying regularity of the complex automation." Discipline was needed to produce goods on time. To orient the hands to this routine, rules became the norm: "Work rules, formalized, impersonal and *occasionally printed*, were symbolic of the new industrial relationships."[41] No primacy for literacy, here, in solving the most difficult of capitalism's conundrums.

To "educate" the workers was necessary. But it was not an education in reading and writing, but

> the need to educate the first generation of factory workers to a new factory discipline, [part of] the widespread belief in human perfectability... but one of their consequences was the preoccupation with the character and morals of the working class which are so marked a feature of the early stages of industrialization.[42]

This view resembles rather closely that of many North American manufacturers, yet their desire for provision of schooling and the timing of provision made for one crucial difference.

Thompson focuses more closely at the importance of time in the transition to the factory, the place of precise and mechanically-maintained clock-time. Whether or not literacy was needed to tell time, "the bell would also remind men of [time's] passing.... Sound served better than sight, especially in growing manufacturing districts." The first generation of factory workers was taught the importance of time by its masters. But there was an area to which the school could contribute; as we remarked above and as Thompson notes as well, schools could be useful in circulating "time-thrift." Charity schools, for example, were praised for teaching industry, frugality, order, regularity, and punctuality. By the time a child reached six or seven years of age, he or she should be "habituated, not to say naturalized, to Labour and Fatigue;" the socialization of the children of the poor should commence at age four. The parallels between the rules of the school and the rules of the factory must not be overlooked either. "Once within the school gates, the child entered the new universe of disciplined time . . . . Once in attendance, they were under military rule."[43]

Some Englishmen, along with Ryerson, were aware of the values of the school. Its importance in the accommodation to the factory was certainly not in terms of literacy or skills, but in morals, discipline, and social values. As R. P. Dore concluded for a different culture, Tokugawa Japan:

> But what does widespread literacy do for a developing country? At the very least it constitutes a training in being trained. The man who has in childhood submitted to some processes of disciplined and conscious learning is more likely to respond to further training, be it in a conscript army, in a factory, or at lectures arranged by his village agricultural association.[44]

Training in being trained, as Dore aptly puts it, is the crucial job preparation and the problem for industrialism. The English examples have been very instructive in this manner, yet the North American experience differed greatly in timing and the sequence of events. England industrialized well before literacy reached universal proportions (not much beyond a 40 per cent "threshold"); education seems not an integral part of the transition, and there is no role for a lag-time for educational investments. The transition to the factory itself was far from easy – marked by riots, strikes, disruption, luddism, Chartism.

On the contrary, North American development, particularly Canadian industrialization, came comparatively much later. Importantly, it followed the establishment of systems for mass elementary education, though not much secondary schooling, and the attainment of new universal levels of literacy. As well, I would advance the hypothesis that in North-America the transition to industrial capitalism was a smoother one.[45] There is, I would now suggest, an intimate connection between the timing of mass educational provision and the subsequent patterns of industrialization. Schooling, in this formulation, paved the way for the economic transformation and here is the function of lag-time at the elementary level. This is the purpose of education of which Ryerson and other middle-class reformers spoke; this is how they sought to control the masses in the cause of productivity and national development.

To do so, it was essential to break pre-industrial work habits, to "Canadianize" the immigrant worker, removing him from his traditional origins and patterns. As might be expected, the transmission of literacy's cognitive skills was of secondary importance. Yet literacy, in virtually all cases, came with schooling and had its uses, some of which labour grasped. Print had important socializing functions; literacy served to regularize behaviour and to discipline man. In the North American case, education could replace much of the coercion of English labour to strict factory rules and internalized self-discipline. As J. F. C. Harrison has argued, "the process of assimilation was closely related to the spread of literacy . . . ." And, in the long run, he concluded, education was much more effective in instilling the necessary discipline.[46] Provision of mass schooling; the working class's acceptance, though a questioning one, of them; increasing rates of attendance; and compulsory education all featured in this direction; promoting discipline, moral values, and the "training in being trained" which mattered most in the preparation of a modern industrial workforce. These were the purposes of the school.[47]

Working Class Housing in a Small Nineteenth Century Canadian City: Hamilton, Ontario 1852-1881

Michael J. Doucet

One way to isolate the degree of stratification in any society is to compare the housing occupied by the various components in that society. To date, however, research into housing conditions in the historical city has focused almost exclusively upon the inhumane conditions to be found in the worst sections of large cities at particular points in time, an approach that can be traced to the work of nineteenth century social critics such as Engels, Dickens, Mayhew and Riis.[1] Re-examinations of working class housing conditions by historians have also been carried out within this relatively static and isolated framework. Thus far we have been able to gain some insight into the state of working class housing in Great Britain, North America and Scandinavia.[2] Unfortunately, however, we still have a great deal to learn about changes in the relative condition of working class housing throughout the nineteenth century, differences in housing conditions among the various segments of the working class, and housing conditions in smaller and newer cities.[3]

The purpose of this study is to examine some characteristics of housing in a small, nineteenth century Canadian city – Hamilton, Ontario. We are interested in the extent, type, condition, and location of working class residences and the changes over time in these variables. Moreover, we will compare the characteristics of working class housing to those for the housing of other classes to determine if this society became more or less stratified, in terms of its housing stock, over the study period. The years surveyed are 1852 to 1881 and the manuscript Assessment Rolls for the City of Hamilton form the basic data source for the study.[4]

Founded in 1813, Hamilton attained city status in 1846 and by 1852 was home to just over 14,000 people. By 1881, the population had increased more than one-and-one-half times to 36,000. Much of this growth was related to industrialization, particularly due to the emergence of Hamilton as a rail centre in the 1850s. The railway brought ancillary industries to the city, especially in the fields of metal working and metal production. Moreover, the railway signalled the dawning of a new age in the organization of work settings. In 1852, no shop in Hamilton employed more than 100 people; indeed, only nine of the 282 establishments enumerated in the census of that year employed more than twenty hands. Thousands, however, were engaged in the construction, operation and maintenance of the railway and by the end of the study period firms employing more than one hundred were common in Hamilton.[5]

Not only did the population and industrial base of Hamilton grow between 1852 and 1881, but as one might anticipate, the built-up area of the city also expanded considerably. Figure 1 depicts this physical expansion process.[6] In 1852, the built-up area radiated out from the city's main intersection, King and James, toward the east, south-east, north, and north-west. Large tracts to the north-east and south-west, however, were either completely vacant or in agricultural use at that date. During the study period, most of these areas became at least partially developed, and, by 1881, only about 6 per cent of the blocks in Hamilton were without some development.

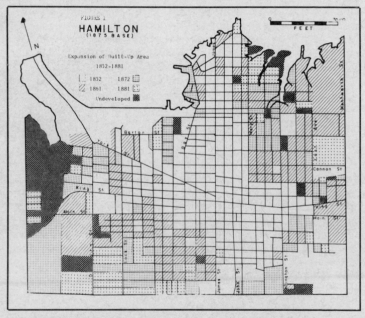

Hamilton did not experience a uniform rate of growth between 1852 and 1881. The march of progress received at least one serious setback; the panic of late 1857.[7] The effects upon Hamilton were both devastating and prolonged. One observer noted:

The loss of 25 per cent of our population, a decrease of 50 per cent in rentals and a continuous three years of stagnation in all descriptions of business – attended with the closing up of nearly all of our factories, were circumstances well calculated to dishearten the most hopeful and destroy belief in the prestige of our city. The proud motto it had assumed – "I Advance" – must have seemed a burlesque to strangers when they saw the city retrograding at an alarming pace.[8]

As we shall soon see, the depression which followed the panic of 1857 had some interesting consequences for Hamilton's working class and their housing.[9]

For the historical geographer, indeed, for all who study the structure of past cities, it is important to consider not only the realities of the place in question but also the images that people held concerning that particular place.[10] In this regard, nineteenth century attitudes toward housing conditions and environmental quality become as important as the spatial extent and economic functions of the city. Evidence relating to these issues is still scant for Hamilton, but there are some threads that we can grasp which help us to understand what it was like to live in that city. For example, although recently settled, Hamilton was not without housing and sanitation problems. In 1852 it was reported:

> During the last three weeks a number of cases of sudden death have been reported, and we believe that there is not room to doubt that some of the mortality is to be ascribed to Asiatic Cholera. In almost every instance, however, the disease has been contracted in low and filthy places, in which it is surprising that human beings could exist at all.[11]

Concern over the sanitary state of the city periodically surfaced whenever the threat of an imminent epidemic was apparent. In reality, however, all such considerations were subservient to the overall goal of 'Progress.' Even the Board of Health, the body charged with looking out for the well-being of the populace, could, in all seriousness, report:

> It is pleasing to note that the industries of the city appear in a prosperous condition, giving employment to our working classes, and thus indirectly promoting health.[12]

Further evidence of the supremacy of civic progress emerged any time the question of industrial pollution was raised. The interests of business were always placed above those of individuals, especially those of the poor. In 1881, for example, those who protested the night-time operation of a noxious and noisy iron foundry in an essentially residential area were reminded:

> The common law requires a distinction between a nuisance in a manufacturing town or city and a nuisance in a village chiefly composed of residences and stores, and the distinction

is a just one. The work of a manufacturing city must be carried on. It is [in] the interest of the community that it should be, even if it does cause some people inconvenience. The man who cannot bear that inconvenience must remove from it, instead of having it removed from him.[13]

Although a small city, even by nineteenth century standards, Hamilton was, nonetheless, a city of contrasting residential and social conditions. On the one hand, the press could uncover a house that had

> ... long been the resort of the lowest and most abandoned creatures of both sexes; the victims of poverty and vice have both taken advantage of the cheap rents and squalid tenements; and the place has been for months, aye for years, one of the most loathsome dens which the imagination can conceive. The inmates have long been the terror of the neighbourhood – and yet this house is situated near the centre of the city, and is, we believe, the property of men who are rich, and who could afford to allow their barrack to remain idle unless respectable tenants offered themselves.[14]

Squalid tenements were not common in Hamilton, however, nor did they occupy large portions of the built-up area. In large measure this must have been a function of the size of the city. Population simply did not exert enough pressure on the supply of land to make high density development attractive to builders. In fact, it was not until the 1870s that the city had spread out to such an extent that all her citizens could no longer walk to work and a street railway service was deemed necessary.[15]

In common with all nineteenth century urban places of respectable size, then, Hamilton had some housing and sanitation problems. Parts of the city remained poorly drained and unhealthy at least until the end of the century. Yet, because of the relatively small size of the area involved and because of the lack of political power among those who resided in such areas, the realities of these problems could not only be ignored, they could be completely masked by the images created by the city's boosters. The local press led the parade and quickly printed the favourable comments of visitors to the city. In 1860, only 10 per cent of Hamilton's dwellings were constructed of stone, yet one traveller wrote:

> Hamilton is a beautiful town.... There are many beautiful private residences in and about Hamilton. They are built upon the elevated grounds in the rear [south] and to the west of the town.... The substantial drab-coloured limestone of the mountain furnishes the material for most of these houses, and, chiefly in the Anglo-Italian style of architecture, a style exceedingly appropriate to the climate and mode of living of

their occupants. Surrounded by fine lawns and gardens, their effect is delightful.

People obviously saw, or perhaps were shown, the houses that they wanted to see. Moreover, the plight of the destitute could also be conveniently ignored in the rhetoric of boosterism. Haley Bamman has given us some insight into the extent of the relief work carried on by one organization, the Ladies Benevolent Society, between 1846 and 1862. Hundreds of people received assistance from this one group alone during this period, yet the editor of the *Spectator* could totally ignore the poor, even during a depression, in the interests of creating a favourable image of the city. One English visitor was reported as writing:

> Though Hamilton runs not to fashions and frivolities, it can, nevertheless, put on a very gay appearance when it likes, and I must own that even among the very lower orders of the working people, I have not seen one during my three days of stay here who has not been cleanly and comfortably clad.

There was no room for the poor in the boosters' images of the city.[16]

While some members of Hamilton's working class were the periodic recipients of philanthropic gestures, assistance was given only to a category of people known as the "deserving poor."[17] The vast majority of the working class had to fend for themselves. This was especially true in the matter of obtaining living quarters. There is little evidence that the city's industrial entrepreneurs constructed dwellings for their employees, as was the case in other places.[18] Nor were building societies of much assistance to Hamilton's workers. They were soon recognized as tools for the middle class. "What is the purpose of Building Societies?" wrote one Hamilton correspondent, "Simply this. To make money out of the poor, the needy – the unwary."[19]

The housing of Hamilton's working class citizens must be viewed before this background of processes, events and attitudes. It must be seen within the context of the overall growth and development of the city, the upswings and downturns of its economy and the philosophy of social assistance of its leaders.

The information contained within Hamilton's manuscript Assessment Rolls can tell us a good deal about the nature of housing in the city. Designed primarily as land taxation records, the Rolls were carefully organized by parcels of land. For occupied lots information was recorded pertaining to the individual or individuals residing on that property (for example, name, age, and occupation). Since the Assessment Rolls also provided data relating to the value, location and, sometimes, the medium of construction for all dwellings in the city, it was possible to study some aspects of the housing conditions of the assessed residents of Hamilton.[20]

Our investigation focuses upon a number of specific occupations that could be identified on the Assessment Rolls of 1852, 1861, 1872-3 and 1881.[21] Four elements of Hamilton's working class population were selected for study; namely, labourers, railway workers,[22] moulders and shoemakers. These four groups provided a cross-section of the various components of the city's Victorian working class. Labourers were the largest element in the unskilled and unorganized segment of the labour force. Railway workers encompassed a broad range of skill, organization and income levels, and were employed in the largest single industry in the city. Moulders and shoemakers were examples of occupations that had organized and unionized at an early date;[23] however, the former were found in relatively large work forces even in Hamilton's early foundries,[24] while the latter were representative of a trade that shifted from an artisanal to an industrial activity between 1852 and 1881.[25] In addition to these four groups, for comparison, statistics were also compiled for three other assessed occupations – clerks, to represent the middle class, and merchants and lawyers, to represent Hamilton's elite. Taken together, the seven occupations accounted for about 30 per cent of the assessed residents of the city in each of the years of the study.[26]

TABLE 1
Size of Selected Occupational Groups
Hamilton, 1852-1881

Occupation	1852		1861		1872		1881	
	No.	%	No.	%	No.	%	No.	%
Labourers	374	15.5	631	19.0	1153	17.7	1001	13.4
Railway Workers	–	–	64	1.9	112	1.7	166	2.2
Moulders	28	1.2	30	0.9	163	2.5	171	2.3
Shoemakers	121	5.0	78	2.3	205	3.1	184	2.5
Clerks	143	5.9	139	4.2	345	5.3	364	4.9
Merchants	74	3.1	71	2.1	95	1.4	122	1.6
Lawyers	18	0.7	34	1.0	30	0.5	46	0.6
Totals	758	31.4	1047	31.4	2103	32.2	2054	27.5
Assessed Population	2412		3324		6517		7477	

By comparing workers' housing to that inhabited by the middle and upper classes we hope to be able to pinpoint changes in the relative position of the working class within nineteenth century Hamilton's social structure. To accomplish this, the analysis will focus on a number of the characteristics of the housing occupied by the city's different classes; namely, the relative value of the dwellings, the level of home ownership, the type of housing and the location and degree of concentration of that housing.

It is revealing to compare the value of the housing occupied by different groups in a city. Due to the fact that the Canadian monetary base was changed from pounds sterling to dollars in

TABLE 2

Index of Relative House Values for Selected Occupations

Hamilton, 1852-1881

Occupation	1852	1861	1872	1881
Labourers	39.4%	57.2%	48.6%	46.7%
Railway Workers	–	120.7	78.2	64.6
Moulders	53.4	100.0	78.1	65.4
Shoemakers	64.1	82.2	63.3	75.3
Clerks	95.4	156.1	129.0	120.0
Merchants	197.2	368.9	366.7	326.9
Lawyers	151.2	400.3	302.6	390.6
Average Assessed House Value for Entire Population	£21	$46.	$974.	$1131.

1857^{27} and because of obvious changes in the rate of assessment over time, an index had to be created so that the figures from the various years could be compared. Table 2 presents the results of the calculation of this index, which relates the average value of the houses occupied by the members of each occupational category to the average value of all occupied homes in the city. Our four working class groups displayed index values which, with the exception of the 1861 figures, revealed that they resided in houses that were assessed at values well below the average figures for the entire city. This contrasts very sharply with the figures for merchants and lawyers. Clerks fell in between the poor and the elite in terms of the assessed value of their homes, although the values for clerks were much closer to those of the working class than to those of the well-to-do. While all groups, except railway workers, displayed higher index values in 1881 than they had in 1852, the most interesting point to be observed in Table 2 is that the differences between the values for the rich and those for the poor increased tremendously during this interval. Clearly this points to an increasingly stratified society.

Peak index values for all seven occupations occurred in 1861. This was largely a consequence of the Depression of 1857. More than 21 per cent of Hamilton's housing stock was vacant in 1861.[28] Of these unoccupied dwellings, almost three-quarters were cheap, frame structures. The exclusion of these houses from the calculation of the average value of occupied homes served to greatly inflate this figure for 1861; yet, at the same time, the temendous decline in rents (see page 84) meant that individuals could afford to live in better houses. Furthermore, students of residential mobility have frequently noted that, among the working class, those with the greatest amount of employment and economic security were most likely to remain in a given place for some length of time.[29] If this was also the case in Hamilton, and there is no evidence to suspect otherwise, then, many poorer members of the city's working class must have migrated during the depression.[30] Those who could afford to remain, and those who came to the city during the depression, found themselves in a buyer's market. Hamilton's workers were probably better housed in 1861 than at most other times during the nineteenth century. By 1872, however, the housing situation had been brought under control once more and the *Spectator* could report:

> For the last few years the increase of people coming to reside in the city is almost unprecedented in the annals of young cities. Last spring such was the demand for houses that many families had to leave in consequence of being unable to obtain places of residence.... To capitalists a better opportunity could not be afforded to realize good interest on their capital by investing it in the building of blocks of houses that would rent at from $6 to $10 per month. Surely we have, in Hamilton, men of sufficient courage and determination to devise some means to supply the demand for dwelling houses either by private speculation or joint stock companies.

A housing shortage, then, was viewed not as a tragedy to the workers, who were always squeezed out in such situations, but as an impediment to the progress of the city and as a marvellous opportunity for adventurous capitalists. "A standing evidence of the steady progress of our city," proclaimed the *Spectator*, "is the difficulty of obtaining residences."[31]

We know little of home ownership patterns in the nineteenth century city.[32] The figures for Hamilton (Table 3) reveal a tendency toward increased levels of owner occupancy over time. Within this framework, however, some of the selected occupations operated in different ways.

The figures for labourers, for example, were unexpectedly high, especially for 1881.[33] We do know, however, that a large proportion of the labourers in 1852 were Irish Catholics[34] and that Catholics, as measured by support of Separate Schools, continued to account for a sizeable percentage of labourers in 1881 (Table 4). Thernstrom has argued that the desire to own a home, no matter how meagre, was very strong among immigrant Irish labourers who resided in Newburyport, Massachusetts between 1850 and 1880.[35] Our Hamilton data lend support to his thesis.

TABLE 3

Proportion of Owner-Occupiers for Selected
Occupations

Hamilton, 1852-1881

Occupation	1852	1861	1872	1881	% Change 1852-81
Labourers	19.5	14.7	20.8	29.8	52.8
Railway Workers	—	7.8	15.2	16.3	109.0
Moulders	25.0	13.3	15.3	22.2	− 11.2
Shoemakers	18.2	25.6	19.5	35.3	93.9
Clerks	10.7	13.0	8.6	17.3	61.7
Merchants	33.8	33.8	30.5	47.5	40.5
Lawyers	44.4	35.3	53.3	56.5	27.3
Total City	26.5	25.6	23.7	30.5	15.1

TABLE 4

Seperate School Supporters for Selected
Occupations

Hamilton, 1881

Occupation	Percentage	Relative Representation*
Labourers	38.7	2.3
Railway Workers	13.1	0.8
Moulders	32.7	2.0
Shoemakers	18.2	1.1
Clerks	6.3	0.4
Merchants	2.5	0.1
Lawyers	4.4	0.3
Total City	17.1	

*Relative Rep. = Proportion of Selected Group/Proportion in City

Of the four working class occupations under study in this paper, the railway workers displayed the lowest degree of home ownership. Some railway workers, for example, rail layers, held positions which were seasonal at best. Even some of the skilled workers did not have a great deal of job security. For example, when officials of the Great Western Railway decided that the company should begin to build its own locomotives, a representative of the local press warmly praised the scheme and declared:

> There are two seasons of the year when traffic on the Great Western is very large, rendering it necessary to employ a large force of men in repairing, &c.; during the intervals between those busy periods, the workmen are comparatively idle, thus necessitating the discharge of the men, or some other employment of a profitable kind .... As an economical scheme, the construction of engines in the Company's works is to be commended; besides, it gives steady employment to the best workmen, whilst it is for the interest of the Company that frequent changes among the workmen are prevented.[36]

If the employment security of the railway workers was as tenuous as the above comment implies, then the low incidence of home ownership among the members of this occupation is not surprising.

Moulders, like railway workers, exhibited home ownership tendencies which were well below those found in the city as a whole, especially from 1861 onwards. As their numbers grew, they fell farther and farther behind the elite of the city. Langdon has argued that the coming of industrial capitalism to central Canada in the 1860s, created a large, self-regulating, impersonal labour market which undermined job security and undercut the wages of employees, especially if they were skilled.[37] Hamilton was an important centre in this process and her moulders, as skilled workers, could not escape its consequences. Thus, the industrial capitalist system did not help them to increase their home ownership levels at rates that matched those for the well-to-do.

Shoemakers were also skilled workers, subject to the effects of industrial capitalism. Yet their home ownership patterns were very fluid. This was probably partly a consequence of the changing fortunes of the trade as it underwent industrialization. Also, the term 'shoemaker' encompassed a rather broad range of economic levels, from shoe dealers and shoe factory owners down to salaried employees in such concerns, with the old-style independent cobblers somewhere in between. These various groups would display quite different tendencies toward home ownership. Unfortunately, it is virtually impossible to sort out these differences from the Assessment data. Perhaps, by 1881, the shoe factory employees had ceased to call themselves shoemakers and had opted for a new title such as operative or machinist, for increased occupational specificity was yet another consequence of industrialization.[38]

In terms of home ownership patterns, Hamilton's clerks did not occupy the expected middle ground. Rather, they displayed even less tendency to own homes than did some of the working class occupations. To a large degree, this reflected the fact that many of them lived at or above the shops and offices in which they were employed.[39]

As we might have expected, the elite groups among our selected occupations displayed very high levels of home ownership. Yet, even here, there was some erosion following the panic of 1857. Merchants appear to have held their own between 1852 and 1861, while lawyers declined. In relative terms, however, lawyers experienced less of a decrease than either labourers or moulders.[40] Furthermore, by 1881, the owner/occupancy patterns for both merchants and lawyers had already reached levels that were not attained by the entire population until the boom years following World War II.[41] Thus once again, but with the exception of shoemakers, differences between working class and elite had increased over the study period.

TABLE 5

Housing Types for Selected Occupations

Hamilton, 1861

Occupation	Brick or Stone	Frame	Shanty	Other	No. of Houses
Labourers	7.8%	88.4%	3.4%	0.0%	585
Railway Workers	24.5	71.4	2.0	0.0	49
Moulders	10.7	89.3	0.0	0.0	28
Shoemakers	12.3	87.7	0.0	0.0	73
Clerks	60.2	39.8	0.0	0.0	83
Merchants	86.2	13.8	0.0	0.0	65
Lawyers	81.8	18.2	0.0	0.0	33
Total City	27.0	71.4	1.0	0.6	2955

Unfortunately, information relating to the medium of construction of Hamilton's dwellings was recorded only on the 1861 Assessment Roll.[42] These figures have been summarized in Table 5. While it would be unwise to press such static figures too far, several things are obvious. First, in a year when rents were extremely low, the working class occupations, with the possible exception of some railway workers,[43] were unable to afford to live in homes constructed of brick or stone. Moreover, two groups, labourers and railway workers, together occupied more than two-thirds of the city's shanties. Clearly, it was the working class who resided in the poorest homes in Hamilton.[44] The elite, on the other hand, overwhelmingly lived in brick and stone houses; and, as we have seen, many were imposing enough to merit the critical acclaim of visitors to the city.

Throughout the study period, Hamilton remained a city of predominantly single family homes.[45] To be sure, there was some doubling up of families, even periods of severe housing shortage; but the tenements of the larger, older cities of Britain and North America were not at all prominent, even in the working class areas of Hamilton.[46] The city's workers may have been better and less densely housed than those of such places as London, New York and Montreal, but very real differences in the quality of housing for the rich and the poor still existed in Hamilton.

Since residential patterns in Hamilton were remarkably complex, to discuss changes in the residential location of the working class it is necessary to create a number of different measures of these patterns.[47]

Initially, we can gain some insight into the degree of residential clustering within each of the selected occupations by compiling statistics for the blocks occupied by each group. These figures have been summarized in Table 6. Obviously, the size of the respective group is a factor in such calculations. For example, members of the largest group, labourers, were most likely to reside upon blocks occupied by at least five others of the same occupation; while lawyers, the smallest group, were most likely to be found on blocks occupied by no other members of their occupation. Sheer size of group was not, however, the only factor involved. Neither merchants nor lawyers resided more than five to a block in any of the years of the study; yet, railway workers and moulders, the groups which were closest in size to the merchants, did.[48] The elite occupied larger dwellings and larger lots than the poor; [49] therefore, even if the sizes of the two groups had been directly comparable, their residential densities would have been quite different and the disparities between rich and poor, expressed in the figures of Table 6, would have remained about the same. The figures for clerks reflect the nineteenth century custom for them to live at or above the shops of their employers.

Sociologists have long been interested in the study of differences in the residential locations of various groups in the twentieth century city. To this end, they have developed a number of measures to enable them to uncover degrees of isolation between groups within the residential fabric of the city. Two of the most widely utilized of these measures are the Index of Segregation and the Index of Dissimilarity.[50] In the former "the residential distribution of a given group is compared to the residential distribution of all other groups taken together, ..." while the latter "measures the extent of non-overlap in the pattern of residence of any two groups, and ranges from zero to one hundred."[51]

TABLE 6

Measures of Residential Clustering for
Selected Occupations

Hamilton. 1852-1881

Occupation	1852				1861				1872				1881			
	1	2	3	4	1	2	3	4	1	2	3	4	1	2	3	4
Labourers	53	3.1	10	45	55	3.2	10	40	67	4.1	6	56	62	3.4	8	45
Railway Workers	–	–	–	–	12	1.5	50	10	15	1.8	46	25	21	1.7	39	4
Moulders	8	1.6	43	0	6	1.4	57	0	20	1.9	31	16	23	1.6	42	5
Shoemakers	33	1.6	38	6	17	1.3	56	0	27	1.8	31	6	25	1.6	42	3
Clerks	29	2.2	29	28	19	2.0	29	28	36	2.3	21	25	38	2.0	25	9
Merchants	21	1.5	48	0	14	1.4	56	0	16	1.4	49	0	16	1.6	34	0
Lawyers	8	1.0	100	0	8	1.2	75	0	6	1.2	80	0	9	1.1	78	0

Note: for each year four columns of data are presented. These are
headed:

1. Per cent of developed blocks occupied by each group
2. Average per occupied block
3. Per cent living on blocks not occupied by others with the same
   occupation
4. Per cent living on blocks with at least five of the same occupation.

Put another way, the Index of Segregation denotes the proportion of a given group that must move in order to make its distribution identical to that of the remainder of the population. The Index of Dissimilarity, on the other hand, indicates the proportion of a given group that would have to relocate in order to make the distribution of that group identical to that of a particular other group. For each of the selected occupations, the two indices have been calculated for each of the years of the study, and the results have been recorded in Tables 7, 8 and 9. Developed blocks formed the units of analysis for these calculations.[52]

TABLE 7

Index of Segregation* for Selected Occupations

Hamilton, 1852-1881

Occupation	1852	1861	1872	1881
Labourers	26	25	22	22
Railway Workers	–	41	37	35
Moulders	42	43	33	33
Shoemakers	28	35	28	30
Clerks	17	18	14	14
Merchants	36	41	39	41
Lawyers	45	45	46	45

*Based on residential patterns in the occupied blocks of the city.

Some interesting shifts can be seen in the values for the Index of Segregation over the study period (Table 7). Index values for labourers, moulders, and railway workers declined; those for shoemakers declined after peaking in 1861. This may, at first, seem surprising in light of our knowledge of the increasing stratification of society during the last half of the nineteenth century; but we must always be aware of general development trends in the place under study and of the limitations of our data. For Hamilton, several things must be considered. First, employment opportunities, especially in the larger industries, continued to disperse throughout the study period.[53] This caused some scattering of the residences of the working class. Furthermore, the population of our working class occupations expanded much faster than undeveloped blocks could be added to the city.[54] Thus, a larger working class population was being forced into a relatively smaller area. Finally, by defining developed blocks as those with at least one occupied dwelling, we have not been able to control for subsequent infilling on blocks that were not fully developed originally. Taken together, these three factors meant that the distribution of labourers, railway workers, and moulders became more similar to that of the *entire* population between 1852 and 1881.

TABLE 8
Index of Dissimilarity for Selected Occupations

Hamilton, 1852 and 1861

Index of Dissimilarity

	Occupation	1	2	3	4	5	6	7
1	Labourers		—	43	32	26	40	45
2	Railway Workers	41		—	—	—	—	—
3	Moulders	45	47		41	42	41	48
4	Shoemakers	34	44	40		28	40	46
5	Clerks	24	40	42	35		36	45
6	Merchants	44	47	46	43	41		46
7	Lawyers	46	49	45	45	45	38	

Note: 1852 figures above the main diagonal
1861 figures below the main diagonal

TABLE 9
Index of Dissimilarity for Selected Occupations

Hamilton, 1872 and 1881

	Occupation	Index of Dissimilarity						
		1	2	3	4	5	6	7
1	Labourers		37	36	32	21	44	48
2	Railway Workers	36		40	42	37	44	48
3	Moulders	33	33		36	33	43	48
4	Shoemakers	33	38	35		27	38	46
5	Clerks	22	35	33	30		38	46
6	Merchants	47	47	45	44	41		38
7	Lawyers	48	48	45	46	45	37	

Note: 1872 figures above the main diagonal
1881 figures below the main diagonal

The pattern for shoemakers was slightly different. A high proportion of old-style artisans characterized the shoemakers of 1851. Many of these operated shoe shops that served quite localized populations, resulting in a reasonably even distribution of shoemakers throughout the population. Their numbers were eroded by both the panic of 1857 and by the rise of industrial capitalism, in the form of the large boot and shoe factory. Shoemakers, therefore, became less ubiquitous in the years prior to 1861. After that date, the distribution of shoemakers performed more like those of the other working class occupations, that is, more like the population as a whole. This trend for shoemakers and the rest of the selected working class occupations need not, however, imply that the city was becoming more homogeneous. In fact, as we shall soon see, just the reverse was the case.

Segregation index values for merchants increased during the study period. By 1881, more than 40 per cent of them would have had to move in order to bring their distribution in line with that of the remainder of the population. Values for lawyers remained constant and high. Clerks, on the other hand, displayed the lowest values of any occupation. This pattern of high values for both rich and poor and low values for the middle class has been found elsewhere.[55]

While the Index of Segregation has shed some light upon the residential patterns evolving in Hamilton between 1852 and 1881, the Index of Dissimilarity is even more revealing, for it clearly points to an important indicator of the increasing stratification of its society; namely, the development of the segregated city. Tables 8 and 9 present the values for this index for the four years of the study. It will be useful to describe some of the patterns in detail. Let us first compare the distributions of labourers and lawyers. In 1852, 45 per cent of either group would have had to relocate in order to create equal distributions. By 1861, this figure had increased to 46 per cent and by 1872 to 48 per cent, a figure that was to remain constant between 1872 and 1881. Thus, the distributions of these two occupations remained quite different throughout the study period and, in fact, became less similar over time. If we next examine the figures for labourers and moulders, a quite different pattern emerges. In 1852, 43 per cent of either group would have had to move to make their distributions identical. This figure increased to 45 per cent in 1861, a consequence, no doubt, of the depression, but declined to 36 per cent by 1872 and still further to 33 per cent by 1881. These two working class occupations had residential distributions that were much more similar in 1881 than they had been in 1852.

It is, therefore, instructive to summarize the changes in the values of the Index of Dissimilarity for the selected occupations in terms of the relationships between and within classes. For example, eight unique pair groupings can be created between the selected elite and working class occupations; yet, in only two instances (railway workers vs. lawyers and moulders vs. lawyers) was there any evidence of increased similarity in the residential patterns of the pairs over time. Even so, none of these eight pairings had index values below 44 by 1881. Lawyers and merchants, on the other hand, became more similar in terms of their residential locations between 1852 and 1881. For the six distinct working class pair groupings, only one case (labourers vs. shoemakers) of increased residential dissimilarity could be isolated, and it represented a rather slight change. Finally, during the period under scrutiny, the distribution of clerks became more similar to every working class group, save shoemakers, less similar to that of merchants and remained stable but very different from that of lawyers. In summary, the occupations constituting the working class tended to become more clustered together residentially. The elite also became more similarly distributed with respect to each other. Rich and poor, however, exhibited less similar locational patterns in 1881 than they had in 1852. Generally speaking, the middle class became more like the working class than like the elite in terms of residential location.

While, in most cases, the direction of change in the values of the Index of Dissimilarity points to a more residentially segregated Hamilton, it must be admitted that the magnitude of the changes was often quite small. This reflects the complexity of the society under study, especially as revealed by such a fine level of analysis as was employed here (specific occupations over a set of individual city blocks). To date, few researchers have had the opportunity to work with such disaggregated data. Perhaps, however, given the problems associated with understanding the meaning of nineteenth century occupational titles, this level of analysis is too fine to uncover clear trends between different classes. If, for example, we group together the four working class occupations and calculate the Index of Dissimilarity between this aggregation and one composed of lawyers and merchants, we can obtain somewhat more convincing evidence that Hamilton became more residentially stratified over the time period. Between these two groups, the index values rose from 36 in 1852 to 41 in 1861 to 42 in 1872 and to 44 in 1881. When we combine this pattern with those discussed above, it becomes more evident that Hamilton's residential structure was not the same in 1881 as it had been in 1852. We can, however, say little regarding the overall significance of the changes suggested by these statistics until we have comparable data for other nineteenth century cities. Nonetheless, the trends uncovered for Hamilton force one to presuppose that that city had begun to develop more homogeneous residential districts at quite an early date.

As we have seen, Hamilton became more residentially segregated during the years covered by this study. At the same time, however, the residential locations of the rich and the poor also altered. A useful measure of these changes is the location quotient which is employed to indicate whether a given attribute is under-represented, evenly represented or over-represented with respect to the overall distribution of the population as a whole, within any set of sub-areas of a city or other political unit.[56]

The values of the location quotient can be readily mapped and such maps can be utilized to pinpoint areas in which a given attribute (for example, the number of labourers or merchants) is highly conspicuous. It will be sufficient to discuss the values of this measure for the years 1852 and 1881 and for two aggregate groups, the working class and the elite. Furthermore, in addition to the maps depicting the values of the location quotient, maps illustrating the percentage distribution of the two aggregate groups have also been prepared.[57]

For the working class, the period from 1852 to 1881 was one in which there was a marked shift in residential location. In the former year, Hamilton's workers had been highly over-represented[58] in the south-eastern portion of the city (Figure 2). By 1881, however, the area of highest over-representation had become the city's north end (Figure 3), a region that was fragmented by rail lines and rail yards[59] and which, even at this relatively late date, contained considerable expanses of low-lying, poorly drained land.

The location quotient merely identifies the relative representation of a group in each of the selected areal units of the city. It tells us nothing about the actual numbers involved. Yet, maps of the percentage distribution of the working class (Figures 6 and 7) support the trends suggested by the location quotient maps. For example, in 1852, just over 30 per cent of the working class resided in those zones which were located south and east of Hamilton's main intersection, the junction of King and James Streets. Only about 14 per cent of the working class lived in that area in 1881. [60] The northern fringe of the city,[61] on the other hand, increased its share of the working class from 27 per cent in 1852 to 47 per cent in 1881. In Hamilton, at least, industrialization had pulled many of the working class to the periphery of the city.[62]

During the three decades under investigation, Hamilton's well-to-do consolidated their hold on the choicest residential areas in the city (Figures 4 and 5). By 1881, the zones in which the elite were highly over-represented were almost all located in the southern (south of King Street) portion of the city. This area was well-drained and was largely situated on gently rising ground leading from the heart of the city to the base of the Mountain (Niagara Escarpment), a much pleasanter and more salubrious locale than the poor were discovering on the northern periphery. The actual distribution patterns of the well-to-do support the trends suggested by the location quotient values: for, between 1852 and 1881, the southern half of the city increased its share of the elite from 43 to 63 per cent (Figures 8 and 9). As the city expanded in area, then, the physical distance between rich and poor increased. The well-to-do laid claim to the aesthetically pleasing south end, the poor located to the north, amid the industries and railways and, sometimes, the marshes of the "Ambitious City." The fragmentation of Hamilton along economic and class lines had begun. In the process, the quality of the residential environment must have declined for many of the city's poorer families.

Peter Goheen has suggested that modern patterns of residential differentiation, based upon socio-economic criteria, evolved during the last half of the nineteenth century. His findings, based upon the study of a relatively large Canadian city, Toronto, agreed with those of Warner for Philadelphia. As this study has illustrated, however, this process was not restricted to large urban centres. Industrialization altered North American society in many ways. Most noticeably it changed the scale of production of goods; but it also meant new work settings, a new set of employer/employee relations and an ever widening gap between rich and poor. By 1881, Hamilton had emerged as an important industrial city in central Canada and the consequences of industrialization were visible in its landscape. The railway and the new industries were constant reminders that a new age had dawned.[63]

Housing, too, was changed by the coming of the industrial age, but perhaps in more subtle ways. Between 1852 and 1881, the gap separating the rich and the poor widened. The relative value of the homes occupied by the working class declined. Their propensity to own homes did increase, but, with few exceptions, the differences in home ownership levels for the rich and the poor increased. Clearly, industrial capitalism had not provided a level of wages and job security that would permit and encourage home ownership among Hamilton's workers. Moreover, the working class became more clustered together and, simultaneously, more distant, in physical terms, from the well-to-do. Finally, the poor came to locate increasingly in the less salubrious portions of Hamilton, while the elite pre-empted choice sites in the vicinity of the Mountain. In Vance's words, industrialization meant that

the cellular nature of urban structure was replaced by *urban stratification* wherein the 'means test' came to substitute for the 'place of employment' in determining where within the city a man and his family would live.[64]

Hamilton remained a small place in 1881. It was still a pedestrian city; yet, even though its physical scale had changed but little, social distances had altered noticeably in the years since mid-century.

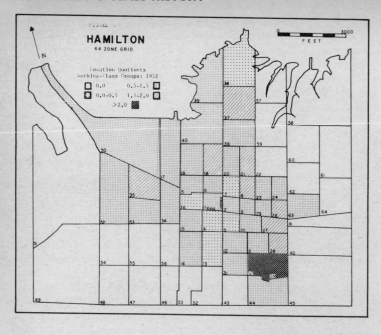

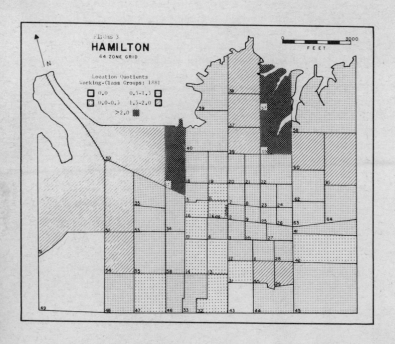

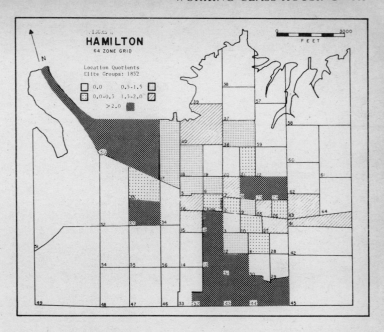

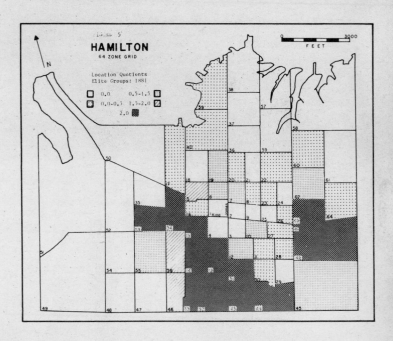

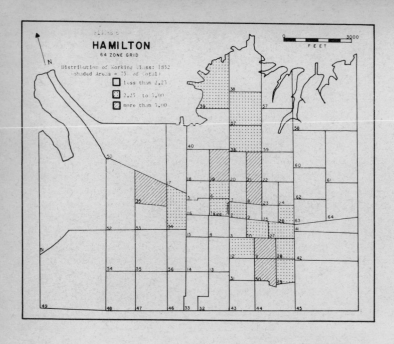

Figure 6

HAMILTON
64 ZONE GRID

Distribution of Working Class: 1852
(Shaded Areas = 75% of Total)

less than 2.25%
2.25 to 5.00%
more than 5.00%

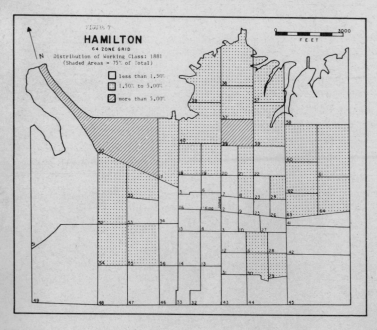

Figure 7

HAMILTON
64 ZONE GRID

Distribution of Working Class: 1881
(Shaded Areas = 75% of Total)

less than 1.50%
1.50% to 5.00%
more than 5.00%

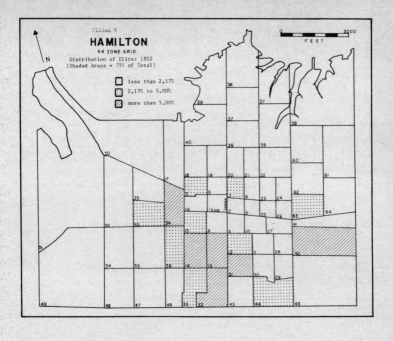

FIGURE 8

HAMILTON
64 ZONE GRID
Distribution of Elite: 1852
(Shaded Areas = 75% of Total)

□ less than 2.17%
▦ 2.17% to 5.00%
▨ more than 5.00%

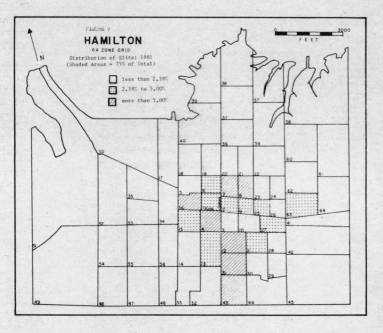

FIGURE 9

HAMILTON
64 ZONE GRID
Distribution of Elite: 1881
(Shaded Areas = 75% of Total)

□ less than 2.38%
▦ 2.38% to 5.00%
▨ more than 5.00%

"Give us the road and we will run it"
The Social and Cultural Matrix
of an Emerging Labour Movement

Bryan D. Palmer

MOB RULE! . . . THE POLICE POWERLESS . . . PROPERTY OF THE STREET RAILWAY COMPANY WANTONLY DESTROYED. With these shrill headlines the *London Free Press* informed the citizenry of the Forest City of the events of the weekend of July 8-9, 1899. Across southwestern and south-central Ontario other newspapers – the *Brantford Expositor, Guelph Mercury, Woodstock Express, Berlin News, Chatham Planet, Toronto News, Toronto Mail-Empire, Toronto Star* – echoed similar sentiments. While the *London Advertiser*, London labour's long-time liberal supporter, refrained from the sensationalist hysteria of the jaundiced press, it too spoke of "Trouble in London" and stressed Joseph Marks' (the city's pre-eminent labour spokesman) restrained plea that, "The lives and property of citizens have to be respected." Excepting the *Industrial Banner*, an aggressive voice of the workingman based in London, the area's press seemed deeply disturbed by the riotous behaviour manifested in London's central business districts on July 8, 1899.[1]

And disturbed they well might have been, for on July 8th London had been the scene of a violent battle which could only be described in terms of "class war." For many months the street railway company and its workers, affiliated with the Amalgamated Association of Street Railway Employees, had bickered, engaging and re-engaging in negotiations. One strike had already run its course, and another was initiated in May of 1899. With this second strike still in progress in July, and with the company manning its cars with non-union, non-resident men, resentment was boiling to a fever pitch. Emboldened by the conspicuous support of the community, and enticed by rumours that the strikebreakers were about to abandon their cars in defiance of the railway management, one thousand working people gathered on the corners of Dundas and Adelaide Streets. When the cars failed to return to the barns, the "crowd" acted in concert: London experienced the trauma of a working class "riot."

Yet the street railway strike of 1898-1899, and its violent offspring, the "riot" of July 8th and 9th, are occurrences of which we know far too little. The strike merits an obscure refer-

106

ence in Lipton's classic treatment of Canadian trade union development and a chapter or two in some dated Masters' theses. Beyond this we know virtually nothing. A recent explication of London's urban evolution, for instance, gives us no food for thought as to why the nineteenth century would close on such a violent note of labour-capital conflict.[2]

Given the paltry state of our knowledge, it is the purpose of this study to examine the milieu in which the street railway strike thrived, and in which the events of July 8th and 9th erupted. To do so is to do nothing less than examine the social and cultural matrix in which a labour movement developed in nineteenth century London, Ontario. For just as the riotous actions of early July flowed directly from the frustrations and inner logic of the strike, the carmen's struggle itself was part of a larger process: the emergence and consolidation of a labour movement. Moreover, as the strike's roots reached far back into London's past, so its impact stretched into the future. In the aftermath of the conflict we glimpse a persistent demand in clashes between London's workers and employers. Workers consciously raised the issue of labour's control, or self-management, over the nature and conditions of work. Although certainly not a local demand, this thrust for control was first articulated in London in 1899, during the street railway strike. The strikers' cry, "Give us the road and we will run it," remained the legacy of the events of 1898-1899.

London, like many English Canadian cities, was peopled by migrants from the British Isles. Early in its development the city lacked the manufacturing drawing power to attract Old World migrants: in 1851-1852 the *Census* revealed that London's population was dominated by native-born Canadians, a situation contrasting sharply with established trends in other urban areas, already experiencing the swelling tide of immigration. By 1871, however, with the expanding labour market bred of economic growth and industrialization, the city attracted newcomers, and the demographic structure reflected this change. Those of English background had risen to prominence, comprising 42 per cent of the population, while the Irish and Scots contingents contributed a further 34 per cent and 18 per cent, respectively. The Anglo-Canadian contours of the city's demographic structure had solidified by 1911, when fully 52 per cent of the community's population was descended from English stock; the Irish and Scots, comprising a further 37 per cent of the population, were prominent minorities, but their presence was clearly overshadowed by the preponderance of the English.[3]

All of this, it can be argued, does not offer any significant deviation from the settlement patterns common to many areas in Canada West. Another variable must be taken into consideration: London was, above all else, a Protestant community. Even given the presence of almost 10,000 Irish in 1911, the city contained only 5,262 Catholics. The large numbers of Presbyterians (8,000 in 1911) suggests that London's Irish were not the Munster or Connaught Catholic peasants whose influx in the 1830s and 1840s supplied the raw muscle needed to construct Canada's canals and railways. Rather, London's Irish likely tended to be Ulster Protestants or sturdy Scotch-Irish, men and women reared in the same urban setting which had spawned their English counterparts.[4]

Other sources, more impressionistic than the figures from *Census* tables, but equally enlightening, also reinforce our conception of London as a community characterized by a marked degree of ethnocultural consensus. London's "dangerous classes," for instance, clearly came from the lower percentiles of the socio-economic hierarchy, but they did not appear to be drawn from any social or ethnic stratum which contrasted sharply with the city's demographic profile. (The only alien element that managed to appear conspicuously on the listings of those arrested and jailed in the years 1893-1906, was a group of Chinese convicted *en masse* on gambling charges). London also seemed to lack any structured residential segregation rooted in poverty and/or ethnic affiliation: with the passage of time came a certain rigidification of neighbourhoods and enclaves, but as late as the turn of the century London still lacked an area which could properly be termed a ghetto. Equally striking was the absence of traditional Protestant-Catholic strife at a time when religious conflict appeared endemic throughout urban Ontario. While Orange and Green brawled in the taverns and on the streets in Hamilton, Galt, and Toronto every July 12 and March 17, an atmosphere of fraternal benevolence prevailed in London. The city's Orangemen often found the outlying agricultural districts more congenial to their cause than the inner city: on July 17, 1889, for example, three London Lodges celebrated with a parade in Exeter, thirty miles north of the city. Michael Cross has noted that "Orangeism was weak not only where Catholics were decisively strong but also where they were so few in number as to provide no threat to Protestant hegemony." For London, the latter was most emphatically the case.[5]

If the city exhibited a remarkable ethnic and religious homogeneity, it also showed a cultural affinity of a particular sort, tinged with the traditions of dissent and a persistent, if mellowed, nonconformity. Dominating the institutional structure of London's churches were the faiths which had long-ago broken with the stale and acquiescent ritualism of the Anglican

Church: Baptists, Presbyterians, and Methodists supplied the bulk of London's denominational adherents. Lurking behind these established bastions of nonconformity were the more fervent sects – Christian Workers, Non-Conformists, New Church, Universalists, Plymouth Brethren – whose very names attested to their estrangement from the parental ecclesiastical bodies: these are E. J. Hobsbawm's and Liston Pope's "labour sects." And even the Anglican Church, in which London's Irish were disproportionately prominent, became, through a process of the Irish Protestant clergy's hostility to anything remotely Catholic, "marked by a sympathy for Calvinism, by an intense love of simplicity in worship,... and by a Protestantism stiffer than that of any other brand of Anglican communion."[6]

It was this fervent Protestantism, pietistic and evangelical, which tempered much of London life in the nineteenth century. While the nonconformist churches, as institutions, settled into obsequiousness, servile and deferential towards their "social betters," men's minds and consciousness retained much of their forefather's passion. For the pietist, religious conviction, rooted in the egalitarianism of the congregational brotherhood, was no narcotic forestalling social change, but a spur to action. The establishment of a Protestant Orphan's Home and the construction of an Asylum for the insane, for instance, emanated directly from the intense pietism of the community. For the workingman, too, this religious fervour brought tangible gain. In the ubiquitous uproar over the desecration of the Sabbath, London's labouring people came to associate their interests with those of the sabbatarians. For, if even the Sabbath could be debased to the level of all other days, London's working men and women could look forward to seven days of toil, rather than their customary six. And they saw no benefit in that.[7]

The most active of Protestant causes was not sabbatarianism, however, but its scrappy sibling, the temperance movement. In London, the Temperance Coffee House of Market Square was long regarded as a local institution worthy of any visitor's attention; that same building often served as an informal gathering place for the city's industrious labourers on a Saturday afternoon. Diverse segments of the local populace energetically supported the "cold water" cause, and no movement was so willingly endorsed by the local press. Temperance societies and organizations seemed to spring from London's soil: as early as 1851 the community had been the recruiting grounds for the Sons of Temperance; in the 1870s the Red Ribbon Society boasted a membership of over 3,000; and in 1876 London gained international prominence when the United Temperance Association of Canada established itself in the city. Dedicated to "the elevation of... intellectual character, [the] cementing...

[of] the bonds of the common brotherhood of man, [and the] cultivation [of] feelings of mutual respect," the temperance advocate found his staunchest support among that strata of the working class – the artisans and skilled craftsmen – whose historical commitment to self-help, mutual aid, and egalitarianism made them pillars of an emerging labour movement. And, indeed, it was among London's artisans that we find the traditions and heritage of the free-born Englishman, reared in the context of an active Protestantism, most vibrant.[8]

The historic importance of the skilled craftsman has long been recognized: in Britain and France artisans gained an early reputation as political activists and radical democrats. This penchant for activism crossed the Atlantic with the British migrations of the eighteenth and nineteenth centuries; it soon manifested itself in the United States and Canada. Standing in the midst of that "rich, shadowy Dickensian understory of artisan toil, high aspiration, self-education, impecuniosity, eccentricity, and sub-parliamentary political activity..." the skilled mechanic was most certainly "an uncommon common man."[9]

Although the later decades of the nineteenth century were years in which handicraft production was consistently being undermined, the artisan "manufactory" remained an ubiquitous, albeit declining, presence. In London, where the foundries and factories of the East end attained an early pre-eminence, innumerable craftsmen, aided by apprenticed journeymen, practised the "mysteries" of a trade mastered decades in the past. Often large concerns, such as Imperial Oil, retained the services of artisans whose knowledge and expertise proved invaluable. Leeman Crawford, carriagemaker, was just such a figure: self-employed owner of his own small business, he was also retained by Sarnia oil concerns to construct made-to-order vehicles. Even among London's Irish, where one would expect to find an abundance of the unskilled worker, skilled tradesmen predominated. If the Anglo-Protestant contours of London's social structure appeared pronounced, the resiliency of artisan modes of work was equally striking.[10]

While the craftsman's role in the city's productive output was undoubtedly great, it was his influence in the institutions of social and cultural life that was most noteworthy. To glimpse this phenomenon we will examine the role of the artisan in the city's friendly societies and Mechanic's Institute, for it was these corporate bodies which epitomized the British craftsman's traditions of self-help, mutual aid, and cooperation.

Perhaps the most striking aspect of later nineteenth century popular culture was the omnipresent friendly or benevolent society. Between 1874 and 1905 no less than sixty-four such organizations petitioned the County clerk for incorporation rights. The city hosted a number of annual conventions of the Ancient and Honourable Fraternity of Free and Accepted Masons, but other societies also found the area attracting. Londoners remained prominent figures on executive boards of many national and international organizations: Antwell Fleming, an apprenticed printer, and B. W. Greer, a prominent Forest City carriagemaker, for instance, functioned within the hierarchy of the Independent Order of Foresters. The city's penchant for association even extended into a more jocular vein. A motley crew of soldiers, printers, and cabinet-makers, dubbing themselves the "Hellfriar's Club," engineered a series of innocent house break-ins in the 1860s. Corresponding with the local press, these pranksters – with the pseudonyms "Slippery Jack" and "Korn Kob, jun." – focused their ridicule upon a social stratum they blithely pegged "the mushroom aristocracy."[11]

Yet, if the friendly society was a potent force in the social lives of London's citizens, we have still to ascertain who comprised the societies' membership. Like most questions concerned with the social/cultural lives of working men and women, the issue defies a precise and simplistic answer: membership listings are inevitably scattered and incomplete. The occupations of those applying for membership in the Forest City Lodge #38, of the International Order of Oddfellows, 1857-1866, for instance, failed to indicate a homogeneous working class base. Clerks, salesmen and merchants were the most prevalent occupational categories culled from the membership applications. Nevertheless, such figures distort the social composition of the fraternal society, for in totalling a diverse number of artisan occupations, we find that the vast majority of applicants seeking entrance to the I.O.O.F. came from the skilled trades. Another listing, published in 1894, detailing the occupations of the membership of St. John's Lodge #20, Ancient Free and Accepted Masons, revealed a similar tendency. Ambivalence characterized the occupational structure of the friendly society's membership, but it was ambivalence dominated by the numerical presence of the artisan.[12]

If the membership listings fail to establish conclusively the primary role of London's artisans in the city's benevolent organizations, other realms of inquiry produce less ambiguity. The *City Directories* listed the area's societies, along with the principal officers: secretaries, treasurers, recorders, scribes; and the more exotic Grand Templars, Most Wise Sovereigns and 32nd Degree Eusibius'. In this critical stratum of functioning officers, members of the skilled trades were most abundant. In 1880, the officers of the Loyal Lodge #5772 of the Canadian Order of Oddfellows, John Day, Samuel King, and W. H. Phillips, were employed in the crafts of tinsmithing, carpentry, and watchmaking. A local chapter of the Knights of Pythias was headed by tinsmith John Maker and painter Richard Poulton in 1898. And in 1913 the Chorazin Lodge #190 of the I.O.O.F. was represented by two carpenters: G. J. Lonfield and Fred Watkinson. In many societies it was men like these who served as secretaries and spoke from the rostrum. In other areas too, the friendly society appeared as part of a larger context in which the traditions and culture of the nineteenth century artisan loomed large. With their elaborate reliance upon ritual the societies pointed to the prevalence of pre-capitalist traits within their midst. Even the language of the friendly society, a complex amalgam rooted in the terminology of the skilled trades, reflected the shared bond between the craftsmen and the associations in which they figured so prominently. Schooled in the rites, rituals and mysteries of apprenticeship, the artisan had carried age-old traditions into the fraternal orders.[13]

Rivalling the friendly societies as a potent force within the artisan community was the local Mechanic's Institute. Historians have been quick to point to the dominance of the crusading "middle classes" within these early agencies of adult education, and there is some truth in this interpretation. Eleanor Shaw, chronicler of the London Public Library, reiterates this theme of the presence of the propertied elements in London's Institute. Yet questions of control are seldom so easily resolved; indeed, a study of London's Institute reveals that the skilled workingman often exercised a degree of independence in his role within and relationship to the local Institute.[14]

Originally established in 1835, the Institute floundered and then revived in January of 1841, when fifty-eight citizens banded together for the "mutual dissemination of knowledge." The original constitution, stating that "not less than three-fourths of the officers shall be practical artisans and mechanics" (Article 8), attested to the tradesmen's attempts to retain their hegemony within the Institute's halls. Yet, it was an ineffectual measure, and as early as 1851 "A Mechanic" voiced disgust with the dominance of a clique catering "to party spirit and class interest." Deploring the gross underestimation of the intelligent artisan's capabilities, this disgruntled mechanic stressed the unnecessary prevalence of non-working class elements in positions of authority. A study of the 1851-1872 membership listings confirms his charges, but also points to the strength of the skilled tradesmen as regular patrons of the Institute's reading rooms.[15]

With the closing decades of the nineteenth century the Mechanic's Institute declined. Other halls – those of the trade union, the temperance society, and the fraternal order – came to function as viable substitutes for the Mechanic's Institute; their rooms were often cluttered with workingmen, attentively present at lectures on topics of interest, or leisurely thumbing the pages of a worn classic. By 1880 not one-fifth of the Institute's membership was drawn from a working class constituency. In 1889, the Trades and Labour Council formed the "Workingmen's Free Library" and initiated a campaign to establish a free public library. Successful in their venture, the city's labour movement was represented on the Library Board by Joseph Marks, a former tinsmith turned labour journalist. Upon the establishment of the Library in 1895, the Mechanic's Institute donated its 3,000 volumes to the new institution and disbanded. Abandoned by those for whom and by whom it had initially been set up, it withered into oblivion.[16]

The historical development of the London Mechanic's Institute remains representative of the ambivalence characteristic of so many nineteenth century workingmen's institutions. Dominated by propertied elements (Article 8 had only a very brief practical influence), the Institute was nevertheless a bastion of the artisan penchant for adult education and scientific knowledge. With no other vehicle capable of satisfying their thirst for knowledge, skilled tradesmen were content to tolerate the irksome presence of patronizingly antagonistic class elements. By the 1880s however, other movements, causes, and institutions had arisen, and the mechanics bolted, asserting their autonomy by leading the struggle for a free public library. Steeling the skilled worker in the lessons of self-help and mutual aid (as well as stressing the gains to be gleaned from literacy), the Mechanic's Institute, like the friendly society, was a "nursery for the industrious classes" of the community. Lessons learned in its halls would not be forgotten in later years.

We have ranged over a broad terrain – from the ethnic composition of the social structure, through the prominence of a dissenting Protestantism, across the reformist movements bred of evangelical fervour, and into the cultural institutions of London's artisan community – and we have unavoidably fragmented too much. What has perhaps been distorted by the above analysis is the unity of the whole, the subtle, but pervasive, interconnections linking the various strands of London's ethnocultural milieu. What we have is not isolated movements, institutions, and cultural forms, but a matrix in which distinct strains coalesced and fused, building upon and borrowing from common traditions and assumptions.

We find, for instance, that the Mechanic's Institute held its early meetings in the Episcopal Methodist Church. One of our first references to the temperance sentiment that would prevail in later decades was " "Nemo, Junior's" assault on the Mechanic's Institute, where, he contended, one could not engage in intelligent discourse without being bombarded by vitriolic denunciations of intemperance. While fraternal and reform societies shared a common legacy of ritual, regalia, and moral righteousness, they also merged in their militant commitment to democracy and egalitarianism. Note the Oddfellows purpose:

We aim to abolish all considerations of wealth or poverty in our fraternity; to make all feel that as Odd-Fellows, at least, they are not only brethren but equals.

And the Ancient Order of United Workmen, by imposing "no religious test other than a belief in the Deity," functioned within a tradition of radical dissent central to the nonconformist impulse. But the most potent of traditions, as the Workmen's motto "Alterium alterius auxilio eget" emphasized, was that of mutual aid:[17]

'In union there is strength,' is a common axiom .... A single individual if he labor with a will, may accomplish much in the field of fraternity, but a host, united in solid phalanx in the service of Benevolence, may revolutionize the world.

Throughout the growth of this complex social and cultural milieu, the "rights of free-born Englishmen" consistently surfaced as critical determinants. In welcoming the North American St. George's Union to London, site of the society's twelfth annual convention, the *Advertiser* paid homage to this phenomenon: "...wherever the standard of civilization, Christianity and civil liberty is planted, there have always been found, and always will be, men with English blood in their veins." London's workingmen had been successful in their efforts to transplant the liberty tree. The soil that nurtured its growth would prove equally favourable to its offspring, a labour movement moulded in the image of the British artisan.[18]

The 1860s, a decade which saw Canada emerge as a nation and industrial capital begin to establish itself as a hegemonic force, witnessed the first rumblings of discontent from Canadian labour. In London, as in other North American urban settings, the workingman's fight against the impersonalization of the emerging market economy was championed most ardently by the skilled tradesman and his craft union. The International Union of Iron Moulders was the first such organization to come into being in the Forest City (1859), and was soon joined by the Bricklayers Protective Association, founded in 1863. But the most vigorous of early unions was the Typographers, established in the late 1860s by four London printers: Thomas Coffee, Archie and Alec Bremner, and John Dewer. Those forces driving the workingman to organize may well have been diverse and variegated, but the *Rules of the Amalgamated Society of Carpenters and Joiners* seemed to capture the essence of these early institutions:

The Amalgamated Society of Carpenters and Joiners has for

its primary object the raising of the status of the artisans engaged in these trades, and generally to improve the conditions under which they shall labour.

Within this context, it was the woodworker's motto – "United we stand; divided we fall" – which pointed to a significant current of thought linking many of these early organizations, that of cooperative enterprise.[19]

We should hardly be surprised to find the cooperative impulse strong among London's workingmen. No strain within the British labour movement, in which many of London's craftsmen must have been reared, had been so pronounced, and we have noticed its presence in the rise of the friendly society. In June of 1867 a number of the city's men acted out this attachment to mutual aid. William Fairburn, tailor, William Scott, carpenter, William Phillips, shoemaker, Robert Richie, machinist, and ten other craftsmen united "to carry out the principles of cooperation between seller and purchaser." Temperate, suspicious of credit, fearful of monopoly, and rigidly adhering to the tenets of democratic organization, these skilled workers saw their chance to transcend the perils of a market economy. While their action was a bold attempt to retain some measure of autonomy, the impersonality and vicissitudes of the market proved too formidable an opponent. By the mid-1870s the Cooperative Association was a dying venture; the impulse, however, lived on, and was to resurface periodically.[20]

Throughout the 1870s, while other urban areas were confronted with the earnest activity of an emerging national labour movement, London appeared rather calm and unagitated. While reform thrusts and attempts to consolidate craft union memberships were prevalent, there appeared to be little concerted action among the city's workingmen. The Nine-Hour movement, often seen as the critical component of labour's activity in the 1870s, gained no foothold in London. Indeed, the major events appeared to be a successful labourer's strike in July of 1872 in which "the men went back to work . . . at the advance of one shilling a day," and the Moulder's picnic, held at Port Stanley, which attracted over three hundred people.[21]

A lack of overt conflict is, however, a poor gauge from which to infer a lack of discontent. The shoemakers seemed relatively placid throughout the 1870s, yet the community's cordwainers flocked to London Lodge #242 of the Knights of St. Crispin. The presence of the Crispins, more than the absence of explicit confrontation, articulated the craft workers' estrangement from the new industrial order. Threatened by the rise of "greenhands" (non-apprenticed shoemakers), attempting to create a unity of action among the city's cobblers, and adamant in their right to exercise control over their craft through the consolidation of an international shoemaker's organization, London's cordwainers were perhaps the embodiment of the artisan response to industrial capital. Turning to the moral economy of a world long lost, the Crispins insisted that labour was the foundation of all social well-being, and "was entitled to ... government protection and encouragement." When such support failed to materialize, the shoemakers embraced cooperation as a panacea capable of remedying their present situation.[22]

The declining status of the cobbler's trade, the more generalized demise of the boot and shoe industry and the drastic impact of the depression of 1873-1877, hit the Crispins especially hard. Their staying power was understandably reduced and, like so many of London's craft societies, they died in the hard and hungry years of the late 1870s. But if the Knights of St. Crispin disappeared, the loss of the shoemaker's institutional garb was not as significant as the legacy left to future toilers: in later decades and more turbulent times the cordwainer, that most ubiquitous of labouring intellectuals, would continue to be a central spokesman for London's working class.[23]

Out of the depression-riddled organizations of the late 1870s surfaced the city's first real labour movement. With the upturn in the economy of the 1880s, London, like so many Canadian cities, experienced an unprecedented growth in union membership; from this flowed a heightened militancy. In regular columns – "Work and Wages" and the "Knights of Labor Corner" – the *London Advertiser* linked the community's wage earners to developments of national and international importance. Co-ordinating labour's upsurge was the Trades and Labour Council, founded in 1884. Led by R. H. Hessel, a carpenter active in South end fraternal organizations, the early Council was comprised of the Cigarmakers Union, the Typographers, and the Iron Moulders. The years 1886 and 1887 stood out as particularly acute; strikes by foundry workers, carpenters, bricklayers and hod-carriers precipitated a previously unknown class polarization of the city. Hessel reminisced on the angry response of the business community: "I was told by one prominent merchant while in his store buying overalls that the trade unionists should be run out of the city." And in June of 1887 the Western Ontario Builders Laborers further angered London's anti-unionists by assembling in the city to urge "the systematic enforcement of the boycott against firms who employ non-union men and foreign labourers at a lower price per day than [a] union workman is paid." Reflecting the increasing consciousness of organization which permeated London's wage earning class, these developments were part of a more particular process of growth – the phenomenal rise of the Knights of Labor – which stimulated labour's upsurge further still.[24]

The role of the Knights of Labor in the city's growing labour movement is one more area of central importance about which we know all too little. We do know that at least seven Local Assemblies were active in the Forest City between 1882 and 1890. Moreover, when London's workers testified before the Royal Commission the influence of the Knights appeared to be paramount. Not only were local Knights prominent as speakers, but the issues and grievances which the Order raised across North America received special attention. And in their comments on the benefits of cooperative association, London's workers articulated the revival of mutual aid which flowed directly from the expansion of the Knights' ranks.[25]

The vitality of the Order's presence was most vividly revealed by a gathering of working class and pro-labour elements in July of 1886. Held under the auspices of the Iron Moulders Union #47, Knights of Labor, this public show of strength was the city's first labour demonstration. With total attendance estimated at between 8,000 and 10,000, the event was described in exuberant terms: "largest demonstration ever held in Canada"; "an immense turnout of workingmen"; "over 4,000 unionists in line"; "formed an unbroken line from Ridout Street to Queen's Park." Heading the workingmen's entourage was Mayor Hodgins and the local aldermen; we thus glimpse the socio-political bond binding the wage earners and the locus of community power which was so characteristic of nineteenth century cities.[26]

Captain Trevellick, a well-travelled spokesman for the Knights, addressed the throng. In his speech, the reformer/ unionist tied the city's organizational spurt of the past years to two critical components of London's ethnocultural matrix. By emphasizing the "duty of the workingmen to educate themselves," Trevellick reasserted the artisanal commitment to self-help and self-education. Finally, although the organizer was an advocate of greenbackism and the eight-hour day, he chose to stress yet another reform note:

In watching the procession, which he was told had numbered 4,019, he thought that of all that vast number there was not one drunkard. He did not want to disparage the cause of Christian workers or of the temperance advocates in Canada ..., but he was free to say that the Knights of Labor had done more to make men sober than any organization that had ever existed in America.

To this the unionists responded with "Loud Cheers!"[27]

The Knights were not destined to sustain their gains of the 1880s. A host of factors – employers' hostility, the economic downturn of the early nineties, craft union opposition, and leadership and organizational ineptness all contributed to the

Order's demise. In London the Local Assemblies held their membership with great tenacity, but by 1892 much of their activity had ceased.[28]

Once again, however, this institutional failure was perhaps less significant than the persistence of the workingman's cultural heritage. Manifesting itself in the establishment of the *Industrial Banner* in 1892, and in the emergence of the "Radical Club," a meeting place for the city's artisan activists, the skilled tradesman's radicalism remained amazingly resistant to corrosion. In the aftermath of the demonstration of 1886, one offended workingman expressed his dissatisfaction with the editorializing of the *London Free Press* (this was, we should remember, the era of Haymarket, May Day, and the mass strike):

> I have been watching the editorials of the London Free Press ... and I think they should bring the blush of shame to every lover of British fair play. Does it imagine that there are no avenues of information other than its own columns, that it insults the intelligence of its readers by such twaddle.

Signed "Decency," the letter articulated the free-born Englishman's dedication to his rights as man and citizen, a devotion to "fair play" that brought the skilled worker increasingly into conflict with his employer. For when "fair play" was transgressed upon, as it so regularly seemed to be in the mills and shops of the new order, the artisan had the inclination to act. Moreover, he saw his actions as part of a legitimized right, and often drew other segments of the working class and the community into battle with him. It was this confluence of class and culture which the street railway strike would make abundantly clear.[29]

No municipal concern was so characteristically the scene of labour-capital conflict and public protestation as the nineteenth century street railway. From Waco, Texas to Winnipeg, Manitoba, employees and "the interests" battled in a series of violent turn-of-the-century upheavals. To the public, antagonistically anti-monopoly and totally dependent upon railways for transportation to and from places of leisure and toil, the fare and the regularity and quality of service were matters of utmost importance; municipalization was an overly popular panacea. If Hamilton, Philadelphia, Brooklyn, Toronto, and countless other North American cities witnessed the motormen's struggles for a better life and a better wage, the conflict in London was equally as vehement.[30]

London's street railway was established in 1873. Led by John Carling, five prominent businessmen secured rights to the city's streets for fifty years; during the next two decades their horse-drawn cars did considerable business, but with Toronto's system exhibiting the benefits of electrification, talk of modernizing the London system was widespread. Local entrepreneurs, however, lacked the capital and expertise essential to the electrification of the roads. A Cleveland interest, Everett and Grace, was thus allowed to purchase a majority stock holding in the company, and on September 13, 1895, the city's first electric car started on its route.[31]

By 1896 the serenity which had distinguished labour-management relations on the horse-drawn system had disintegrated. The Cleveland interest's practice of importing workmen infuriated the resident carmen; differential rates of pay for regular and relief men, rigid discipline and the Company's unrelenting demands further fueled the employees' discontent. The motormen formed a branch of the Amalgamated Association of Street Railway Employees and on October 28, 1898 they struck.[32]

The strike quickly attracted the sympathy of the public. Five thousand Londoners gathered at the Princess Rink to express their contempt for the company. Prominent speakers assured the men that God was on their side, demanded that the workers be treated "as men, and not as slaves" and depreciated the "monopoly crushing these men." The *Industrial Banner* aptly described the gathering as "a magnificent testimonial to London's sense of British fair play." As the strike progressed, community support stiffened: local shopkeepers refused to service non-union workmen; fraternal orders – Orangemen, Woodmen, Masons, and Orient Club – popularized the slogan "we walk to protect labour"; and local trade unions were generous in their financial backing. Few segments of London society visibly supported the corporation.[33]

With this web of legitimization extending across the city, violence against the Company seemed inevitable. Cars and their non-union motormen were mercilessly pelted with assorted paraphernalia; women hurled abuse at the drivers and yelled that "they would not ride as long as a 'scab' was at work." Austin Addison, a street railway operative who chose to break ranks with his former fellows, was the target of particular revilement. Children hounded him in the streets shrieking "Scab! Scab!"; he was often accosted in alleyways and darkened streets; even his young daughter was assaulted, run over by a bicycle driven by classmates. Reporting these incidents, the *Free Press* wailed that "the people have been led into giving open approval to disorder." Anarchy seemed imminent.[34]

Eventually this widespread support won the day for the carmen. Drastic losses in revenue and threats to company property and personnel eventually brought President Everett to London to implement a settlement. The agreement, signed on November 11, 1898, was looked upon as an important victory for London's workers:

It was a warning to the trusts that the patience of the people has reached its limit; that the wage earner has rights that capitalist organizations must respect. It was a magnificent tribute to London's sense of British fair play, an outspoken verdict that no company or corporation could afford to ignore.

Only the future would tell how attentive the Everett group would be to such a warning; whether "British fair play" would continue to reign.[35]

As the winter and spring months of 1899 passed, it appeared that the Company was doing everything in its power to nullify the agreement of 1898. Grievances lingered, yet the company, led by Manager Carr, brazenly refused to accommodate the men, concentrating instead on insisting that employees remain loyal to the company and disband their union. The carmen's anger escalated and amidst the rain and thunder of the afternoon of May 22, 1899, the cars returned to their barns. A second strike was underway.[36]

Once again an irate citizenry gravitated to the striker's cause. And again, the traditions of the Old Country seemed to feed the community's sympathy for the workingmen: a procession heading towards a meeting at the Grand Opera House broke into a chorus of "Rule Britannia"; minister and mayor deplored the men's "un-English" treatment and the moral turpitude of the Company. Fraternal organizations, led by the Sons of England, once more joined the union carmen, and across Southwestern Ontario the wealthy outsider, "Boss Everett," became the focal point of a vicious harangue. Thousands thronged to the Jubilee Rink to hear Joseph Marks chronicle the struggle "against a company composed largely of American capital." With community consensus so clearly in their favour, the motormen gained a confidence and zeal seldom attained by striking workmen.[37]

The carmen's original act of defiance was to run buses along the routes serviced by the Company's trolley cars. While this measure provoked the management, it provided little gratification for the angry workers and they soon turned to more illicit tactics. John Garnett, chairman of the strikers' committee, was incarcerated, charged with placing torpedoes on the tracks; a similar fate befell Winfield Armstrong, apprehended while planting explosives on company property. Local judges, however, were reluctant to convict: William Nelson, a moulder at the Stevens foundry accused of hurling a bolt at a streetcar driven by the infamous Austin Addison, was acquitted; charges against a trio of London workingmen, arising from their disorderly behaviour while yelling "Scab!" and "Rats!" in the street, were similarly dropped. The city's police chief, throwing up his hands in despair, expressed open dissatisfaction with the Magistrates' policy of acquittal.[38]

By mid-June, the stage had been set for a violent conflict. Manager Carr, in letters to the *Free Press* and Garnett, stressed that the strikers' demands infringed upon rights long held to be the sole prerogative of management. Tension mounted in the city as the strike drifted into an impasse from which neither party could retreat. Men brawled in the streets and in the Chamber of Commerce aldermen hotly debated the issues of the strike. When massive demonstrations, 3,000-4,000 strong, failed to break the deadlock, the city's wage earners, in a desperate burst of frustration, took matters into their own hands.[39]

Friday night (July 7) and Saturday morning rumours had circulated that the strikebreakers were about to abandon their cars and make common cause with their striking antagonists. A crowd gathered to encourage such defiance and assembled in front of the Company's offices. When "scab" motormen began to comply with the crowd's chants to "Return to the barns!" Manager Carr ordered all drivers, upon pain of disciplinary action, to return to their routes.[40]

The crowd immediately surged forward, cohesive and disciplined, directing its anger against the company and attempting to protect its members from arrest or attack. Trolley cars were pulled down; car windows smashed; chandeliers and cash registers systematically destroyed. Along the routes arsonists lit deserted streetcars with the flames of working class rage. In a strategic encirclement of key streets the crowd took possession of the entire east end of the city. With local police apparently powerless, the Mayor read the Riot Act and summoned the militia from Windsor. Not until two o'clock, Sunday afternoon, were the streets cleared and some pretense of order restored.[41]

While precise data is unavailable as to who actually "rioted," the evidence suggests that the "rioters" were drawn from a wide cross-section of London's wage earning class. One elusive rock thrower was described "as a man well up in years, bearing the marks of respectability." Prior to the actual outbreak Wesley and Harry Scott, locally employed teamsters, had been brought before the local Magistrate for disorderly conduct and threatening a constable with a revolver. And those arrested during the mêlée reinforce our contention that it was the city's respectable workingmen that wrought havoc in London's streets: John Dare, a motorman charged with disorderly conduct; William Nelson, a moulder whom we have met before, arrested for assault; a printer, William Taliferro, incarcerated for rioting; and Fred Goodacre and Hugh Day, two striking motormen unlucky enough to be caught in the streets.[42]

Ironically enough, London's wage earners, spurred to greater militancy by community support, alienated many non-working class elements with this show of rowdiness. The business community, glimpsing "the swinish multitude" in action, inched then galloped into the open arms of the company. Judges soon began to convict; acquittals grew very rare. When the city council condemned the actions of "the mob" and local politicians refused to endorse strikers' meetings with their presence, the union was left without that critical component of "substantial" support which it had so long enjoyed. Over the difficult autumn months of 1899 the union attempted to hold out, but by mid-November the strike had functionally terminated.[43]

All was not lost, however. London's labouring men and women continued to reiterate their allegiance to the rights of free-born Englishmen, rights they felt had been trampled upon by the local police, the imported militia and the Street Railway Company. In a procession mocking the propertied elements' repression of the "riot", London's moulders and cabinetmakers, attired in mourning clothes and bearing coffins, ridiculed Hellmuth Ivey (the Company's lawyer) and T. C. Smallman (a resident director of the Street Railway) with banners proclaiming "We must defend our city," "To Hell-muth Ivey: Do Send for the Guns," and a casket labelled "For a Small-man." The *Motorman and Conductor* proclaimed that "if President Everett thought that by getting the militia out he could scare Johnny Cannuck into submission he was very badly mistaken." But if the allegiance to Englishmen's age-old rights remained uppermost in the collective consciousness of London's workers it had been elevated to a higher plane. From the back of a crowd an unidentified individual cogently expressed the aspirations of his class. With the cry "Give us the road and we will run it," London's workingmen posed the issue of the strike as one of collective working class management over the processes of work. It was this thrust for control, the direct legacy of the motorman's struggle, which dominated the local labour movement in the aftermath of the years 1898-1899.[44]

Steeped in the culture of the nineteenth century artisan, drawing moral strength from their Protestantism, London's wage earners turned instinctively to the remnants of social life brought from the New World to the Old in the face of a rampant capitalism. Yet the institutions and forums of intellectual intercourse, which had played so vital a role in the life of the skilled craftsman, proved outmoded in the midst of industrial capital's relentless onslaught. They were the institutions and ideologies of the era of transition; with capital so firmly entrenched they came to reflect an increasing ambivalence. Thus the friendly society degenerated into insurance agent, the Mechanic's Institute became little more than another lever for suppression rather than social betterment, "Blue" or "Saint Monday" gave way to the temperance society and the institutional structure of dissenting religion became undermined by a newer and more vibrant Christianity.

Assimilating many of the features and roles of these earlier institutions and traditions – mutual aid, self-help, cooperation, piety, political activism and the rights of free-born Englishmen – and filling a void in the workingman's social and intellectual existence was the emerging labour movement. In the aftermath of the street railway strike its influence became truly pervasive; the *Industrial Banner* could write that the labour movement was "a machine that reaches and penetrates to every portion of [the city], . . . unceasingly working, . . . watchful and awake . . . to work for a common cause." Referred to as a "new Christianity," a "new Democracy," a "new philanthropy," a "new political economy," the labour movement finally stood on firm ground; the process of emergence had given way to consolidation.[45]

Within this consolidated labour movement the thrust for labour's control over the processes of work, originally amplified by the striking carmen in 1899, became increasingly prominent. Tailors, foundry workers, bricklayers, boilermakers and seamstresses all utilized the strike and the slow-down to secure, or retain, some measure of control over their lives in the factory, shop or mill. And in 1913 the stogiemakers, their craft assaulted by the unskilled hand and the mould, the market for their wares collapsing, walked out of one local shop demanding a committee of workmen to regulate hours and conditions, as well as the right to formulate policies of hiring and firing.[46]

But the most vivid testimonial to the wage workers' commitment to the tenets of labour's self-management was the "London Experiment," a cooperative toy factory established by the Trades and Labour Council. The factory, which marketed its wares across the nation, began production to alleviate the unemployment which ravaged the city in the recession months of 1908 and 1909; it employed over sixty craftsmen during its brief lifespan. Arguing that "the largest possible measure of liberty is not incompatible with the operation of an efficient system from which the best results shall accrue," the workmen of the "London Experiment" blatantly rejected the rigidity of factory discipline. With its democratic organization and efficient production, the toy factory articulated the viability of working class self-management of the productive process. As such it was a fitting symbol of the extent to which the motor-men's cry, "Give us the road and we will run it," had permeated the ranks of labour. Workers' control had become the logical extension of the rights of free-born Englishmen struggling in the context of industrial capitalism; it had, in short, become the aspiration of a class.[47]

The Last Artisans : Toronto Printers, 1896-1914

Wayne Roberts

"Alex Corbett is in town!" noted a Star reporter in the spring of 1909. He had cornered the old-time typo, one of the last of a vanishing species, as he waited to hop the next freight out of town. Alex was not averse to passing a little time reminiscing about the old days. Philosophically, he recalled the life and times of itinerant printers like himself, who worked the rush jobs a few days or weeks at a time, in small-town offices.

When Alex embarked on his career, around the time of Confederation, a printer was still master of all the jobs in a print shop. Moreover, he was an important personage in the community, patronized by preachers, school teachers, beneficent old ladies "and the solicitous community generally . . . ." He could tell them more "of the inside doings of 'sasiety' and of the eccentricities . . . of the editor than anyone else and therefore was entitled to respect." In recent years however, he was finding it harder to get work. The typesetting machine had displaced the hand compositor and there was very little "straight matter" to be set. But when there was work, and if Alex happened along, he would take a temporary job. And so after a few days work as the Junction, he moved on, watching for "the next turn of fortune's wheel."[1]

Although some of the props of the traditional artisan may have been whittled away in the twentieth century, there were still places for rounded tradesmen like Alex. "I want a good, reliable, competent, all-round printer," one ad read. "Steady job for a capable man. Must be steady and clean compositor, able to make up, run presses, etc . . . . One who could do a little local reporting, estimating and soliciting jobs, ads and subscriptions preferred."[2] The mechanical improvements in the printing trade that made people like Alex obsolescent as a social type did not eliminate the need for all-round skilled printers. It just made them harder to find.

Old members of the craft, steeped in the traditional training, were uneasy about the new generation of workmen that were being produced. Waxing on the theme "we wish to excell in our craft," veteran William Powell urged a thorough and vigorous union-backed program of technical education. "Not a few . . . have, at some time or other, been called upon to perform some one thing in the composing room that they had never come in

125

contact with sufficiently before, and how embarrassing it was to them – honest employees – who wished to do a fair day's work and to uphold the best traditions of our craft . . . ," he lamented.

He recognized that typesetting machines had revolutionized important facets of the trade. But, by an ironical dialectic, "this, in its turn, has made a demand for the all round man in both the newspaper and job rooms, until today I venture the assertion that the just mentioned class of printer is the scarcest of all. The printer who can impose a form, set a neat job and ads, and employ the products of the machine to the best advantage, is the man of today and the future."[3]

The mechanization which ravaged the integrity of so many artisanal trades was not as brutal in the case of printing. Its imperatives may have been restrained somewhat by the health of the industry. For a printing centre like Toronto, employment expanded considerably after the turn of the century. Typographical union membership, always corresponding closely to the number employed in the trade, rose from 574 in 1900 to 882 in 1907 and to 1200 in 1914.

More important, competition between publishers was shielded by Toronto's domination of the publishing market and the obviously enormous locational advantages inherent in city dailies. The industry did not require the all-out war against the rights of employees as was the case in internationally cost-competitive industries like the iron and steel industry. It was not that difficult for the owners of city dailies to band together and arrive at a common rate of pay and standards.[4]

The inroads and demands of mechanization were uneven. In some cases, they generated new skills and specializations like lithography and electrostereotyping. They never totally displaced the need for old skills, although command over them may no longer have been a daily necessity.

Thus the printers were not a beleaguered craft. The artisanal character of their occupation was in large measure retained and safeguarded. This accounts for the artisanal mentality which continued to hold sway among printers and to determine their outlook and actions. It is this outlook, more than anything else, that explains their behaviour.

Of course their craftsman's pride was hurt by the occasional snub. "Some people still do not appreciate our share in educating the multitude," one printer complained. Apparently a new clerk, in receiving his job instructions "was particularly enjoined to keep the side door closed during working hours, so that the intelligent comps inside would not be disturbed by newsboys and bums. But the foreman had a fainting spell when the aforesaid clerk wanted to know how to distinguish between bums and printers."[5]

But the printers' outlook was not shaped by dejection or status deprivation as some fashionable interpreters of the labour movement assert. On the contrary, the printers faced the world with great self-confidence and a measured sense of self-worth. They welcomed the public attention frequently fondled on them, modestly noting that it was based on the fact "that members of our craft here are no different from those the world over for eccentricities of genius and all the concomitants which go to perpetuate the traditional craft-fellowship of all disciples of Gutenberg." Their confidence was well merited, for Toronto's printers were a remarkable group of men. This can be seen most easily by the career patterns many of them followed. The striking printers from the *News* who founded the *Evening Star* following a dispute over the introduction of machines provide a dramatic illustration of their capabilities. Of those who signed the first editorial manifesto of the new paper, Ross Harkness claims "scarcely one failed to leave his mark in the world of politics, business, journalism or printing. From them came two Mayors of Toronto, a publisher, manager of a provincial daily, a sales manager, three reporters, and four superintendents of newspaper plants in Toronto, New York and Detroit."[6] Harkness neglected to mention that one also became a senator.

Printers did not seem surprised at the prominence that awaited some of their membership. In an 1895 motion of congratulation to Prime Minister Bowell, they noted that he was "a fellow craftsman, one who always prided himself on being a printer." They took no more awe at James Boyle, a printer of the seventies who became secretary to the American governor and later President, McKinley. And they noted with pleasure how Billy Cullin became King's Printer in B.C., how veteran Bill Powell became editor of the *Aylmer Reformer*, how Charlie Hinds became proprietor of the *Lumsden News Record* and mayor of the western town to which he emigrated.[7]

On the other hand a reversal of the argument about status anxiety in favour of an overview of the printers' attitudes as rooted in relative privilege does not explain much. Printers were not relieved from the problems that other workers faced in this period. An analysis of twenty-seven randomly selected printers in 1905 showed that only five were homeowners. The rest were tenants or boarders. The assessments on all their residences were quite modest, ranging from $400 to $2000, with most of them somewhere in the middle. Conditions for all of them appeared to be quite crowded. The only possible indicator of reasonable status is that they all appear to have municipal manhood franchise.[8] While the printers were certainly relatively well-off, they were by no means an aristocracy and their relative position in the working class is not an adequate explanation of their behaviour.

Nor were the printers distinguishable by ethnicity or country of origin, in any extraordinary sense. Although most appeared to be Protestant, they were spread over a number of denominations; Methodist, Presbyterian and Church of England (in that order). Most printers were recruited from a relatively parochial labour pool, coming in their overwhelming majority from Toronto and Ontario. There were none from Britain between 1896 and 1900. Thereafter members originating in the British Isles trickled in until 1905 and outnumbered new members from Toronto only in 1913, by which time the character of the craft was well established. British immigrants never came close to equalling the combined total of new recruits from both Toronto and Ontario as a whole. Furthermore, of the 196 British immigrants who came after 1900, only seventeen had previous union experience. They can hardly serve as the basis for the explanation of the union norms of Toronto typos.[9]

The printers were not distinguished then by their unusual ethnic or national background nor by an unusual command over wealth or an unusual decline in status. Rather, they were distinguished by the lingering integrity of their craft and the lasting tradition of the artisan.

Even by purely quantitative measurements, this is the outstanding characteristic of their trade. Generational inheritance, a common indication of a closed and traditional artisanal occupation, was markedly high. Sometimes, inheritance even involved actual place of employment. Bob Wilson, for instance, left the Methodist Bookroom after seventeen years, bringing "to a close a family connection of about 50 years, his father and grandfather having been employed there".[10]

But the most important reflection of their artisanal frame of mind is in their attitudes – their attitudes to their work, attitudes to their workmates, to their union, to their employers and to society at large. All of these are related in some coherent manner to the artisan mind.

The most obvious measure of this consciousness was the almost entrepreneurial pride they took in the quality and control of their work. In making his case for the union sponsorship of training schools. Powell insisted on the union's responsibility. "The work of the composing room is our business. To no one else can we depute it. It is absolutely ours. The talk of running another man's business will not hold. It is ours; we learned it, and must control it. . . . "[11]

Of course, modern conditions made it difficult to sustain that pride. The slovenly manner in which papers were produced had to be taken up in one of the "good and welfare" discussions on the agenda of union meetings. They felt that "the Art Preservative was deteriorating under the present system of rush" and urged members to take special care of quality rather than quantity.[12]

The sense of pride in their work is perhaps most clearly revealed in the name for their basic unit of organization – the chapel. Certainly, it matched the sense of purpose that their work was imbued with. As William Taylor, the Toronto Typographical Union's own poet, put it:

We pass Assyria, Egypt, Greece and Rome,
Where intellectual giants built a home;
But all their labors only helped to fence
The king's, the priest's, the soldier's consequence;
The common herd, the people, bore the brand
Of deep seated ignorance on brow and hand;
But Gutenberg's great light dissolved hell's gloom
That caste had spread on earth for labor's doom.
Rejoice! Bold Typos! Nobly play your parts,
Defend 'the Art Preservative of Arts',
We lead the van in war for Liberty
And guard the precious boon Equality,
So let us not forget Fraternity;
For universal brotherhood we strive,
And keep the grace of charity alive
Another era dawns upon the world,
The rings and money kings will soon be hurled
From self-elected thrones – their mills shall cease
To grind up flesh and blood for chariot grease.
May capital and labor join and say:
"A fair day's labor for a fair day's pay"
So said the MAN whose Word our laws inspire:
"The laborer is worthy of his hire".[13]

The pride in craftsmanship was inculcated and reinforced in various of the union's rituals and paraphernalia. This pride was linked up with a sense of social service and duty corresponding to the trust embodied in the trade. The letterhead on their stationery boasted of their union's tasks ranging from provision of homes and sanitaria for the aged and sick to the making of better citizens. A new member, even before pledging himself to maintain the rates of the unions, had to plead his desire to be "more serviceable to my fellow craftsmen."[14]

The initiated craftsman was provided with a code of social and craft obligations. The preamble to the constitution defined their purpose:

To establish and maintain an equitable scale of wages and

protect ourselves from sudden or unreasonable fluctuations in the rate of compensation for our labor; and protect, too, just and honorable employers from the unfair competition of greedy, cheap labor, huckstering rivals; to defend our rights and advance our interests as workingmen; to create an authority whose seal shall constitute a certificate of character, intelligence and skill; to build up an organization where all worthy members of our craft can participate in the discussion of those practical problems upon the solution of which depends their welfare and prosperity as workers; to foster fellowship and brotherhood, and shield from aggression the isolated and defenceless toiler, to aid the destitute and unfortunate, and provide for the decent burial of deceased members; to develop and stimulate, by association and social converse, those kindly instincts of humanity that most highly adorn true manhood; to encourage the principle and practice of conciliation and arbitration in the settlement of differences between capital and labor; to incite all honorable efforts for the attainment of better conditions of labor – shorter hours, increased privileges, and greater enjoyment of the ennobling ammenities of life ... to defend the defenceless, befriend the friendless, and in all charity inculcate lessons of justice and good will among men.

The union motto pledged: "United to support; not combined to injure."[15]

This artisanal package provided for everything from uplift fellowship to practical protection. The sense of class it embodied was pluralistic and rooted in a benign sense of a proper relation between a workman and his employer. If this relation were violated by caste pretense or huckster competition, it could provoke bitterness. But it did not turn the printers' sense of class into a Marxist one, a sense of class based on the inherent conflict between worker and employer over the division of surplus value.

This important distinction in the concept of class is partially revealed in the tasks printers imposed on their union. The printers set limited tasks for their union. "Much of our year's work," the union president reported in his annual report for 1899, "has been of a routine character. Many matters of apparently small moment in themselves have been amicably settled in as quiet a way as possible. Big questions as a rule don't pay and we should therefore be pleased that we have none to settle and hopefully look to the future for a similar fortune for years to come."[16]

Their union was certainly not designed to encompass all in

the trade. Many were rejected for incompetency. Moreover, the whole stress of their union method placed the bulk of responsibility on the individual craftsman's honour and ability. Charges would be brought on a member for conduct unbecoming a union man for violating the union scale if he only took what the employer offered. Appeals frequently came in from old or non-English members asking for permission to work under scale; permission which was granted unevenly, but which never provoked an investigation of why senior members should face wage reductions as the reward for a life's labour.[17]

The threat of competition from fellow workmen was what brought them into the business of active union organizing. In 1903, "Two Stars", the union's journal correspondent, called for the appointment of a Canadian organizer who could scour the small plants and towns for members. "Through this policy," he felt, "all outside competition would be removed, and the employers would be unable to draw on these places for help in time of trouble, and our scales would be negotiated in a much easier manner."[18]

There is considerable other evidence of the remnants of the artisanal tradition. The union's recreation program resulted from an intimacy that could not have been shared by workers in an impersonal shop. They sponsored regular outings, sports events, concerts and the like. All was not concerts and picnics, of course. The landlord of their union office at one time had to threaten to take possession immediately if disorderlies were not barred from attending. And the practical joke, of elaborate complexity, was often resorted to and was generally tied into the trade.[19]

On the other hand, the company was good enough for some sacred ceremonies. "A most pleasant interruption to the routine of the daily rush of business took place a week since in the composing room of the Star," it was reported, "The parties most concerned were Frank Hyland, compositor, and Miss Margaret Hamilton, copyholder. Their fellow employees were equal to the occasion and presented the newly married with a handsome and substantial present." And in between these extremes was a wide variety of printers' union clubs, concerts, banquets and picnics.[20]

Their annual concerts were always popular. As well, they allowed for the display of some native talent. One concert, reported as "the best program ever put on in Massey Hall" featured the Crescent Male Quartet, three of whose members were typos and the daughter of a prominent typo singing an aria. These talents blossomed in less auspicious circumstances. One initiate, obviously unaware of the proverbial versatility of the "comps" made a bet at a banquet that no comp could play as well as the excellent orchestra they had hired. "Well, the surprise of his life was then and there. Borrowing a violin from a member of the orchestra, John J. Thompson, of the *Evening Telegram*, and who is also chief of the fire brigade there, went through such famous scores as 'Cavaliera Rusticana,' 'Bloemliede,' and the Strauss waltzes varieting between renderings by giving popular themes of the 'Down on the Suwanee River,' 'Annie Laurie' and the 'Home Sweet Home' variety." As for the inexperienced comp, "the subsequent toast at his expense caused a heavy financial hemmorage on his part, but was right royally liquidated. 'Smoke up'."[21]

Athletics were also a specialty. A Labor Temple Bowling League was formed in 1904 to pit printers of one shop against another and remained vital throughout the period. They were confident of taking on printers' baseball leagues from across the continent. Most of their local's team members played semi-professional on the side and their coach not only played semi-pro but also doubled as a sports correspondent for the Saint Louis *Sporting News*. In local circles they were regular victors in the Labor Day Parade sports competitions. And they had to do it by winning in all the speed sports "We did not enter a team for the tug of war as we were short of heavyweights."[22]

Picnics were well-organized and elaborate, including ferry rides, bands, and athletic competition. It would be impossible to list all the picnics, the journal correspondent admitted, now that their popularity is revived. "These outings do a lot of good in a social way and enable families of employees to become acquainted; besides, the employee and employer are able to meet and see the human side of one another – and the time clock isn't working."[23]

Another reflection of the artisanal origin of the union's character was its well-developed benefit features, including even a retirement home for senior printers. As well, the union had many occasions to congratulate itself on the breadth of its sympathies expressed on a purely informal basis. After giving $1000 for the final mortgage on the homestead of the deceased T. C. Vodden, a longtime active unionist, they rejoiced; "In these days of x-ray investigations of fraternal society death claims and employers liability dodging, it surely is gratifying to note the action taken by a body of organized workmen." In the case of craftsmen who died penniless, the union took responsibility for burial.[24]

Death was an important occasion for the printers, and the

deceased's fellow tradesmen were a regular part of the ceremonies. The following is a typical death notice: "The funeral of the late John H. Lumsden, formerly a member of TTU No. 91, took place on Tuesday and it was very largely attended as the deceased was very popular. A delegation from 91 was present, as were many old time typos." Certainly the death of printer union activists evoked the most solemn of resolutions and praise of union and craft activity. Even these were formulated according to the traditions of union resolutions.

Whereas the great architect of the Universe, in his infinite wisdom, has severed earthly ties and called from among us our brother and fellow worker, Edward M. Meehan, a firm union man in all that the name implies, and who never shirked the duties of any office he held, therefore be it resolved ... Mrs. Meehan, the members of Toronto Typographical Union, no. 91, extend to you their feelings of supreme sorrow in the death of your dear husband. If God has plucked the devoted helpmate from your home, it is for a purpose none of us dare divine. He alone can pour balm upon your crushed heart. The holy joy is yours of knowing that angel eyes will watch for your coming and that your devoted husband will receive you when 'life's day is done'; May almighty God console you in this dark hour of your tribulation.[25]

The final indicator of the artisanal character of the trade and its tradesmen can be found in the working conditions which earned the typos a real reputation. The typos worked in small shops, most of which employed between five and fifteen men. Apparently they even had authority to deny access to the composing room to all non-tradesmen, even supervisors. One dismayed employer sent a letter to the union executive inquiring about some of the union prerogatives and found out the following. A compositor working six successive days cannot be laid off until all accumulated matrices have been set. A man simply has to tell his foreman that he is going off work and cannot be discharged even if he brings no proof of sickness. A man can't be discharged for incompetency without notification. A regular can go hunting for a few months, as long as he has arranged for a substitute. Even if the substitute quits, the man's job is guaranteed.[26]

Much of this power was achieved by having the foreman as part of the union. Several cases occurred where foremen fired or harassed printers only to have the union pull rank on him. The foreman had to join the union and obey it. His only recourse was to appeal the decision of the local to the international. Several foremen and employers learned this to their chagrin in this period.[27]

The employer was, of course, far from defenceless, and the union was far from a bully. In some cases the union was very cautious about enforcing regulations. At one point it decided not to uphold the eight hour law in the *Star*, hoping that the situation would right itself. The union might find an issue "not opportune to enforce." But if the matter was serious, as for example the discharge of an employee, there would be no hesitation in voting a strike. Pro-strike votes of 210-5 were not an abnormality in these cases.[28]

How did mechanization affect this classical artisanal trade? The 1890s saw the introduction of typesetting machines and a series of scuffles over the issue. Major employers refused to confer with the union over wages or prices, difficulties coming to a head after the *Telegram* settled. The *News* locked out its men, who retaliated by establishing the *Evening Star*. Within a month, however, a proposed agreement was being discussed by the union's secret strike committee and the company. The results of this bargaining, which also involved the arbitration of former printer E. F. Clarke, M.P. saw the *News* emerge as a fully union office. Union men were to be trained at the new machines. The union then spent several months congratulating itself on its unprecedented victory. "Never we believe since the memorable date of 1872 has the union come through such a crisis as it has in this year! And in the end,...we have lost nothing and gained everything," the executive reported to the annual meeting. They had established their first machine scale. The only bad taste was the unemployment of many of their members, a problem they hoped would soon be solved.[29]

They managed similar victories in 1892 against the Star Plate Co. and the Presbyterian Office, both of which threatened to man their new machines with non-union girls and both of which were humbled by their inability to operate their machines without the aid of the striking printers.[30]

By 1899 it appeared that problems were being resolved and unemployment was down.

The life of gentility and leisure that some of us were obliged to lead is in danger of being abruptly terminated if things keep on improving... In fact scarcely a day passes but the daily papers advertise for a 'printer,' 'a man to take charge,' etc. One in the *Globe* a short time ago read: "Wanted—all-round printer—book and job, able to do 'local'; when necessary; must have a knowledge of shorthand and bookkeeping and be able to 'play in the band.'"

"It's no wonder" the reporter concluded "the boys are shy of 'leaving' the business."[31]

It was this continued need for all-round and experienced printers that gave the printers their leverage. They attempted to add to it by adjusting to new technology through technical education. This was the particular passion of local president William Powell.

The days of typesetting by hand are numbered—in fact it will in a very short time be a lost art—and the 'handy man' will be in great demand. More especially will this be the case when advanced machinery reduces the price of composition. More printing will then be done than ever before and it is for us to see that the men who are displaced by typesetting machines are in a position to take up the other branches of the trade.[32]

Mechanization was continued in the twentieth century as a number of publishers switched to machine typesetting, reminding the "old time orthodox comps that they are becoming obsolete in their methods." But the major problem was limited to unemployment, which was reported as chronic, due to the new machines. But even this was temporary as the printing industry picked up in the new century.[33]

Following the strikes of the 1890s the union was able to deal with the problems of mechanization by the updating of members' skills and by some shrewd bargaining, and jockeying of timing and strength. The executive admitted one year that it had been a warm year despite the fact that little of note had been accomplished. But their critics "forget the fact that during the machine transformation a good deal of shifting was done, which allowed some abuses to creep in which it has been the province of the present executive committee to have remedied, and the abuse levelled at the committee in some quarters is but evidence of the sincerity with which they are performing their work."[34]

The major questions that had to do with mechanization rarely centred around machinery or principle *per se*. Rather they dealt with side effects, all of which were handled by an elaborate labyrinth of ritual carefully designed to facilitate consensus. This strategy on the part of both sides was based on mutual recognition of relative strengths and weaknesses. It came to characterize dispute settlement in the industry and thus removed the dramatic issue of technological change from the centre of labour-management relations. Presumably it was also removed from the centre of the printer's mind as a factor in his consciousness. Indeed, to the extent that the adjustment to modern technology affected the world view of the printer, his experience would tend to reinforce his craft-learned sense of good employee-employer relations, his respectability, and his gradualism. This perhaps explains why printers who became involved in independent labour politics were also identified with the more moderate currents on the left.

Two major negotiation issues surfaced as a result of mechanization; apprentices and matrices. Both of them were dealt with in a calculating, rational and bargain-conscious manner.

The apprenticeship question went hand in hand with the challenge to the artisanal character of printing and was always considered an important question and posture for the union. In the first place, it threatened to upset the equilibrium of advantage between shops. When the union allowed a boy to work a machine at the *Globe*, Hamly Bros. immediately protested. "I desire to give our men notice that I may be compelled to do likewise as no one office should have an advantage over any other," they argued.[35]

The inadequacy of the apprenticeship system also threatened the integrity of the craft and the certification of the union as a licence of competency. The union had no response when employers charged that the union membership was designed merely for self-protection and was no longer a certificate of competency. It was not the employers themselves that were at fault but the system. The prevalent atmosphere of greed led the boys to leave their station before fully learning the trade simply to get more money. The employer, for his part, tried only to maximize the profitability of the boy.

In desperation the printers were forced to agree that for the time being they were compelled to take in all members who had completed the appropriate number of years, regardless of competency. They remained wary of the consequences. As late as 1907 they feared that, "in a few years at the most, we believe, our art will be represented by specialists and incompetents, and the workmen who will be capable of doing any work that comes into a composing room will be almost extinct."[36]

They also feared the problem of cheap competition. At one point they seriously considered a modified version of the indenture system with the printer as one responsible party to ensure proper attention. This would meet their "earnest desire to see the boys turned out better printers, and to remove in a large measure from the reach of employers the club they had used in the past when adjusting wages and hours – viz – that our union was not all composed of competent printers."[37]

Finally they had an obligation to the boys. As Powell argued in a presidential address: "We should guarantee that they receive justice in the profession they have chosen and not leave them to the unscrupulous capitalist, who, for the sake of a few paltry dollars, keeps them at some menial branches of the business at which they have become adept, blasting their lives to further advancement among their fellows."[38]

Despite artisanal anxieties, pieties and rhetoric, the 'boy problem' was solved by hard contract negotiation. There was only one strike over the issue and that took place in a small shop where one pious owner was apparently more guided by the Almighty than by adherence to union rules. The union succeeded in keeping boys off the machines until 1903 when they conceded to allow them to practice during the last three months of their five year apprenticeship. They gradually moved to have the apprentice issue included in general contract bargaining and forgot their schemes of indenture. In 1911 there was a complaint from a chapel chairman that a twenty-five-year man was being used only to deliver messages. But there was no other complaint until 1914 when there was fear that apprentices were not being interviewed after their first year. The introduction of machinery did not affect the labour pool by destroying the distinction between apprentice and journeyman printer. By this measure of deartisanalization, the craft passed into the modern age with a minimum of trouble.[39]

The other battleground over the results of mechanization was the matrix law or 'dead horse,' which concerned the manner in which ads were to be set. This was a gut issue which severely affected the employment of printers. In 1899 it was considered that "the most important business was passing a law doing away with the custom of borrowing, swapping and 'stealing' plate matter between the different newspaper offices. It is claimed that the enforcement of the much needed legislation will give employment to at least twenty-five or more men each week." In this pioneering work of featherbedding, the typos again showed their penchant for negotiating the byproducts of mechanization in a manner acceptable to both publishers and printers and resolving tensions by jockeying concessions rather than resorting to confrontation. The law was refined in 1908, permitting mat from recognized ad agencies to be reprinted without being set, but the onus of proof was on the publisher. There appeared to be no resistance on the part of either side. By 1914 a tour of union officials through Toronto news plants concluded that the matrice laws were being followed everyplace but one and that one promised to correct himself.[40]

The pattern of negotiation on issues unconnected with mechanization was even smoother. All the papers were willing to accept the 1898 scale, although there was some give and take on the question of the apprentices' occasional use of machines. The union resolved to prepare for the next session of bargaining by learning to put out the paper in eight hours.[41]

In 1900, although some matters were not resolved, a printed

agreement was arrived at without difficulty. The 1901 agreement was worked out very elaborately, negotiations being carried on between representatives of all the printing trades and all the employers. It was reported that their joint sessions were very sophisticated and never in any danger of a deadlock. Both sides were anxious to reach agreement without recourse to arbitration.[42]

In 1902 there was some trouble with Eaton's, which was employing its own printers to put out catalogues. When they failed to uphold union conditions, those connected with the printshop walked out, including the non-union bindery girls. The strike was fought vigorously by a secret strike committee with the endorsation of a 208-2 strike vote. The printers won the battle of public opinion. The Methodist Bookroom refused to do Eaton's work. The local weeklies supported the printers and scorched the dailies for their silence on the matter. The printers popularized their boycott with a bicycle parade. The union felt it had "a thousand, more or less, aces up our sleeves" and felt that the circulars and boycott were only getting "the branding irons heated thoroughly." They carried the campaign to the small towns and cut even further into Eaton's trade. They spread the message "as to the disreputable methods pursued by Tim [Eaton] and his departmental trust to defeat and prostitute the principle he and his psalm singing sycophants so earnestly put forth to the gullible section of the community.... To save his dividends, poor old Tim had better put his philanthropic endowments to that of paying living wages to those who create his wealth." After a seven-month battle the strike was ended with a compromise, whereby union rates would be paid, but the printers would have to work the same hours as other Eaton employees.[43]

The printers had shown themselves well prepared to handle a strike with a major capitalist and to have a good command over the community resources to carry it through. But the strike was not one which generated divisions across the class lines in Toronto or had any lasting effect on their consciousness. In the midst of it, they carried on their negotiations with the newspapers and won major wage increases without any indication of tension.[44]

For a while it looked like the relations between printers and employers in 1904 were heading toward crisis with both sides initially talking very tough. But before long the bravado gave way to major concessions and a satisfactory arrangement was made. The printers were saving themselves for the 'eight hour' battle.[45]

The International's campaign for the eight hour day was the subject for a great deal of war whooping, but the struggle was resolved outside of Toronto, since Toronto typos were prohibited from joining in by their contract. They secured a 100 per cent effective eight hour day without a struggle. Toronto printers took the opportunity to scoff at the dismal science of economics and note that it "no longer scares anyone but professors," but their victory did not flow from any local struggle.[46]

The only tension in the 1907 negotiations arose from the fact that the international representative signed the contract without the approval of the local. Although this caused a great deal of heat at the time, the local did not even appear to make an appeal.[47]

The 1907 agreement ended in 1912 and the printers looked for a major wage increase. Although the bargaining lasted for a considerable time, and there were major conflicts over the proper arbitrating body, not one day was lost in strike. It seems that no one even entertained the idea of a strike.[48]

Thus we can see that the printers' form of class consciousness was not learned on the picket line. Nor was it learned under fire in solidarity with other trades. They themselves did not have to rely on class solidarity to win their battles. Although they appreciated support for the label, they did not carry on a prolonged flirtation with it as a means of buttressing their strength. After the battle of the nineties, it was not much on their mind.[49]

In the terms of their relations with other tradesmen, they had a reputation that was not always deserved. A probably wider-held view was expressed by a machinist's official who had just lost some members to the printers. They had been "forced to join that most arrogant and malodorous of all labour bodies," he thought. Indeed they were not inordinately loyal even to other members of their own trade. They were slow to establish relations with other printers and did not establish a provincial body of printers until 1911. They threatened to withdraw from the local labour council if the Printing Pressmen were admitted. And although they supported the federation of different printing trades in 1894 and threatened to strike if a Web Pressman was replaced with a nonunionist, they were opposed to any principle of solidarity stikes that might unduly tap their power when there was a little prospect of victory. They often got exasperated at the other printing bodies for their inability to pack a punch at negotiations and got tired of dragging them along. Their relation to the federated council of printing trades became very tenuous after 1912 when latter were racked by secession and enormously weakened for collective bargaining.[50]

Their record in regard to the general labour movement was also mixed. It was only under protest that Foreman Parr allowed strike-bound Gurney ads to be set in the *Star* in 1902. They made frequent donations to bodies of striking workmen across the continent. When the 1904 butchers' strike against meat-packing magnate Joseph Flavelle extended to a boycott of his newspaper, the *News*, the printers reacted stridently. Local 91 deigned to intervene on behalf of the butchers only after they had begged forgiveness for their failure to consult the printers before declaring the boycott.[51]

But if there were warts on their record as trade unionists, their reform credentials were almost impeccable. They were consistently active in the local labour body, providing it with many executive members and presidents over a long period. On some occasions they almost totally dominated its leading bodies. Even with the Hare Spence proportional voting system of the local council, the typos were consistently elected. The printers had a simple explanation for that: "No system, however complicated, can prevent the printing industry from being recognized."[52]

They were well-known advocates of several reform schemes. In 1892 they endorsed a very elaborate scheme of proposals ranging from demands to increase the circulating medium; to restriction of undesirable immigration, particularly Chinese labour; to contract labour for public works; to opposition to property qualifications in the holding of municipal office. In 1899 they affiliated with the newly formed Civil Progress Association. In 1900, they passed a referendum 198 to 68 in favour of independent labour political action. They persisted in this later and urged a constitutional amendment on the local labour council, forcing its officers to support candidates endorsed by the body. They also adopted for themselves, and pushed on the Ontario Parliament the "Hare Spence" system of voting, a system of proportional representation that gives better odds to minority parties. All was not liberalism on their side, however. The following resolution was moved by printer-socialist Jimmy Simpson, and passed unanimously; that the immigration of Sikhs and their wives to Canada "would inevitably lead to a lowering of the standards of living of the great army of workers, would create an undesireable moral atmosphere, and would ultimately impair the present and contemplated social order."[53]

These reform policies did not violate their other positions or characteristics. As artisans searching for an equilibrium, they naturally would favour a system of proportional representation. As respectable workmen, they would naturally look forward to a pleasant working relation to some body such as the Civic Progress Association. As worker-citizens, they naturally favoured the opening of politics to the workingman. As representatives of a distinct but not necessarily antagonistic social labour they felt entitled to separate representation in Parliament. And as artisans eager to control the labour pool, they were naturally hostile to immigration. Their politics came as naturally to them as their entertainment program.

The printers' experience and consciousness was virtually unique. Skilled workers as a whole in the building trades and especially in the metal trades did not fare as well under the battering ram of mechanization.

But they were even unusual in the printing trades. The Printing Pressmen, one of the specialty trades created by modernization, were just as jealous of workplace control. But they shared none of their reform aspirations. Striking moulders who came to the Pressmen for assistance were reminded "that we are not a public auction." It was moved and seconded of a resolution from the Toronto Federation for Majority Rule that "it be put in the waste basket."[54]

The stereotypers and electrotypers, another recent trade, shared the benefit features of the typos, but their fraternity had none of the printers' breadth. Their major competition for meetings was the fraternal lodges, despite the fact that the smiles that came out of a union meeting showed that "the fraternal organization [the union] is the best investment that a man can make." They were full of good humour, practical jokes and trade stunts, Sports reporting and the snipes that were made at individuals made their journal resemble a proletarian social page.[55]

The bookbinders who shared with the printers in longtime artisanal tradition were not as able to control the labour pool or exert the bargaining power of the printers, partially because of internal discord and partially because of an inherently weaker bargaining position.[56]

It was only the printers who retained the majority of the traits of the old artisan and were able to successfully adapt them to the modern world. That is why they are so distinctive.

The printers can be seen as the progenitors of the modern labour movement; their pioneering efforts at self-organization, their heralding of major labour goals such as the nine and eight hour day, their penchant for reform in general and independent labour politics in particular. They were very conscious of this pioneering role they played and frequently "freely indulged in" their past role "with pride and satisfaction." But sometimes their identification with these broad labour movements might have been casual rather than causal. Certainly in the developing movement for independent labour and socialist politics fostered by the estrangement of social classes, their style of class consciousness did not establish them as pioneers. On the contrary their world view grew out of a workplace ecology and craft norms that stood in striking contrast to the experience of most workers. They practised the class consciousness of the "producing" artisan not that of of the wage earner alienated from his product. They were, however, an adornment to these developing expressions of the labour movement. It is ironic that as an adornment, they were more like an antique.[57]

Ethnicity and Violence:
The Lakehead Freight Handlers Before World War I

Jean Morrison

Between 1902 and 1912, freight handlers at the Canadian Lakehead conducted a series of six strikes, which twice erupted into gun battles between strikers and company police, against the railways. While the causes of unrest which led to the strikes can be stated with little difficulty, the same cannot be said of the violence. All immigrants, the striking freight handlers of Fort William and Port Arthur came from many European countries as well as from the British Isles. But while the strikes themselves were conducted by workers of several national origins, each case of violence involved only those strikers from Italy and Greece. Workers from England and Scotland, who had played a leading role in many freight handlers' strikes in the past, not only had no part in the violence, but they deplored it. This difference between southern Europeans and the British in the conduct of their labour disputes suggests some relationship between ethnicity and violence. The problem now is to define that relationship.[1]

In the early twentieth century, there was little doubt in English-speaking Canada that ethnicity and violence were intertwined. The orderly evolution of Canadian society as a natural and inevitable process based on British precedent was a salient tenet of British Canadian mythology which looked on past and present turbulence as deviations from the norm, fomented by non-British elements. The ethnic composition of those who took part in the many violent labour disputes reinforced the idea that violence was an alien import to Canadian society and its British institutions. In the trial of the Deprenzo brothers, accused of attempted murder in the riot between striking coal handlers and Port Arthur police in 1912, the presiding judge expressed the prevailing attitude:

The point that he emphasized was that those foreigners must not be led to believe that they can take the law in their own hands, throwing aside the measures provided by civilized society for the punishment of crime. If this condition was once allowed civilization would descend to barbarism.... The point that must be brought home to these people was that violence in any form will not be tolerated in this country regardless of any customs or usages prevailing in Russia, Finland, Italy or whatever country the foreign element comes from.[2]

Other opinion leaders revealed their own special interests by analysing the cause of violence in slightly different ways. Well-meaning Protestant clergy and laymen looked to the immigrants' lack of "Canadianization" as an ever-present threat to the social order. Where Canadianization succeeded, industrial peace among immigrants followed. With the establishment of the Methodist Wesley Institute in Fort William's coal docks section after the violent freight handlers strike of 1909, the result, thus, was no further labour trouble by "the foreigners at the head of the lakes"[3]

In high levels of government, fears of imminent social conflict were voiced by the Deputy Minister of Labour, William Lyon Mackenzie King, but for him its source lay in class rather than in ethnic struggles.

King's horror of "the possibilities of civil conflicts begotten of class hatreds" led to the enactment of the Industrial Disputes Investigation (or Lemieux) Act in 1907. Directed toward the achievement of industrial harmony, the Act made mandatory the conciliation of labour disputes prior to strikes or lock-outs in such industries as railways, coal mining, and public utilities. Department of Labour officials, not surprisingly, found the explanation for violence at the Lakehead not in ethnicity, but in the failure of foreign workers to invoke the Act.[4]

By tracing violence partly to the failure of immigrant workers to become organized and thereby to follow proper procedures in handling their grievances, the Port Arthur Trades and Labor Council indirectly linked violence to ethnicity. Generally, however, the Council and labour sympathizers placed the blame on the policies and practices of the immigrants' employers, the railways. Some link between ethnicity and violence, then, was not in dispute among such bodies as the courts, the churches, the government or the trade unions. Their disagreement lay in the definition of that link.[5]

Just as no simple solution to this problem presented itself then, neither does a solution become evident now. One line of enquiry is suggested by recent examinations of the differing ways in which peoples of diverse cultures have responded to industrialization. Reaching beyond the trade union and the radical party to the many faceted life and culture of workers, social historians in the *genre* of E. P. Thompson have enriched our concept of "labour history" by treating it as an integral feature of the society in which it evolves. Regardless of national origin, proletarians undergo similar class experiences, yet their differing historic and cultural traditions make for differing kinds of responses to these experiences.[6] In England, a distinctive and disciplined working class had emerged by 1832 with characteristics observable in the Lakehead freight handlers strikes some seventy years later.

The situation in the United States was quite different. As the American industrial machine required continual infusions of fresh manpower at least until the First World War, the business of making proletarians out of pre-industrial peoples in every generation made for severe discontinuities in the making of the American working class. The analysis by Herbert G. Gutman of the recurrent tensions created by the re-introduction to the work process of first generation proletarians from within and without the American social fabric has given a deeper dimension to our understanding of the complex inter-relationship of working class with immigrant life. The conflicts within American labour history are not only those of the normal disruptions of industrialization, but represent a clash of cultures created by waves of immigration of non-English-speaking peoples from abroad.[7]

While the Canadian experience duplicated neither that of the English nor the American, it contained many features of both. ("Canadian" in this context, of course, means English Canadian.) The English and Scottish traditions created out of generations of experience with industrialism lent a definite cast to the Canadian working class, especially in its trade union manifestation. But other ethnic groups, formed an integral part of its development as well. Working class and immigration history "intersect" in Canada, as in the United States. We can see this particularly in the wheat boom era when massive infusions into the Canadian working class by navvies from many European cultures led to the grave social and industrial tensions for which the social gospellers sought remedies, and which manifested themselves in such violent eruptions as the Lakehead freight handlers' strikes.[8]

Any analysis of the relationship between ethnicity and violence, however, must consider factors other than those relating to the doubly painful adjustment of first-generation proletarians to industrialism and of foreigners to a new society. E. P. Thompson defines the working class in terms of its ongoing relationship with other classes expressed in "action and reaction, change and conflict." The role of the employers, the work process itself, and the community in which these interactions occur all impinge on the ethnicity-violence equation. Beyond the local community was another variable, the increasing intervention of the state in labour relations. Examining the context of the violence, then, becomes equally as essential to an understanding of its source as does isolating the responses of differing ethnic groups to the work process.

Known as the Lakehead, this context comprised the two municipalities of Fort William and Port Arthur, both dependent economically on the railways which had introduced the foreign sub-cultures into their midst, and both dominated socially and politically by an English-speaking middle class. In simplified terms, a triangular relationship had been created involving the railways, their employees and the local community. The economic significance of freight handling at the Lakehead and its social ramifications thus provide the background for the strife it engendered. Each municipality originated as a point of transshipment between the Great Lakes navigation system and the vast hinterland to the north west, Fort William in the early 1800s as the inland capital of the North West Company, and Port Arthur in 1857 as the starting point of a wagon and water route from Lake Superior to the Red River. In 1875, the Canadian government chose Fort William as the starting point of the Canadian Pacific Railway's line to the west, and in 1902 Port Arthur became the Lake Superior terminus for the Canadian Northern Railway.[9]

During the wheat boom era, the economic life of the communities centred around railroading and shipping, and around the seemingly endless construction of rail and shipping facilities, all designed to stimulate the grain trade from the west and the flow of manufactured goods, raw materials and immigrants from the east. Although the Lakehead became world-famous for its enormous grain-handling facilities, its function as a freight handling centre was equally as important. Longshoring, including freight handling, probably accounted for the largest single occupation. As their work consisted in transferring goods from ships to the freight sheds and thence to the freight trains, freight handlers were variously referred to as dockers, porters, truckers, or longshoremen and came within the jurisdiction of the International Longshoremen's Association. Other categories of longshoremen included grain trimmers, rail handlers and coal handlers. The freight handlers were part of that vast reservoir of cheap labour brought to Canada from Europe during this period by transportation companies or immigration agencies for work on the hardest, heaviest and most precarious jobs. Depending on the season, each railway employed from several hundred to over one thousand men in its freight sheds alone. The essential role played by the European navvy in the development of the Lakehead as a shipping centre may be seen in the population statistics for 1913. By then, the non-English-speaking inhabitants accounted for about one-third of the population of each city.[10]

The freight handlers came from Italy, Greece, Finland, the Austro-Hungarian and Russian Empires, and at times, from the British Isles. While the predominant nationality at both railways seems to have been Italian, the Canadian Northern sheds in Port Arthur also used considerable numbers of British. Although the British performed manual labour alongside the Europeans, the advantage of literacy and the English language enabled them to advance to higher status jobs as checkers, clerks, or supervisors, or to move on to better positions elsewhere. Such skills also enabled them to organize their fellow workers into unions. At the Canadian Northern sheds, it was the British who assumed leadership in strikes; at the CPR's, the Greeks and Italians usually took the initiative, but as shall be seen, in quite different ways.

The manner in which European nationalities developed their own sub-cultures as havens against what they found to be alien structures is a well-known feature of North American society. To the despair of the Protestant clergy and laity, immigrants at the Lakehead, as elsewhere, clung to such Old World institutions as churches and fraternal societies to preserve their only source of dignity, their culture heritage. To cope with exploitation and socialization, they also created new defensive mechanisms. The influence of culture on this process is shown in the marked differences between the behaviour of pre-industrial peoples from northern and southern Europe, particularly if we contrast the transformation by Finns of their literate and Protestant European heritage into highly organized and politicized activities in North America, with the adaptation of cultures based on illiterate, Catholic societies. Considered as the "aristocracy" of the immigrant population at the Lakehead, the Finns, however, had no important part in the freight handlers disputes and therefore do not come under the purview of this paper.[11]

Lacking the class conscious ideology of the radical Finns, the Italians developed their own sense of "community control." As far as possible, they unofficially governed and policed themselves within the confines of the local jurisdictions. Instead of calling on the police to settle quarrels amongst themselves or with other nationalities, they would refer to their own leaders, many of whom appear to have been members of the "Black Hand" which operated within the Italian community as an almost quasi-government organization. Although this name conjures up visions of the Mafia, its purpose probably was more the protection of immigrants than the practice of extortion. Keeping weapons for self-defence was another Italian practice. When defending their livelihood in strikes, using guns and "taking the law into their own hands" would be resorted to only naturally.[12]

Anglo-Saxons generally held all southern Europeans in low esteem for their allegedly volatile nature; the Greeks, however, earned a lasting reputation among all nationalities for their fiery qualities which, combined with the custom of carrying knives, became known as a major cause of disturbance at the freight sheds. But the non-passive reaction of Greeks to their role in the Canadian industrial process cannot be explained by personality alone. As the following account shows, the response of Greeks workers to industrialism in their homeland around the turn of the century was little different from the response of their fellow countrymen to the same process in Canada a decade later:

> It was neither class tradition nor organization, but simply the natural tendency of the Greek worker to oppose all kinds of oppression, coupled with a growing realization now of his importance in the industrial revolution, that sought expression in action: his first impulse to strike without organized leadership was not only a manifestation of national character but also a demonstration of strength.

This description applies to Greece; it is equally applicable to the freight handlers' strikes in Fort William.[13]

Just as Europeans in Canada fought social injustice in their own ways, so did the British who, regardless of political persuasion, sought out their traditional working class institution, the trade union. A good example of this is the young Scottish immigrant of Conservative learnings, Lauchlan Torrie, who without prior trade union experience nevertheless responded in the ways of his class to intolerable conditions at the Canadian Northern freight sheds in Port Arthur by organizing a union in 1907. The traditions brought by the British were based on "the rhetoric of the free-born Englishmen." No matter where born in the Empire, Britons believed in "British fair play" and it was something to which they were automatically entitled. Canadian or British-born, Conservative or socialist, English-speaking trade unionists at the Lakehead would invariably include appeals to "British fair play" when seeking a hearing from employers or the public. This report of a British trade unionist's address to striking freight handlers in 1907 is but one example of this attitude:

> He was always led to expect, he said, that men were all free wherever the Union Jack flew, but he did not think this was the case with the men employed by the CPR.[14]

If the British entertained no doubt about their "rights," they did have conflicting views on the nationality question. As internationalism had always been a strong component of the British labour movement, particularly in its radical wing, the British at the Lakehead accepted the "international" nature of the unions they found or formed in Canada as incipient expressions of future working class solidarity. This attitude, however, conflicted with a strong prejudice among most English-speaking workers about the foreign-born. Most British and Canadian workers shared the dominant notions of Anglo-Saxon superiority which the threat of cheap, foreign labour only magnified. Protection from the foreign-born thus became an inducement to join unions.[15] Far-sighted trade unionists recognized that greater security could be derived from organizing the foreign-born than in excluding them from the labour movement. Their success, however, was limited and not only by attitudes within the American Federation of Labor craft unions. Part of the problem lay with the difficulty of organizing first-generation proletarians handicapped by enforced mobility and language barriers. But the real impediment to permanent unions of immigrant workers lay elsewhere. The railways had the means through their transportation facilities and their strike-breaking apparatus to ensure the non-unionization of their freight handlers.

Another way to maintain a reserve of cheap labour was through substandard housing. "Immigrants are encouraged to come," noted the *Social Survey of Port Arthur* "but little thought is taken for their housing and living conditions." Freight handlers, like other foreign-born workers, settled mainly in the "coal dock section" of each municipality. Fort William's, in particular, developed into a distinctive, cohesive community sandwiched between the CPR tracks and the freight sheds, coal docks, railway yards and grain elevators then lining the Kaministikwia River. In Port Arthur, the geographical separation of freight and coal handling operations led to a more diffuse foreign community, as did the greater distance between residential quarters and the freight sheds. As suggested below, these geographical differences may partially explain the differing nature of the Fort William and Port Arthur freight handlers strikes.[16]

The immigrant districts were similar, however, in their location on low, swampy land completely lacking in drainage or sanitation, and in their congested housing conditions. Abhorred by the middle class, substandard housing enabled the immigrant to save enough money to buy his own "shack" or to send money back home for his family's support. The seasonal nature of longshoring and other occupations normally reserved for foreigners led to enforced mobility which conflicted with the desire for stability as shown in their returning summer after summer to the Lakehead. Although their living conditions were conducive to social unrest, the immigrants began to develop a stake in their own communities and hence in their jobs. This longing for permanency in their lives helps explain the tenacity with which the freight handlers fought their strikes.[17]

Just as the nature of freight handling helped shape the crowded immigrant communities, it also created the conditions allowing for industrial strife. Before the age of mechanization, freight handling required vast quantities of manual labour in the trans-shipment of goods from ship to shed to freight train, but it required this labour in varying numbers at irregular times. The freight handlers focused their grievances not only around low wages, but long, irregular hours of work. For most of the period, the basic hourly rate remained at $17\frac{1}{2}¢$ an hour. (For the sake of comparison, the lowest rates for "rough" labour won by the iron workers and carpenters unions in 1903 were $22\frac{1}{2}¢$ and $25¢$ an hour respectively.) The normal working day at that time was ten hours, but normal days were rare, for the amount of work depended on the arrival of ships. With "five hours work one day, no work the next, and eighteen hours the next," freight handlers took as much work as could be endured to compensate for lost time and low pay. The hiring system through which the railways regulated their labour pool also contributed to uncertainty and violence, for every time a ship came in more men than were needed fought one another "in an awful crush" to grab the metal disk giving permission to work.[18]

Another means by which the railways exercised control over their labour force was the bonus system. The bonus was a small amount varying from $1¢$ to $2\frac{1}{2}¢$ an hour over the regular wage held back for payment at the close of navigation to those who remained on the job for the entire season. By requiring the men to be always available for work, whether or not there was any, or sacrifice the bonus earned, the system limited the freedom of the freight handlers to seek better employment while at the same time ensuring a stable work force for the railways.[19]

Given these conditions, it is hardly surprising that a continual state of labour unrest existed at the Lakehead freight sheds. Details of early strikes unfortunately are obscure, yet it is possible to discern in them the pattern of future developments. In 1902, a strike at the Canadian Northern's sheds in Port Arthur ended with the arrival of an imported gang of Italian strike-breakers under the escort of ten special constables. In 1903, another strike of the Port Arthur freight handlers ended with the reading of the Riot Act, the arrest of the "ringleader," the firing of those involved, and the "dispersal of a crowd of Italians." The evidence suggests that both strikes were sparked by unsuccessful union drives of the United Brotherhood of Railway Employees in western Canada in 1902, and the campaign by A.F.L. organizer, Harry Bryan, to extend unionism to unskilled, immigrant labour at the Lakehead in 1903. Imported strikebreakers, private police forces, rioting, and the breaking of unions were to become regular features of the freight handlers strikes of the future.[20]

In the spring of 1906, the chronic unrest at the Canadian Northern sheds in Port Arthur came to a head under the leadership of British handlers. The construction boom in railroad and building which had attracted many British workers to the Lakehead also brought in its wake increased activity on the labour front. Although the British workers who had found employment at the Canadian Northern freight sheds had no association with a union, they joined in the movement for higher wages by circulating a petition which contained a strike threat if their demand for a pay increase was not met. As seen by the formation of a committee of four British, one Italian and one "Russian," representing the major nationalities at the sheds, by the circulation of the petition amongst all freight handlers who gave it their overwhelming support, and by its presentation to management, their methods were based on British constitutional tradition. But the rejection by the railway of the workers' demands, and its threat to put to work sixty-five strikebreakers brought from Winnipeg and to bring in one thousand more in the event of a strike, effectively blocked the British method of solving grievances through the peaceful means of petitioning.[21]

That autumn, the Canadian Pacific freight handlers in Fort William, who had not participated in the earlier disputes, put forth demands similar to those made by the Canadian Northern men a few months previously. But instead of following the British precedent of petitioning, the CPR men presented their demands to the company only after striking without prior warning. Conveying an impression of spontaneity, their methods contrast vividly with the legalistic approach adopted by the Canadian Northern petitioners. Initiated by Italians who reportedly "induced" the Greeks and "Hungarians" to follow them, the Fort William strike apparently lacked formal leadership. Some kind of organization based on the social structure of the coal dock district became evident, however, as strikers exercised control of movement in and out of the area to prevent local inhabitants working at the sheds or leaving for city construction projects. At Port Arthur, the Canadian Northern freight handlers responded by joining the strike. In the two towns, one thousand men were out, all foreigners with the exception of the English-speaking group at Port Arthur.[22]

Attempting to fill the leadership void, the British formed a representative committee of Canadian Northern strikers composed of three English-speaking and two Italians, organized joint meetings with CPR strikers, and admonished against violence. But while orderliness generally prevailed the first day, some incidents with violent overtones did occur. In Port Arthur striking Italians "mobbed" labourers working on the new CPR station and then attacked a constable trying to intervene. In Fort William, a clash between strikers and two CPR policemen followed by singing, shouting and parading through the coal docks district sufficiently alarmed the Port Arthur *Daily News* (October 1, 1906) to describe the events as "a regular reign of terror." These incidents seem to have been exceptions, however, for the *Daily News* also reported that order generally prevailed.

"Strike Breakers Precipitate Violence" is how the Fort William *Daily Times-Journal* (October 2, 1906), described what happened the following day when a special train from Winnipeg carrying strikebearers, railway officials and CPR police arrived at the Fort William freight sheds. In the ensuing battle, Italian and Greek strikers who had run home for their weapons exchanged some hundred and fifty shots with railway police. (That only one constable and two strikers were wounded was considered "little short of a miracle.") With the municipal police maintaining an uneasy peace between the contending forces that night, the situation remained explosive, for the strikers had neither been subdued nor the strikebreakers put to work.

Much to the displeasure of the railway, the Fort William Mayor, E. S. Rutledge, refused to read the Riot Act, to call out the militia, or even to demand additional volunteer policemen. Instead, he chose to act as mediator. The resulting settlement which included abolition of the contentious bonus system and a new base rate of 22½¢ an hour instead of the former 17½¢ represented a victory made possible, it seemed, by the use of force against the strikebreaking apparatus of the railway.

At Port Arthur, the Canadian Northern men succeeded as well in preventing imported strikebreakers from being put to work in the sheds, but by quite different means. Here the logistics of the situation made it possible for the Italian strikers to meet the train carrying strikebreakers, who were also Italian, and who learned for the first time of the strike's existence. The press reports how the newcomers joined their fellow countrymen's cause "without intimidation" and then marched up town to the cheers of the strikers into the care of the Italian community. Whether derived from class or ethnic loyalties, this display of solidarity led to the Canadian Northern's failure to break the strike and to a settlement similar to that won in Fort William.

Why the violence in Fort William and not in Port Arthur? The non-violent policy of the British-dominated strike committee undoubtedly influenced the strikers of all nationalities in Port Arthur, while the logistics of the situation facilitated persuasive methods instead of force. In Fort William, on the other hand, the proximity of the freight handlers' dwellings to the freight sheds enabled the immigrants to resort to their time-honoured self-reliance in matters of self-defence. But the use of force by the CPR strikers must be seen not only in relationship to their ethnicity but in context of the inflammatory situation created by the CPR. Unlike the Canadian Northern Railway, the CPR displayed both belligerence and provocation in importing strikebreakers guarded by armed police in the face of a determined throng of strikers who had no penchant for the British policies which prevailed in Port Arthur. There, where the situation was conducive to alternate means of stopping strikebreakers, strikers of the same national origin had no need for violence.

To the English-speaking community, however, there seemed little doubt about the relationship of ethnicity to violence. Even prior to the shooting, minor skirmishes in both towns had provoked this editorial commentary in the *Daily News* (October 1, 1906):

... for a community of British citizens to have to submit to the obloquy of insult and armed defiance from a disorganized horde of ignorant and low-down swashbucklers and peanut vendors is making a demand upon national pride which has no excuse.

The paper went on to suggest that the strike had been prompted in the first place by the rumour that both railways intended doing away with Italian labour. Could Italians, Greeks and Hungarians ever become good British citzens, it asked, or should "brawny English-speaking men and youths" be induced to take their place? Replacing the foreigners in the sheds by British or even "Finns, Swedes, Scandinavians, and others of like sturdy races, all of whom are regarded as permanent and order-loving citizens" had become an attractive objective for the English-speaking community and the railways alike.

At the beginning of the 1907 shipping season, the CPR revealed its assessment of the ethnic question by refusing to hire Greeks or Italians, by replacing them with some seven hundred freight handlers of English, Scottish, Polish and Hungarian origin. While the Canadian Northern re-employed its strikers of 1906, both railways reneged on the wage settlement and reintroduced the bonus, this time of 1¢ an hour.[23]

Insisting that they were "victims who had been enticed into this country under false representations," the British at Port Arthur responded to this quashing of the previous year's gains by organizing their fellow workers into the International Freight Handlers and Warehousemen's Union. The enthusiasm generated by the union's demands for wage increases and overtime pay was such that, without union sanction but "by their own free and sensible will" the men refused to unload a ship on a Sunday at the regular rate. When the Canadian Northern replied by firing L. Torrie, the young Scottish president of the union, the freight handlers stopped work in a body. With the union unprepared to lead the strike which, moreover, was illegal under the provision of the recently-passed Industrial Disputes Investigation Act requiring conciliation before strikes by railway employees, Torrie urged the men to return to work, but in vain. Reluctantly, the executive assumed leadership of the strike begun by rank-and-file of all nationalities while cautioning them not to break the law but "to be gentlemen and to make every act one that would reflect credit on themselves."[24]

Over in Fort William, meanwhile, the British replacements for the Greeks and Italians succeeded in extending the strike to the CPR sheds. But united action by an unseasoned group of several hundred workers from several national origins proved impossible. While the strikers vacillated, the CPR put to work a labour force available in the community and broke the strike. The strikebreakers were none other than those Greeks and Italians whom the railway had refused to re-hire just a few weeks previously for their role in the strike of 1906. Attempts to convince them to join with the strikers failed: "The Englishmen, they claim, had no scruples about going to work when they were shut out and they certainly do not intend to turn around and help them when they are shut out."

The CPR thus broke the strike by playing off one nationality against the other. Over in Port Arthur, the Canadian Northern also succeeded in defeating its strike, this time importing strikebreakers in sufficient numbers to demoralize the workers and preventing the strikers from contacting them. With the defeat of the strike came the defeat of the union and the dismissal of all union spokesmen. In 1906, violence had created a demand for the employment of British workers, but in 1907, the railways rejected British trade unionists and their methods, thereby recreating the conditions leading to violence.[25]

As it turned out, the battle of 1906 had been a mere dress rehearsal for that which occurred during the 1909 CPR freight handlers strike in Fort William. Led by the Greeks and Italians as in 1906, the strike appeared to be a spontaneous and leaderless "demonstration of strength," for the men still had no union and had given no warning to the company. The immediate posting of pickets and obvious preparations for a "long siege," however, suggest both premeditation and some internal though perhaps informal structure.[26]

From the beginning, the CPR accused the Greeks of precipitating the work stoppage and of intimidating the other nationalities into joining them. While some English-speaking checkers later expressed fear of the Greeks and "their long sharp dirkes," the union of the Europeans throughout the strike does not indicate Greek domination. Neither does the representative nature of the strike committee nor its choice of an Italian interpreter as spokesman. With the arrest of a Greek freight handler for carrying a revolver, the solidarity of the strikers and their "community control" philosophy became apparent in their insistence that the offending policeman himself be arrested and that the strikers had the same right to be armed as the police. With the erection by the CPR of a long barricade of freight cars between the sheds and the residential quarters in preparation for the arrival of strikebreakers coming from Montreal, a "pitched battle" seemed inevitable.[27]

The anticipated happened on August 12 with the arrival by train of thirty heavily-armed CPR policemen from Winnipeg as an advance guard for the strikebreakers. The detachment's appearance at the CPR bunkhouse near the entrance to the sheds had a predictably electrifying effect on the strikers crowded around the intersection. When the strikers' warning not to leave for the sheds was defied, the shooting began. Driving the police back into the bunkhouse during the half-hour gun battle, the strikers would have stormed it but for the persuasions of the small municipal force. The railway policeman now virtually prisoners of the strikers, the local force maintained an uneasy truce until relieved by the militia some hours later.[28]

Although eye-witnesses differed as to which side fired first, most commentators – from Fort William's chief of police to the deputy minister of labour – later placed the ultimate blame for the riot on the CPR for the provocative manner in which it had introduced its forces into an explosive situation. But could the CPR's deployment of its police be considered as merely the "immediate cause" of the violence? To Colonel S. B. Steele, the officer commanding the forces on duty in aid of the civil power, the violence had been the direct result of the strikers being foreign. As District Officer commanding Military District Number 10, Steele was sufficiently impressed by the strength and defiance of the strikers to order seventy regulars of the Royal Canadian Mounted Rifles down from Winnipeg to supplement the one hundred and fifty men mustered by the local militia. By the strike's conclusion, Steele had become convinced that the immigrant population represented a perennial source of violence. Accordingly, he recommended to headquarters that the local militia be strengthened "owing to the very great number of foreigners in the two cities of Fort William and Port Arthur," and that the permanent force in Winnipeg be increased in the event of more than one such emergency occurring in the district simultaneously. For Steele, the role of the military had thus become not one of defence against foreign foes abroad, but one of defence against foreign foes at home.[29]

This equating of the immigrants to an enemy alien force within the Canadian social fabric became apparent during Steele's pacification campaign. Until the strike ended on August 16, Fort William's coal docks district must have resembled occupied territory as the combined force of over two hundred soldiers armed with fixed bayonets tried to enforce the submission of a hostile, immigrant community. Reports of foreigners cowering in the presence of the military to the contrary, the freight handlers exhibited their defiance by refusing to return to work.[30]

One cause of this intransigence was the CPR's announcement of a permanent ban on Greek workers for their role in the strike and the riot. "The two hundred Greeks are an impossible, dangerous and disturbing element," CPR general manager G. A. Bury proclaimed, to which Fort William's chief of police, W. A. Dodds, added, "Of all the European polyglot, the Greeks are by far the most dangerous and difficult to handle." In reply to this attempt to divide them on the basis of nationality, the strikers convened a "conference of all nations" which pledged that none would return to work unless all were taken back.[31]

In the meantime, various individuals and groups within and outside the community had been stirred by the riot into seeking explanations for the violence more fundamental than the provocations of the CPR police or the temperament of the southern European. Although civic officials and the local and national press generally condemned the foreigners for "taking the law into their own hands," some among them offered criticisms of the strikers' working and living conditions. One of the most important interventions came from the Port Arthur Trades and Labor Council which first came to the aid of the strike committee to lend it "something like discipline." The council passed a stinging resolution condemning first the CPR for "sending armed special constables in the midst of between six and seven hundred offended and angry workers, knowing that many of those workers were armed," as well as "the practice of calling out the militia to shoot down their fellow workers in times of trade disputes." The resolution also called for government investigation of the freight handlers' working conditions. But before the Deputy Minister of Labour F. A. Acland's arrival in response to this request, the strike had ended. The failure to break the workers' resistance through intimidation had left one means to end the strike, conciliation under the terms of the Lemieux Act. With the backing of the railway and the military, Fort William Mayor L. L. Peltier succeeded in persuading an assembly of the entire coal docks community of five thousand inhabitants that its best interests lay in the strikers invoking the Act and returning to work to await the results.[32]

The adverse publicity given the freight handlers' conditions, the desire of the Department of Labour to prove the effectiveness of its legislation, and the importance to the national economy of preventing further shipping tie-ups, all contributed to the sympathetic understanding of the strikers which prevailed during the conciliation board hearings. If the conciliators linked ethnicity to violence it was not to the innate qualities of certain nationalities, but to their ignorance, as foreigners, of Canadian law. If only the freight handlers had been aware of the Lemieux Act, the argument ran, and had asked for conciliation instead of striking in the first place, the violence and the bloodshed could have been avoided. The strikers also concurred in this view, pleading ignorance of the law and promising to abide by it in the future. They, too, traced their actions to their national origins, for in striking as they had, "they had acted in good faith, and as they would have acted in their own respective countries."[33]

In this conciliatory atmosphere, the Board handed down its unanimous recommendations which included a wage increase and abolition of the bonus system. Although the strikers' original demands were not met, the settlement seemed like a victory, especially since the CPR took back all the men, including the Greeks on whom it had earlier announced a permanent ban. But just as it had in the spring following the seemingly victorious 1906 freight handlers strike, the CPR had the last word. With the commencement of the 1910 shipping season, the railway again announced that it would employ neither Greeks nor Italians at its sheds. Preparations against further trouble from the excluded men were announced by the CPR's secret service department:

> The police department of the CPR is organized this year, and just now enough constables could be mustered to compete with a company of soldiers, let alone a bunch of foreigners who would not stop running if they saw a red coat walking down the coal docks street.[34]

For the Greeks and Italians, then, conciliation had been a farce. When military might had failed, the government and the railway had joined in using the Lemieux Act to force the men back to work. And now a lock-out prevailed against those who had initiated the strike. In fulfilling its purpose of maintaining social order, the Act had been used not only to defuse an explosive situation, but retroactively to break the strike as far as the Greeks and Italians were concerned.

Labour riots involving immigrants in 1912 and 1913 reinforced public belief in the affinity of certain ethnic groups for violence. In the 1912 strike by employees of the Canadian Northern Coal Dock Company of Port Arthur, whose number included discharged CPR freight handlers, a lone picket's attempt to block two local strikebreakers ended in a bloody mêlée between five city policemen and perhaps one hundred Italian residents of the coal docks districts of both cities. During the 1913 street railwaymen's strike, immigrant sympathizers of the English-speaking strikers overturned a street car driven by local strikebreakers as it proceeded along the boundary of Fort William's coal docks district. This led to the arrest of a rioter, a rush on the coal docks jail to free him, and the police firing into the crowd, killing an Italian onlooker. Each time, rioting had followed warnings from English-speaking trade union and socialist leaders to avoid violence.[35]

On both occasions, the southern Europeans had followed behaviour patterns quite similar to those displayed in the earlier freight handlers strikes. But was this seeming affinity for violence derived from ethnicity itself, "characteristics in the blood" to use Gutman's phrase, or were other factors involved? Part of the answer lies in the transition process of first-generation proletarians to industrialism which always carries within it elements of violence. But this is not the entire answer, for non-industrialized peoples from Finland and the Austro-Hungarian Empires took part in the same strikes as the Greeks and Italians, yet refrained from violence. These groups did not escape conflict in their encounters with industrialization, but they handled it differently, depending on their cultural heritage and their objective situation.

It is hardly necessary either to document the unruliness of first-generation proletarians in Great Britain, or the turbulence of its industrial revolution. Even after British workers made themselves into a disciplined class and had acquired a reputation for their law-abiding conduct, they still encountered violence in their labour disputes both in the old country and in the dominions. Such violence, however, was largely initiated by capital or the state. For the British workers in the Lakehead freight handlers strikes, such provocation was generally absent.

Neither did the southern Europeans automatically engage in violence. We have only to recall the 1906 strike in Port Arthur when freight handlers behaved differently from those of the same nationalities in Fort William. During another freight handlers' strike in 1912, there again was no violence even though many Canadian Northern strikers had participated in the CPR strike of 1909. This peaceful behaviour on both occasions *may* have been the result of British leadership; more critical was the absence of provocation by strikebreaking. In 1906, the strike-breakers at Port Arthur had been won over; in 1912, few were available in that year of a national labour shortage. Strike-breaking inevitably produced violence; significantly, in the freight and coal handlers strikes. However, this violence was aimed not at the strikebreakers themselves, but at the private and municipal police forces supporting the strikebreaking oper-ations.

The labour and socialist press of the period likened these riots by immigrant labourers to the revolts of oppressed peo-ples. Commenting on the significance of the number of strikes by immigrants imported to take the jobs of Canadians, the *Industrial Banner* of September, 1909, contended after the CPR freight handlers strike that "the poor, exploited foreigners had good cause for revolt" and urged they be organized. And after the riot by immigrant sympathizers of the street railwaymen in 1913, the socialist *Cotton's Weekly* of May 22 had this to say:

> How the capitalist press gurgles over the arrival of a shipload of foreigners! How the masters chuckle as they fondly imag-ine they will be able to get cheap labor! ... But they often make a mistake in the spirit of the foreign slave. He gets wised up to the rotten system of robbery and peonage prac-tised on his kind, and revolts with his Canadian brother slave.

This pithy language notwithstanding, perhaps these riots can best be understood as "revolts" by peoples doubly oppressed as wage-earners and as "foreigners," categories in which the Ital-ians and Greeks stood at the lowest level. Industrializing socie-ties have traditionally supplied their needs for unskilled manual labour from pre-moden peoples considered backward and infe-rior to the dominant culture. In the 1830s, the Irish played this role in Great Britain, and during the early stages of industrial-ism in Canada, they played it here, with consequences some-times violent. During the wheat boom period and later, the southern Europeans were amongst those best fitted for this role. Bringing traditions of violence, they came to conditions of vio-lence created by the process of adjusting uprooted peoples to a new work discipline. But with their strange languages, their dark complexions and their non-integrating cultures, the south-ern Europeans were "foreign" and therefore "inferior" in Can-ada in a way the Irish never were. Confirming this attitude were the immigrants' working and living conditions, themselves sources of violence which, when it erupted, reinforced discrimi-nation.[36]

Regardless of the national origin of the participants, violence is always an inherent danger in any strike involving strikebreaking. When ethnicity is a factor, the danger is intensified, particularly when the ethnic groups are those most alienated from society. The railways, however, created the conditions for violent confrontations by transporting strikebreakers under the protection of secret service departments and special police forces. But the strikes themselves were the outcome of more basic policies, those being the refusal of the railway companies to institutionalize labour relations and recognize trade unions. Violence became the only alternative to immigrants facing intolerable conditions. As a consequence, the railways alternated between those who "took the law into their own hands" and those who acted within the law but organized unions. To meet the labour unrest and violence that such policies generated, the government operated two seemingly contradictory agencies; its conciliation machinery and its military forces. The former failed; the latter became a tool for breaking strikes and suppressing the "revolts" of immigrant workers.

Unlike the British, the Greeks and Italians came from societies which offered little experience with either work discipline or with constitutionalism and trade unionism. When the confrontation tactics of the railways met their cultural patterns headlong, the result was violence. A relationship between ethnicity and violence, then, did exist; its source, however, lay in the industrial relations of the railways which had shaped the place of the immigrants in Canadian society.

Class Conflict in the Coal Industry Cape Breton 1922

David Frank

Suddenly the whole country was watching. Alarming reports were coming out of "the Canadian Far East." Sabotage seemed to stalk the eastern edge of the country. Then came Sovietism. Soon the coal mines were shut down, and Nova Scotia was "simply bristling with dangerous possibilities." By the late summer of 1922 more than one-quarter of Canada's army was boarding eastbound trains, fully equipped for battle.[1]

What was happening among the coal miners of Nova Scotia? In March the Minister of Labour denounced them as "un-British, un-Canadian and cowardly." In June the miners proclaimed themselves "out for the complete overthrow of the capitalist system and the capitalist state, peaceably if we may, forcibly, if we must," and all Canadian workers were invited to join in the attempt. In August the coal miners closed the mines, and their disciplined strike became "the most remarkable possibly in the history of Canadian labour disputes." In left-wing circles the coal miners were acclaimed for placing themselves "in the forefront of the radical forces in North America"; in business circles the cry went up for prompt military action to put down a red uprising in the east. What had happened in Nova Scotia's major coal-field? It was "the most menacing industrial crisis" in the province's history, worried the *Halifax Herald.* "Never before since coal mining began in this province has a like mental attitude existed among the workers." "The idea of a class war, rather than a partnership in industry, had taken possession of the mining towns," commented another observer. But perhaps it was J. S. Woodsworth who suggested the most useful way of looking at events in Cape Breton. "What is the root of all this trouble in Nova Scotia?" he wrote, "Bolshevism among the foreign miners? No, that is not an adequate answer, though an easy way of disposing of any industrial difficulty. The miners in Nova Scotia are chiefly of Scotch-Canadian stock and there was similar trouble long before Lenin came upon the international stage. No case can be summed up in a word, yet there is one word that is much nearer than Bolshevism: that is 'Besco'—the common sobriquet of the British Empire Steel Corporation. For years we have been studying the miners and are puzzled because we cannot find a solution to the trouble. Suppose we devote our attention to the other factor. Better still, suppose we study the relations of the two factors."[2]

Under industrial capitalism class relationships are broadly similar from time to time and place to place. But they are never just the same – and they do not have just the same results. For instance, the explosive confrontation between labour and capital in Cape Breton in 1922 emerged from the specific circumstances in the coal industry at the end of the First World War. Two historical cycles intersected. The coal miners harboured their highest expectations at a time when the coal industry teetered dangerously on the edge of collapse. A rejuvenated and aggressive labour movement clashed head on with the anxious new captains of a weakened coal industry. For reasons of their own, each side urgently wanted to change the terms on which labour power was bought and sold in the coal industry. Neither side was willing to yield, and the course of events in the 1920s demonstrated this common stubborness and tested the comparative strength of the two sides. The confrontation of 1922 showed the effectiveness of several sources of strength available to the working class and introduced one of the most sustained episodes of open class conflict in Canadian history.[3]

The First World War was a decisive turning point in the history of the coal industry. The period of rapid expansion ended with the war and the industry began its long decline. The crisis was rooted in the uneven development between regions which characterized the growth of industrial capitalism in Canada. Two aspects of this process shaped the history of the coal industry in Nova Scotia. The division of labour between regions established the Nova Scotia coal industry as a staple exporting industry for the use of central Canada, rather than as an engine of local industrial development. At the same time, the concentration and centralization of economic power delivered control of the industry into the hands of Boston, Toronto, Montreal and London financiers, for whom the fate of the coal industry was only one of a hundred considerations of rates of profit. As a result the Nova Scotia coal industry suffered from two historic weaknesses: distant and unstable markets, and external corporate control. Each contributed heavily to the crisis in the coal industry at the end of the First World War.[4]

The National Policy established central Canada as the main marketplace for the Nova Scotia coal trade, but it did this in an ambiguous and incomplete way. The tariff was never high enough to let Canadian coal compete against imported American coal in the industrial heartland of Ontario. And in Quebec, its major market, Nova Scotia coal faced a continual threat from American producers. Transportation added another handicap: though the water route was relatively cheap, navigation on the St. Lawrence was subject to various natural hazards, including the annual freeze-up. The disruption of commercial shipping during the war completely closed the Quebec market to Nova Scotia coal; the alternative of rail shipments was uneconomic. Wartime demands for coal from the local steel industry and the British fleet compensated for the closing of the Quebec market. But after the war recovery of the Quebec market was slow and inadequate. Overproduction in the American fields led to increased exports to Canada at unusually low prices, and the Nova Scotia coal operators seemed to find the prospect of temporary gains in overseas markets more attractive than a difficult campaign against their traditional rival in the Quebec market. By 1921 sales in Quebec were about 60 per cent less than in 1914. The industry's second major customer, the local steel industry, offered no consolation, for it was undergoing its own economic calamities and working far below capacity. Under the impact of this crisis of markets, coal production and man-days worked by the coal miners fell by one-third between 1917 and 1921.[5]

Meanwhile a second crisis further weakened the coal industry. By early 1921 an ambitious Montreal shipper and financier, Roy M. Wolvin, had skilfully merged his latest personal promotion, Halifax Shipyards, with the whole of the province's inactive steel industry and practically the entire coal industry. The resulting merger, the British Empire Steel Corporation (Besco), at once earned the jibe that it was formed with hydrants instead of hyphens. Large blocks of "watered" stock represented idle or grossly overvalued assets, no new capital was raised, no provision was made for rehabilitation of the war-weary coal and steel industries, and market prospects were painted in deceptively optimistic terms. To still doubts about its flimsy financial structure, to demonstrate the corporation's viability, and to attract new investors, Besco needed to show an ability to return high dividends on its top-heavy capitalization. Within Wolvin's ramshackle merger the coal industry, despite its crisis of markets, remained the strongest and only profit-making sector; as a result the coal industry was assigned the urgent task of generating sufficient earnings to support Besco's unrealistic financial structure. Given the crisis of markets, higher coal prices could not meet this need. And increased productivity was unlikely in an industry which needed development work and suffered from a shortage of experienced miners. In an industry where wages made up about 60 per cent of production costs, the easiest answer seemed to be to reduce wages and increase the margin of profit on the coal operations. Squeezed between falling markets and a rising need for profits, Besco during the 1920s desperately attempted to stave off financial collapse at the expense of the working class in the coal industry. To solve this crisis of corporate welfare, when Besco began discussing its first contract with 12,000 coal mining employees in 1921, the corporation proposed that the wage scale be reduced by one-third.[6]

In the coal industry, as elsewhere, the working class emerged from the First World War with hopes for substantial improvements in their standard of living and with a growing interest in the possibilities of social reconstruction. The longstanding poverty of the mining communities was aggravated by rising prices and unsteady employment at the end of the war. Living conditions in the coal towns drew statements of anger and disbelief from outside investigators and sparked strong demands from the miners' union for better housing and sanitary living conditions. And demands for stricter enforcement of safety regulations and for improvements in working conditions in the mines occupied a large part of union energies at the end of the war. The miners' resistance to the proposed wage reduction became a symbol of protest against all of these conditions and expressed the miners' view that the time had passed when "anything was good enough for a miner."[7]

The establishment of effective collective bargaining in the coal industry provided a suitable instrument for pursuing these goals. In 1917 the formation of the Amalgamated Mine Workers of Nova Scotia, encouraged in wartime by the federal and provincial governments, ended the divisive rivalry between the indigenous Provincial Workmen's Association (PWA), which has been established in 1879, and the more militant international union, the United Mine Workers of America (UMWA), who began to challenge the PWA after the turn of the century. In 1919 the coal miners linked their popular new organization to the UMWA and became District 26 of the international union. Through their union the coal miners almost doubled their wage scale between 1916 and 1921. But in a time of rising prices this was not enough: the miners found they were barely keeping up to the cost of living and often they were falling behind. "We want a better standard to build on than the conditions in 1914," argued union president Robert Baxter in July 1920, when the miners' real wages were 11 per cent less than in 1913. "When we have comfortable conditions in which to live, then we shall have something to keep up to." And he added a warning: "If things do not improve, then we will have the same result as they have had in Russia. It might very easily happen if we do not get what we are asking for."[8]

As the remark implied, the end of the war saw the growth of labour radicalism in the mining districts. The tragedy of the war generated hopes that society might be reconstructed on a sound moral and economic basis, with cooperation replacing profit as the ruling principle in society. "Yes, we have come to the turn of the road," announced the Sydney *Labour Leader* in 1919; "the wagon has been jarred, and, at last the workers are awake. They will not go to sleep again until the day's work is done." A vocal labour press spread radical ideas and encouraged working class political action. The miners elected labour candidates to their town councils, sent four labour members to the provincial legislature in 1920, and enthusiastically supported their secretary-treasurer, James B. McLachlan, when he attempted to win election as a labour candidate to the House of Commons in 1921. The Russian Revolution and the Winnipeg General Strike inspired wide interest and sympathy among the miners. "Bolshevik" ideas were popularized for instance, by Glace Bay writer and poet Dawn Fraser:

In every contest between labour and capital, I am with labour and against capital, first, last, and all the time. And if you ask me what percentage of the actual product of labour capital should receive? I cry loudly none. Damn it. None. But be assured that I class all worthy effort as labour, and summed up my contention simply is: That any person who does not work at all, should not eat at all. Excepting of course invalids and children.

The arrest of leaders of the Winnipeg Strike drew protests and support from the coal miners, and strike leaders toured the coal district. One dramatic indication of the miners' increasingly militant mood came on May 1, 1920, when, in response to an appeal from Winnipeg for demonstrations of support for the arrested leaders, the coal miners closed the mines for a one-day general strike.[9]

The flow of life in the coal mining communities of Cape Breton promoted a spirit of interdependence and cohesion among the population. United in "the largest compact industrial community in Canada," dependent on a single employer, facing common hardships and enjoying common recreations, the coal communities "had what was a togetherness, and one's trouble was the other, one's joy was the other. They were a very close knit people." Culturally the population was strongly homogeneous, and the traditions of Scottish culture and history offered a common bond. The basic pre-industrial Highland stock contributed a scale of moral values against which the "tyranny" and "slavery" of workaday life was measured, as in the words of a Gaelic song written in Glace Bay in 1922:

Oh isn't it a shame for a healthy Gael living in this place to be a slave from Monday to Saturday under the heels of tyrants, when he could be happy on a handsome spreading farm with milk-cows, white sheep, hens, horses, and perhaps a car, and clean work on the surface of the earth rather than in the black pit of misery.

The migration of experienced mineworkers from the Scottish Lowlands at the turn of the century added the ginger of militant trade unionism. With an eloquent blend of Burns, Carlyle, and Hardie, of "scotchie talk," "pit talk," and "clan spirit," leaders like Robert Baxter and James B. McLachlan, who had learned their class consciousness and socialism in the Scottish coalfields, effectively rallied the community around the miners' common concerns. The mining towns themselves were another focus for working class consciousness. These were no simple "coal patches," for with so much of the coal resource lying under the ocean floor the major towns enjoyed a unique permanence as beachheads for the assault on the undersea seams; nor were they simple "company towns," for by the 1920s the town councils habitually challenged the coal operators on various civic issues and in times of crisis actively took the miners' side. Against this community solidarity it was difficult for a corporation to make way. The community regarded the parade of successive absentee coal owners as a "floating element," one local writer explained,

... the industrial population is settled; Cape Breton is its home. Every man has relatives and friends and neighbours. The entire population is with him. The managing operator is the floater. He shifts every three or four years and sees only the dollar in the vision. He has no stake in the community; no love for the people.

Or, as another local observer wrote:

We in Glace Bay are unfortunate in being a one-industry town. Close or suspend operations at the mines and we starve. But before dying we put up a fight, and that is exactly what has happened in this mining area.[10]

An important source of working class unity lay below ground too, in the unusual physical conditions which make up the everyday work of most miners: the wet, the dirt and the darkness, the coal dust and stale air, the ever-present danger and the back-breaking hard work. Robert Drummond, a founder of the PWA in 1879 and an unsympathetic witness to the labour militancy of the 1920s, wrote that the coal miner has "an interesting personality:"

Daily he has to face perils of one kind or another. But he is not flustered, he is without neither hope nor consolation. He derives satisfaction from the knowledge that he is the autocrat of industry. He squares his shoulders and declares that a live collier is better than a dead cardinal. Knowing his power and position he may at times be inclined to be somewhat impulsive. His continual tussle in the mine, with the forces of nature, and the bosses, and out of it with the General Manager, give him an independence which at times is embarrassing to his leaders, his employers and the community.

The hardship and the peril connected with coal mining bred an endemic "radicalism" among the coal miners: "blood on the coal" helped shape the miners' attitudes to the coal operators and helped set the market price of their labour power. The miners' union aspired to win "compensation fully compatible with the dangers of our occupation." Between 1871 and 1939 more than 1,600 men were killed in the Nova Scotia coal mines, an average of about twenty-three deaths per year, but in the years 1914-1921 the average annual fatality rate was more than twice as high, mainly as a result of major mine disasters in 1917 and 1918, which killed 153 men. Pressing the case for nationalization of the mines in 1925, McLachlan opposed any form of compensation for the owners: "The workers have put too much into these mines ... more than all the millions they [the operators] have put in. Over a period of years they have put the money in, the workers have put their blood in it."[11]

The organization of work underground also set the miners apart and helps explain the sense of "power and position" and "independence" described by Drummond. Though machine cutting grew significantly after the 1890s, bringing some new tensions into the workplace, by the early 1920s the traditional organization of work remained basically unchanged. Coal mining was still a labour-intensive industry conducted within the traditional room and pillar geography of the underground coal mine. Before the introduction into Cape Breton in the late 1920s of longwall mining, a rough version of the mechanized assembly line in the coal mines, the coal industry largely escaped the rigorous work discipline associated with the growth of industrial capitalism. In 1922 about half the underground workers did the actual mining and shovelling of coal, about one quarter transported coal within the mines, and another quarter were engaged in ventilation, pumping, roadmaking, and timbering work. In the extensive honey-combed interior of the room and pillar mine, most men seldom saw their supervisors. The actual miners and their helpers worked in distant, isolated locations, while drivers, timbermen, and roadmakers were constantly on the move within the mines. As a result, like the "autonomous workman" in the disappearing crafts, the mine-worker himself retained a considerable degree of control over his work and his workplace. "We built up a certain pride," recalled one miner, "This is *my* mine. This is my *section* of the mine. And you prided on that." In important ways the coal miners continued to regard themselves as "their own men," and felt less responsible to the coal operators than to their own pride in their work, their own ideas about how long and hard a "normal day's work" should be, and their responsibilities towards other underground workers. For about one-third of the miners this independence retained formal expression in the payment of a tonnage rate rather than a daily wage for the coal they mined. In the absence of close supervision underground the miners generated their own rules of suitable underground behaviour to enforce safety, fairness and efficiency in mine operations. The miners also developed a spirited tradition of conversation and debate in the mines. A break in the work – and groups of miners would gather to air common complaints, send grievances to the mine managers, discuss the conduct of operations in the mines, or debate topical issues. The end of the day was one such occasion, one coal miner recalled:

> You'd be sitting down waiting for what they call the trips – a trip of empties, empty boxes or empty cars. They're always talking about McLachlan [the union leader], and this and that, strikes and so on, always.... It was the way since I can remember, and so it was the way with us young fellows too. We had our own interests ... and we'd be thinking of our own way. But nevertheless we'd be listening, and we'd be following them .... We'd be getting our political education from them.

Such talk has always been a basic ingredient in trade union traditions, and together with other aspects of the coal miners' work gave the working class tradition strength and meaning at the workplace as well as at union meetings or in the community at large. Indeed it is not surprising to find the emergence of strong trade union traditions in work situations where the workers had some amount of independent control over the production process.[12]

The buying and selling of labour power causes an ongoing quarrel over the price of labour power in this transaction. As one early writer about working class problems in the Maritimes observed, the price "will lie somewhere between the subjective estimates of the buyer and the subjective estimates of the seller."[13] In the Cape Breton coal industry by 1921 the "buyer's estimate" was shaped by a crisis of restricted markets for coal and a crisis of corporate welfare within Besco. On the other hand, the "seller's estimate" was shaped by enhanced working class hopes and growing labour militancy and radicalism, which both found strong sources of support in the pattern of life and work in the coal communities. In 1920 the inflationary price cycle ended. Prices fell sharply until the middle of 1921 and remained fairly stable at this reduced level for the rest of the decade. Pointing to this sudden change in price levels, in 1921 the coal operators demanded that the miners accept a one-third reduction in their wage scale, a measure which threatened to reduce the miners' real wages to the pre-war level.

But from the miners' point of view, the drop in prices provided a windfall gain in real wages: if the wage scale could be defended against excessive reductions, the miners would win a permanent improvement in their standard of living. In the past it had been the policy of the PWA that the wage scale "must accommodate itself to the state of the trade" and to the ebb and flow of prices, but by 1921 the miners were no longer willing to follow this philosophy. Nor did the miners accept the corporation's argument that lower wages would bring larger markets for their coal. The miners argued that coal prices could be lowered by placing the burden on accumulated surpluses and existing profit margins, not on the wage scale. Production costs might be reduced through elimination of needless officials and exorbitant executive salaries, greater efficiency in mine operations, and a more concerted campaign to recover the Quebec market. Indeed, they pointed out, in a country which imported half its coal supplies, adequate protection of the coal industry by the federal government could easily stabilize the domestic coal industry. In short, the miners refused to offer their wage scale as "economic cannon fodder"; they wanted a "new code of morality" to distribute more fairly the burdens of economic problems in the coal industry. Wages and not profits, they argued repeatedly during 1922, should be the first charge upon the earnings of the coal industry. Also, Besco's notorious financial structure, Wolvin's precarious position in the Canadian financial community, and the corporation's refusal to discuss production costs and profit margins with the miners, all reinforced suspicions that Besco wanted to cut wages for the good of a sickly corporation, not for the health of the coal industry itself. To earn profits on "watered stock and idle junk," the miners' wages were attacked. As it turned out, these suspicions were justified. The Duncan Commission, which closely audited Besco's books in 1925, discovered that in spite of "hard times" the coal mines returned handsome profits and "the operators were not justified in insisting on a reduction of wages in 1922, even in spite of the change which they estimated had come over the market and future prospects by the end of 1921."[14]

No settlement of the dispute was reached before the standing agreement expired at the end of 1921, and the corporation introduced the full one-third wage reduction on January 1, 1922. The union protested that because a conciliation board was being formed to hear the dispute, this unilateral step violated the provisions of the Industrial Disputes Investigation Act. One Nova Scotia Supreme Court Justice agreed and issued an injunction forbidding the wage cut, but the full court swiftly reinstated the reduction before the first payday arrived. In January and again in May conciliation boards supported the corporation's case for substantial reductions; both times the board agreed to take confidential evidence from the coal operators and then ruled two-to-one against the miners, the employers' representative and the government-appointed chairman voting together against the union appointee. By the summer the corporation had modified the original wage cut to some extent, but the miners' resistance had stiffened in the meanwhile and there was still no settlement. When the miners went on strike in August, some 1200 troops poured into the Cape Breton coalfield. More troops and a special provincial police force were held in readiness.

Despite this intimidating display of power and influence on the part of the corporation during 1922, Besco did not triumph in the conflict. The corporation was forced repeatedly to change its terms during the year. The outstanding feature of the coal miners' response to the wage reduction in 1922 was its unanimity. After the first conciliation board's disappointing report, the miners voted only 486 in favour and 10,305 against its recommendations. In March, when union leaders obtained some concessions and urged that a contract be signed, the miners voted 1,352 in favour of settlement and 8,109 against. Even a last-minute compromise, agreed to by the union officers on the eve of the August strike, was repudiated by the miners. By September the miners had managed to transform an average 33.6 per cent reduction in their wage scale into a more acceptable 18.9 per cent average reduction. By resisting the initial wage reduction the miners raised their real wage scale from an average index of 102.0 in January (1913 = 100.0) to 134.7 in September, thus defeating the corporation's attempt to restore real wages to the pre-war level.[15] Moreover, the miners preserved their union at a time when some leaders feared the miners' intransigence would lead to the collapse of collective bargaining in the coal industry. Though they might have accepted a smaller wage cut, the vast majority of the miners plainly found the one-third reduction intolerable. But how were they to enforce this opinion? What were the sources of working class effectiveness in this confrontation?

With sharply reduced rates in effect and working time even

shorter than usual during the winter months, the coal miners and their families quickly felt the pinch of necessity in January, 1922. Union locals distributed their savings as relief, and the company stores advanced goods on credit. One local resolution warned that if the government "wishes to avoid any riot, revolution or upheaval on the part of labour, then they had better provide our idle members with that which is necessary for the upkeep in comfort and decency as becomes a British subject." Strong words were matched with action. When an unemployed miner with nine children was denied credit at the New Aberdeen company store on January 21, the prevailing bitterness in the Glace Bay district erupted in a series of raids on the store. The first was a spontaneous reaction to the denial of credit to the one miner; the men present ordered the store manager aside and "took what they needed. There was no disorder. Only food was taken." In the evening a large crowd gathered, tossed snowballs at the company policeman on duty, then smashed the windows and looted the store. The next night a crowd of some 4,000 people surrounded the store. When several hundred men rushed forward with a shout and attacked the store, a squad of company policemen fired in the air and retreated. A fourth raid was averted by the town police with drawn pistols. The raids did not continue or spread, nor did they recur until 1925. Community opinion distinguished carefully between those who raided "for need" and those who raided "for gain" and regarded this form of direct action as an unfortunate symptom of the deepening distress rather than as an attractive or effective solution to the miners' serious plight.[16]

As the crisis sharpened during the next two months, spokesmen for the coal communities articulated their support for the miners' resistance to the wage reduction. New Waterford Mayor James Ling served as the miners' representative on the first conciliation board, though with no effect on the majority decision. And in March the town councils in four mining towns launched a joint appeal to Ottawa on the miners' behalf. They argued that the miners' wages were too meagre "to provide even the necessities of life for themselves and their families" and noted that malnutrition, sickness and inadequate clothing among children were causing more absenteeism from school "than ever before in the history of the mining towns in this district." The mayors complained that the conciliation board had failed to investigate the impact of its decisions "in the lives of tens of thousands of human beings" and called for appointment of a "competent, independent commission" to visit the mining districts and see "with their own eyes the conditions under which these people are expected to live and bring up healthy families." A solution must be found, they warned, for "matters, too long drifting, may break out into open hostilities. . . . " Petition in hand, the mayors of Glace Bay, Dominion, New Waterford and Springhill arrived in Ottawa at the end of March.[17]

But it was mainly through their union that the miners tried to express their response to the wage reduction. The alternative of going on strike, however, was unattractive, for without adequate financial backing a strike would only invite more hardship and deprivation into the miners' homes. Unfortunately, the UMWA offered no hope of substantial aid for a strike, though this was a major attraction of membership in the international union. In early 1922 the UMWA was bracing for its own fight to maintain the 1921 rates in the American fields and was unwilling to commit resources to a difficult preliminary skirmish in an outlying district. Setting these facts before the miners' convention in late February, union president Robert Baxter concluded that the "whole question resolves itself into one of force."[18] And the miners apparently had little "force" at their disposal. The union executive travelled to Montreal, met corporation officials, and despite sharp differences among themselves, decided to refer a proposed settlement back to the membership. When it came to a vote on March 14, the "Montreal Agreement" was soundly defeated. Apparently the miners had a different opinion than their president about how much "force" was at their disposal.

The ensuing events demonstrated that wage disputes are not decided across the bargaining table alone. Under various names and in various forms, restriction of output, or striking on the job, has been a recurrent form of protest among the working class. In the Scottish mineworkers' tradition it persisted in the form of the "wee darg," as R. Page Arnot has explained:

It had long been the custom amongst the colliers to meet a reduction of wages or other worsening of conditions by a reduction of output, called the 'wee darg'. The 'wee darg' recurred for another generation after 1837, and, though in an altered form, could be found till nearly the present day whenever conditions called it forth. The 'wee darg' was a normal, 'instinctive' reaction to any unfair bargain, especially when trade unions were repressed or not recognized, so that collective bargaining could not take place.

In so complex an industry as coal mining, the notion of a "normal day's work" – "the darg" – was as difficult to measure as it was to enforce. The size of the "darg" was a matter of custom – and of dispute, never more so than when the miners objected to the coal operators' policies. Then came the time to "ca' canny" – go slow – and substitute the "wee darg" for the normal "master's darg." Rooted in the Scottish working class tradition and made possible by the special conditions of underground work, restriction of output came readily to hand as a suitable device for the Cape Breton miners to use.[19]

In January and February 1922 the idea of striking on the job became the tacit alternative to normal strike action. The device answered the need of the moment: unprepared to walk off the job, the miners could still register an effective protest. Moreover, at a time when demand for coal was short, a slowdown would "spread the work around" and help reduce idleness. In January the tactic enjoyed some success at one mine where underground drivers who had been demoted from contract rates to daily wages decided that a "fair day's work" ought to be somewhat less than before this change in their status and earning power. The tactic also gained support as a response to the general wage reduction. In February, a Halifax reporter finally broke the silence about what had been taking place unadvertised for at least a month. "Fabian tactics," he reported,

> had spontaneous growth, arising with the men themselves as their method of expressing dissatisfaction with the wages now in force, and with the same wages in force it is likely that the practice will continue. Beyond question, it has operated to cut down production, in some mines by something like 50 per cent...

After rejection of the "Montreal Agreement" on March 14, striking on the job became an open strategy. Its purpose was to put pressure on the corporation by raising production costs and lowering profits, and at the same time, to dramatize the miners' plight, make their cause a public issue and compel the government to intervene on their behalf. On March 16 the tactic acquired a dynamic public spokesman in the person of James B. McLachlan, the union's fiery secretary-treasurer, who circulated a formal appeal. "War is on, class war," his declaration began; the plan of attack was outlined in detail:

> War is on, and it is up to the workers in the mines of the British Empire Steel Corporation to carry that war into the 'country' of the enemy.... Every contract man who voted against acceptance of the wage agreement last Tuesday should at once cut down his production to a point where he can get about the same wage as the low paid men in the mine, and at the same time see to it that every day paid man takes the full eight hours to land his reduced output on the surface.

As the plan suggests, striking on the job was well suited to conditions in the mines. The chain of operations started at the coal face, and if the coal cutters would "work with their shirts on" and "walk about between whiles," then the pace of work throughout the mines could easily be slowed, especially among the loaders and drivers, the other two major groups of mine-workers. Only the contract miners, who were paid by the tonnage of coal they produced, needed to suffer reduced earnings through the slowdown, but as the best paid workers in the mine, they could afford to sacrifice one-third of their rate. Most mineworkers could "go slow" and still collect their daily wages as strike pay. The appeal of the tactic also had a certain logical neatness: a fair day's work supposed a fair day's pay, if wages were cut one-third then profits should be cut one-third, if the corporation could water their stock then the miners could water their labour.[20]

In the first three months of 1922 coal production was one-fifth less than in the same months of 1921 and one-third less than in 1923, but the significance of this is not clear. We lack adequate records to attempt an exact measure of how widely restriction of output was practised. McLachlan soon after stated that striking on the job achieved dramatic results at Dominion No. 2 and No. 4, where output was said to have tumbled by two-thirds or more and the tactic to have been "down to a perfect science." From here, McLachlan claimed, the campaign "spread to the other mines like wildfire." In 1925 Besco's superintendent of coal mines, Alex S. McNeil, gave a similar estimate to the Duncan Commission: "He thought that the 'strike-on-the-job policy' had been followed 'pretty generally' throughout Nova Scotia, but added that it had been followed most consistently at Dominion's Nos. 4 and 2." The local press was uniformly hostile to the "monstrous proposal," claiming that it was imported from the Old Country or from the IWW and associating the tactic with vandalism and sabotage. The daily newspapers played upon the miners' traditional distrust of shirkers and appealed to their "reputation for honesty and square dealing," and such appeals probably reflected ambiguous feelings among many miners about the morality of the tactic. The local president at Dominion No. 1 resigned because he opposed the general support for the tactic at that mine. But he was the only reported public critic among the miners; it seems that disagreements were suppressed, and it was only after the episode was over that Baxter and McLachlan openly debated the morality and effectiveness of "ca'canny methods." Striking on the job found no reported support at the five mines in the Sydney Mines district, but carried great appeal in the larger south Cape Breton field

At six of the 13 operating mines in this area, including three of the largest producers, there is strong evidence of support for the slowdown strike. Joint meetings of locals in the Glace Bay and New Waterford districts endorsed the policy, and after a stormy debate the union executive officially endorsed the strike on the job on March 23. These endorsements no doubt increased the spread of the tactic among the miners. Given the hostility of the press, the elusive nature of the size of a "normal day's work" and the semi-conspiratorial style of the strike, much support went unproclaimed and undiscovered. Probably restriction of output was supported at least to some extent by most of the more than 8,000 men rejected the corporation's latest offer on March 14.[21]

Whatever its actual extent, the tactic brought results. Though the corporation failed to yield, the political pressure created by the dramatic protest was successful. Twice McLachlan addressed open letters to the members of the House of Commons pointing out the desperate tactics the miners were forced to use against Besco. His furious telegraphic duel with James Murdock, Mackenzie King's novice Minister of Labour, rivetted the country's attention on the controversial dispute. Himself a former labour official, Murdock judged the miners "un-British, un-Canadian and cowardly to pretend to be working for a wage rate in effect while declaring to the world that only partial and grudging service will be given." McLachlan retorted that in the absence of any wage agreement there was "nothing dishonest about it. . . . Our method of fighting this unjust wage reduction is effective and within the law." Their words flew back and forth; the whole country was watching. Spurred on by the growing crisis in the coalfields, the delegation of mayors from the mining towns arrived in Ottawa. But their appeal to the cabinet for a new public inquiry into the miners' case was dismissed. A different story unfolded on the floor of the House of Commons. On March 30 William Irvine, the Calgary labour MP, launched an emergency debate on the crisis in Nova Scotia. The debate revealed considerable sympathy in Parliament for the strike on the job. Murdock defended his earlier views. J. S. Woodsworth, the second labour MP, defended the miners' actions and, as a student of society and sometime longshoreman, informed the House that restriction of output was a "natural, recognized mode of procedure" in Canada, in business, on the farm, and at the workplace. Conservative leader Arthur Meighen condoned the miners' tactic and scolded the government for refusing to reopen their case. And Progressive leader T. A. Crerar suggested the conciliation board be sent to make a more thorough study of conditions in the coalfields. Faced with this united opposition, the minority Liberal government accepted Crerar's plan, with the implicit condition that in return the miners end their slowdown. On April 4 the union executive accepted this solution. The decision on March 30 represented success for the imaginative tactic. By dramatizing their resistance to the wage reduction through the strike on the job, the miners had won national attention, and though the delegation of mayors was brushed aside, the miners' own protest could not be ignored.[22]

An uneasy peace settled over the coalfields. With the resumption of shipping in the spring and the shutdown of the American coal industry by the UMWA's strike there, the condition of the coal trade improved. The miners enjoyed full shifts and steady wages, in sharp contrast to the harsh winter months. When the original conciliation board refused to reconvene, a new board was established. Its hearings were markedly sympathetic to conditions in the mining districts, but the plea for a "living wage" in the form of the 1921 wage scale was no more successful than earlier in the year. Despite critical comments about living and working conditions among the coal miners, the board's majority report recommended almost exactly the same wage scale which the miners had rejected so unanimously in their referendum on March 14. Relying again on undisclosed evidence, the board held that the corporation could afford to pay no more. For his part, the miners' representative stood by the principle that "dividends should be sacrificed before the worker should be compelled to accept less than living wages." Less restrained were the words of the *Maritime Labour Herald*, which reached back to the warrior traditions of the Highlands for its response: the award of the conciliation board "takes the place of the cross dipped in blood as the signal of war. The fight is not against another clan. The fight is directed against as bold a band of cutthroat robbers as ever disgraced a country. So the miners gather to the fight, with weapons the profit gluttons little dream of."[23]

The test of strength was renewed. In June delegates from the union locals met in convention and discussed a policy report which offered a choice between two courses of action:

(a) accept the present conditions with all their humiliation and poverty, and repudiate the sacred obligations which every sire owes to his son; or

(b) reject and fight with all the power that is in us the present conditions and make one bold attempt to hand down to our children something better than a slave's portion.[24]

The miners chose the second course, resolving to sign no contract for less than the 1921 wage rates. By late July, encouraged by the apparent success of the American strike for the 1921 rates, and prodded by the international union not to continue working without an agreement, the miners' locals voted almost unanimously to strike on August 15 unless the 1921 wage scale was restored by that date. The brisk condition of the coal trade now enhanced the prospects of a successful strike against Besco, and the miners prepared enthusiastically for the forthcoming shutdown. Last minute negotiations produced a compromise settlement which the union executive tried to refer to the miners for a vote, but their attempt to postpone the strike on August 14 failed, and the walkout took place as planned.

The strike closed all Besco's collieries in Nova Scotia. Moreover, it was a "100 per cent" strike, a term the miners used to describe the removal of every last union member from the mines, including the maintenance workers. This not only halted production, but it also added the threat of mounting accumulations of gas and water in the mines. Though the tactic was not used in the mines of Pictou County, where high gas levels made it unattractive to the miners, the "100 per cent" strike was universally adopted in Cape Breton. In the wetter mines of this district the corporation predicted the imminent destruction of several collieries and denounced the whole strike as "an insurgent move by men who have overridden law and order."[25] The miners argued that only inconvenience but no permanent damage would result from the mounting water levels in the mines. The tactic expressed the miners' determination to win a suitable settlement – and the threat of flooding promised a short, decisive confrontation.

Armed force was the coal operators' main reply to the outbreak of the strike, a course of action Wolvin had planned the week before the strike began. When the strike started on August 15, Glace Bay's labour mayor, D. W. Morrison, a war veteran and a former miner, twice rejected requests that he requisition troops to deal with the strike, pointing out that there was "absolutely no disorder, much less violence" and troops were "totally unnecessary." But later in the day County Court Judge Duncan Finlayson made the necessary application to the military authorities, and that night troops began embarking at Halifax and Quebec City for the Sydney coalfield. Jeers and stones greeted the first troop train the next afternoon. But although the troops were fully armed and equipped for battle down to the last bayonet and chinstrap, on the whole it was a remarkably peaceful invasion. Except for three people killed at a level crossing by one of the unscheduled special trains en route to the coal district, there were no casualties during the strike. The 1,200 troops occupied the vital Dominion No. 2 colliery, the largest producing mine and the site of the power station for the Glace Bay area mines. Under strict orders from Ottawa to refrain from "active measures ... likely to precipitate trouble," such as escorting strikebreakers, they remained under canvas and made no attempt to replace pickets or take control of other mines. If the troops were supposed to preserve law and order, there was no disorder to command their attention. The use of troops only strengthened the miners' solidarity and marshalled the entire community against the invasion.[26]

A remarkable order reigned in the south Cape Breton field. Some 200 miners and war veterans were sworn in as special town police by Mayor Morrison. Prohibition was never more strictly enforced: the "lid was on tight" as squads of union men raided illegal drinking spots and searched all incoming traffic, including the troop trains, for illicit "scabs and booze." On the road from Sydney the miners erected a barrier across the highway, and all cars were stopped and searched before they were allowed to enter the strike zone. At the mines themselves access was controlled by shifts of union pickets, organized in semimilitary picket companies with elected captains. As the strike progressed, the military discipline grew more overt, and a bugle would sound each morning in the streets of New Waterford to rouse the men for picket duty. Nor was all seriousness: on occasion bagpipes played in the street, and the miners took advantage of a rare summer vacation to visit the prolific blueberry barrens. Except for one short altercation between soldiers and pickets on the night of August 16, no clashes took place between the rival camps at Dominion No. 2; both sides hung over the fences and talked. Reporting the strike for a Halifax newspaper, Dalhousie philosophy professor H. L. Stewart was amazed that "the order preserved by a leaderless multitude has been so perfect. No looting, no drinking, no rioting!" But behind the orderliness he found a "distinctly fierce mood." "This is too quiet," worried another visitor, who sensed something "ominous" about the "deliberate, organized quality" of the strike discipline.[27]

On August 18 the only mass demonstration of the strike took place in the form of a silent semi-military parade of four or five thousand men through the streets of Glace Bay: "no chanting, no disorder, no impressive features apart from the impressiveness of a vast body of men moving methodically and purposefully through the streets of the town." After displaying their marching precision to the troops at No. 2, they completed manoeuvres at the ballgrounds with resolutions of protest against the presence of troops. Meanwhile a flood of other resolutions coursed into King's office in Ottawa. Among them, the Great War Veterans' Association in Glace Bay censured the Prime Minister for "helping Wolvin make a fortune out of starving miners and their families" and appealed for national support for the miners' "fight for a living wage, home and children against stocks, bonds and dividends."[28]

Though Wolvin and the local military authorities appealed for additional troops, naval forces and an air squadron, the federal government denied these requests. In Halifax, however, E. H. Armstrong, the Minister of Mines and Public Works, announced plans for a special 1,000-man provincial police force to wrest control of the mines from the union pickets. But this force was not used in 1922. The intervention of Premier George H. Murray resulted in the corporation's agreement to resume negotiations if the "100 per cent" aspect of the strike was ended, and the maintenance workers returned to the mines on the sixth and seventh days of the strike. Strike discipline continued until the miners ten days later endorsed a new agreement with the coal operators, 7,768 in favour, 2,920 against. Work resumed on September 5. The agreement did not restore the 1921 rates, but it did eliminate a large part of the original wage reduction, especially for the lower paid workers, and the long sixteen-month contract represented a substantial victory for the coal miners. Relying on the general support of the mining communities and on their own latent ability to control production by restricting output or by closing the mines, the coal miners had regularly refused to compromise their demand for a "living wage." Weakened by lack of support from the international union and disappointed by the wavering of a divided leadership at home, the rank and file of the miners themselves provided the main inspiration for the continuing resistance to the wage reduction in 1922. What the Halifax *Citizen* said of the "most unique strike in Canada's history" was true of the whole process of events leading up to the August strike: it was "a solid strike, with leaders ordered to take orders from the rank and file or get off the job."[29] Without this militant pressure from below, exerted on both the coal operators and the union leaders, the issue of the miners' wages would likely have been settled sooner and with poorer results for the coal miners.

The events of 1922 were primarily a campaign of resistance against the wage reduction, but the conflict was also a struggle over the future of the coal industry. The growth of the coal and steel industries in Nova Scotia was "a case of development from without," Harold Innis noted a few years later, and "resistance came, not from the industries as such, but from the workers to whom they gave employment." The miners' resistance to lower wages grew into a challenge to private ownership and control of the coal industry. By August 1922 Prof. Stewart could observe that the miners saw the coal mines as a "high public utility, not owned by any corporation, but owned by the province as a whole, and thus the intimate concern of every taxpayer;" they believed the corporation was betraying this public trust when it placed the good of Besco ahead of the miners' welfare. Wolvin's Besco was never a popular corporation. Attacks on Besco's absentee management and "autocratic methods" were mounted by the local Tory press, and this helped deepen the miners' distrust of the corporation. For instance, in January 1922 the *Sydney Post* complained: "Who ever heard of an efficient management being located 1,000 miles away from the actual base of operations? With such absentee management, even an intelligent discussion of reformed industrial relations is impossible." From the beginning Besco was frowned upon in Canada's best financial circles, and during the 1920s a concerted move was afoot to oust Wolvin from control of the coal and steel industries and install Royal Bank President Sir Herbert Holt in his place. The first open skirmish of this ultimately successful campaign came at Besco's annual board meeting in June 1922, where Wolvin repulsed the attempt by securing increased British backing and reorganizing the board of directors. But the months of visible crisis, manoeuvring and suspense highlighted Besco's instability and undermined Wolvin's authority.[30]

"Cost of production," the *Post* observed in February, "is the pinch of the whole dispute"; only through "co-operation, mutual trust and open dealing" could the miners ever be led to accept "costs of production" as a satisfactory reason for reducing wages. But the corporation stubbornly refused to discuss costs or profits. No presentation of the miners' views at this time was complete without reference to the substantial accumulated surpluses of the coal industry in the years since the war. And when Besco published its first annual report in May 1922, revealing earnings of more than $4.4 million in the last nine months of 1921, resentment grew. Distrust of the corporation's candour led to demands for seats on the Dominion Coal Company's board of directors, in harmony with an early Besco promise to put "Workers on the Directorate." When the conciliation board rejected the miners' arguments that wages should be the first charge on the industry's earnings, a spate of new proposals followed from the union locals, declaring that the only way to free the coal industry from "incompetent private management and overcapitalization" was to cancel Besco's coal leases and have the province run the mines "for the benefit of the people." In February the miners' convention unanimously adopted a demand that the province take over the mines and run them with the participation of the coal miners. In Halifax labour MLA Forman Waye tried to introduce a bill for nationalization of the coal industry should Besco continue to deny "a decent Canadian standard of living."[31]

The proposals circulating in the labour press and debated at union meetings were vaguer and less developed than those in parallel campaigns among British and American miners at this time, but they did reflect the same view that private ownership of the coal mines was wasteful to the country and harmful to the wellbeing of the coal miners. The proposals reflected a growing opinion that it was wrong to assume, as the *Maritime Labour Herald* put it, that "labour will go on labouring, and capital will go on capitalizing, and labour will be willing to go on short rations in order to allow capital to continue augmenting their revenues." By the time the second conciliation board met in May, many miners were inclined to agree with McLachan when he declared: "the miners are going to get a living out of this industry and there will be no peace until they do . . ." A long time socialist, McLachlan argued that "if this system of production and distribution cannot give to the toilers human living conditions – then we are wasting our time discussing wages and hours of labour; we should be discussing the route to a new and better system." In June the miners' convention adopted a policy document which condemned "the pretty state existing among coal miners in Nova Scotia as a result of the efforts of 'captains of industry' to run the coal business." The miners' delegates then adopted a series of radical resolutions, including an appeal for allies in their campaign "to secure for our class . . . the working class of Canada, a living and free access to all means of life in this country." They concluded with the soon notorious declaration:

That we proclaim openly to all the world that we are out for the complete overthrow of the capitalist system and capitalist state, peaceably if we may, forcibly, if we must, and we call on all workers, soldiers and minor law officers to join us in liberating labour.

Bold in its language, the declaration was far from an irrational or gratuitous outcry, for it was firmly rooted in the miners' search for ways to replace private control of the coal industry with social control.[32]

By 1922 the appeal of radical ideas among the coal miners was twofold. Partly it was a tactical appeal: the threat that dire consequences like "Bolshevism" would follow if the miners' just demands were not met. As one local resolution protested early in the year, "Bolshevism is the effect of oppression and tyranny on the part of those in control. . . . Bolshevism finds no soil to grow in a community of working people who have employment at an adequate wage." And partly the appeal was a strategic one: the feeling that if society could not provide men with a "living wage," then it deserved to be rebuilt more soundly. Under the impact of economic and social crisis in the coalfields after the First World War, hopes for social transformation continued to grow and acquire new meaning among the coal miners. As "oppression and tyranny" continued to deprive the miners of a "living wage," the radicalism of the coal miners became less a symbol of protest and more a conscious policy. In the wake of the radical declarations of the June convention, the coal miners showed they were willing to support radical policies and leaders. At the convention the union's divided executive resigned, and the new election in August brought a decisive victory for the "radical" candidates. For the post of secretary-treasurer the miners re-elected McLachlan by a vote of 6,192 to 2,250, and for the presidency they chose a McLachlan ally, Dan Livingstone, over Baxter by a vote of 7,170 to 1,695. The election of the "red executive" marked a clear "left turn" in the miners' affairs. On May 1, 1923, some 5,000 coal miners, headed by their union officers, marched through the streets of Glace Bay behind the "biggest red flag in Canada" emblazoned with the words "Long live Communism." And in the summer of 1923 the coal miners risked their hard-won contract to mount a sympathetic strike to support the Sydney steelworkers and protest the renewed use of troops in industrial Cape Breton. In 1922 the coal miners' campaign was "a fight of patriotic, loyal citizens against industrial tyranny," their goal was an ill-defined "industrial democracy," and one of their rallying cries was "Rule Britannia, Britons never shall be slaves!" But the process of radicalization which had begun was no less authentic for that.[33]

Unlike other factors of production, labour power is not easily regulated by the laws of the marketplace. "Labor, in spite of sentimental objections, is undoubtedly a commodity which is bought and sold," explained University of New Brunswick political economist John Davidson in 1898, " . . . but it is not therefore true that labor is a commodity resembling in all essential respects every other commodity in the market. Labor differs from most, if not all, other commodities in retaining, even under modern industrial conditions, its subjective value to the seller. We cannot separate the labor and the laborer." As E. P. Thompson has pointed out, coal miners have had particular trouble in "comprehending the simplest of propositions as to the market regulation of wages, and they have always clung tenaciously to unscientific notions such as 'justice' and 'fair play'." Caught in a crisis of markets and a crisis of corporate welfare, the owners of the coal industry in Cape Breton attempted to ensure the survival of Besco at the expense of the coal miners, and repeatedly attempted to reduce the miners' wages. When the first of these assaults came in 1922, the coal miners defied the economic orthodoxy that when prices fell wages should fall in step. Instead they asserted a new regulatory principle:

The miners' wages and working conditions have been determined largely by the kind of organization the miners had and whether the tactics applied by that organization were those taught the miners by the coal operators and businessmen or were developed by themselves from their own economic necessities and surroundings.

In applying this guideline and organizing their resistance to the wage reduction in 1922, the miners expressed the cohesion of life in the coal mining communities and the strength of working class solidarity among the coal miners. United against an outside corporation and its allies, the working class found their most effective tactics in the assertion of a latent workers' control over the production process, earning key victories through the strike on the job and the "100 per cent" strike. Agreeing that the coal industry was in poor health, the miners also launched a search for solutions which would promote the prosperity of both the coal industry and the coal miners at the same time. This led them to challenge private control of the coal industry, to propose nationalization and democratic control as the alternative, and to question the capitalist system in general.[34]

What would be the miners' next step? After 1922 it remained to be seen whether the coal miners would again be able to resist renewed corporate assaults on their wage levels in 1924 and 1925. And to what extent would the miners continue to follow the "left turn" they began in 1922? Would the miners complete the transition from their spontaneous radicalism to the establishment of an effective form of radical trade unionism in the coalfields? And to what extent would the government, the corporation and the international union, all alarmed by the events of 1922, allow the attempt to take place?

Ultimately there were no victors in the dramatic and tragic events of the 1920s in Cape Breton. In 1923 the coal miners' union was seriously weakened by the intervention of the international union, the suspension of district autonomy, and the removal of the district's strongest leaders; after the long and traumatic strike of 1925 the union remained largely ineffective until the 1940s. In 1926 the flimsy structure of the British Empire Steel Corporation began finally to collapse; Wolvin was ousted in 1928 and a new coal and steel corporation replaced Besco. The coal industry, propped up by growing government aid after 1927, continued its long decline. The 1920s brought lasting victories for neither the coal industry, the corporation, nor the coal miners. But, as E. P. Thompson writes, it is never safe to assume that any of our history is altogether dead. It tends to accumulate as a form of "stored cultural energy," and from time to time moments of cultural transmission and illumination take place.[35] As the history of the coal miners' revolt against industrial capitalism in Canada is written, we shall find much to learn.

Lawren Harris, Glace Bay, *1921.*

Bibliographic Essay

Abbreviations Used in The Essay

AIHR	Alberta Historical Review
BCS	BC Studies
CCHAAR	Canadian Catholic Historical Association Annual Report
CHAR	Canadian Historical Association Annual Report
CHR	Canadian Historical Review
CJEPS	Canadian Journal of Economics and Political Science
CRSA	Canadian Review of Sociology and Anthropology
HP	Historical Papers, Canadian Historical Association
HS	Histoire Sociale/Social History
JCS	Journal of Canadian Studies
JSH	Journal of Social History
LUR	Laurentian University Review
MQ	Marxist Quarterly
OH	Ontario History
RHAF	Révue d'histoire de l'amerique française
RI	Relations Industrielles/Industrial Relations
SASK.H	Saskatchewan History
UTQ	University of Toronto Quarterly

The history of the Canadian working class has only recently come under systematic study. Nevertheless a literature has been built up over the years. The list which follows is in no sense complete and the material varies widely in quality.

I. OVERVIEWS

Especially noteworthy is the pioneering work of Stanley Ryerson. *The Founding of Canada* (1960) and *Unequal Union* (1968) are brave attempts at a Marxist synthesis. Another pioneer was H. Clare Pentland, whose works include "Labour and the Development of Industrial Capitalism in Canada", (University of Toronto Ph.D. thesis, 1960), "The Role of Capital in Canadian Economic Development before 1875", *CJEPS*, (1950), and "The Development of a Capitalistic Labour Market in Canada", *CJEPS* (1959). A very important local study testing out these interpretations is Leo Johnson, *History of the County of Ontario, 1615-1873*, (1974). See the opposing view presented in Tom Naylor, *A History of Canadian Wealth*, 2 vols. (1976). For new approaches in working class history, see the introduction to R. G. Hann, *et al.*, *Primary Sources in Canadian Working Class History1860-1930* (1973).

Perhaps the best single volume of social history written in this country to date was not the work of historians: R. Cole Harris and John Warkentin, *Canada Before Confederation: A Study in Historical Geography* (1974). Useful collections of articles in Canadian social history, although somewhat disappointing, are Michiel Horn and Ronald Sabourin, eds., *Studies in Canadian Social History* (1974) and S. D. Clark *et al.*, eds., *Prophecy and Protest: Social Movements in Twentieth Century Canada* (1975).

Overviews of working class history are quite weak with the single exception of Michael Cross' source book *The Workingman in the Nineteenth Century* (1974). Among organizational histories of trade union activities are: Harold Logan, *History of Trade Union Organization in Canada* (1928) and his *Trade Unions in Canada* (1948); R. H. Coats, "The Labour Movement in Canada", in *Canada and Its Provinces*, Vol. 9; Morden Lazarus, *Years of Hard Labour: Trade Unions and the Workingman in Canada* (1974); and by Eugene Forsey, his "History of the Labour Movement in Canada", in *Canada Year Book* (1967) and his more interesting "Insights into Labour History in Canada", *RI* 20 (1965). Another category is that of celebrations of workers from writers on the left. It is at its most nationalistic in Charles Lipton, *The Trade Union Movement in Canada* (1973) and Jack Scott, *Sweat and Struggle* (1974). Perhaps the best general work on Canadian labour unfortunately deals only with strike activity in the twentieth century, Stuart Jamieson's *Times of Trouble* (1968). An interesting and brief summary of this work is Lorne Brown, *Breaking Down Myths of Peace and Harmony in Canadian Labour History* (1973), a *Canadian Dimension* pamphlet.

II SPECIFIC NATIONAL STUDIES

Works that try to generalize about more specific aspects of working class history include: A. E. Kovacs, "A Tentative Framework for the Philosophy of the Canadian Labour Movement", *RI* 20 (1965); Eugene Forsey, "The Movement Towards Labour Unity in Canada", *CJEPS* (1958); Martin Robin, "The Working Class and the Transition to Capitalist Democracy in Canada", *Dalhousie Review* (1967). An extremely important recent work is Stephen Langdon, "The Emergence of the Canadian Working Class Movement, 1845-75", *JCS* (1973), republished as a pamphlet by New Hogtown Press, Toronto (1975). Other works on the early period include: the dated *The Knights of Labor in Canada* (1954) by Douglas Kennedy; Doris French, *Faith, Sweat, and Politics* (1962), a weak biography of early Knight's leader D. J. O'Donoghue; and Eugene Forsey, "The Telegraphers Strike of 1883", *Transaction of the Royal Society of Canada*, (1971). Copious evidence on most aspects of working class life in the nineteenth century is offered in Greg Kealey, ed., *Canada Investigates Industrialism* (1973). A collection of useful essays on major strikes is Irving Abella, ed., *On Strike: Six Key Labour Struggles in Canada* (1974). On the industrial relations system, the most famous study is William Lyon Mackenzie King's *Industry and Humanity*, reprinted in 1973 with a useful introduction by David Bercuson. Later studies include: A. E. Grauer, *Labour Legislation: A Study Prepared for the Royal Commission on Dominion-Provincial Relations* (1939); Harold Logan, *State Intervention and Assistance in Collective Bargaining: The Canadian Experience, 1943-54* (1956); and, on an earlier period, Eugene Forsey, "Notes on the Dominion Factory Bills of the 1880's", *CJEPS* (1947).

A question which has generated much recent controversy is international unionism. The oldest work on the subject is Harold Innis, ed., *Labour in Canadian-American Relations* (1937). Works supporting international unions are: C.B. Williams, "The Development of Canadian-American Trade Union Relations: Some Conclusions", *RI* 21 (1966) and "The Development of Relations between Canadian and American National Trade Union Centres, 1886-1925", *RI* 20 (1965); John Crispo, *International Unions: A Study in Canadian-American Relations* (1967) and *Role of International Unionism in Canada* (1967). Also: Eugene Forsey, "The Influence of American Labour Organizations and Policies on Canadian Labour", in Hugh Aitken, ed., *The American Economic Impact on Canada* (1959); J. T. Montague, "International Unions and the Canadian Trade Union Movement", *CJEPS* (1957). The nationalist position is argued by: Robert Babcock in *Gompers in Canada: A Study in American Continentalism Before the First World War* (1974), "Sam Gompers and the Expansion of the AF of L into Canada, 1882-98", *RI* (1972), and "Samuel Gompers and the Berlin Decisions of 1902", in R. A. Preston, ed., *The Influence of the United States on Canadian Development* (1972); Irving Abella in *Nationalism, Communism, and Canadian Labour* (1972), "Lament for a Labour Movement", in Ian Lumsden, ed., *Close the 49th Parallel* (1970), and "American Unionism, Communism, and the Canadian Labour Movement: Some Myths and Realities", in Preston, *The Influence of the United States on Canadian Development;* and Gary Teeple, ed., *Capitalism and the National Question in Canada* (1972).

III WORKING CLASS POLITICS

Perhaps the most work relating to labour has been done in the field of working class politics. Much of it is flawed by the political assumptions of the authors, be they social democrats or communists, who all too often have projected values onto the working class rather than studying its political behaviour. Studies of working class politics in the late nineteenth century include: Donald Creighton, "George Brown, John A. Macdonald, and the Workingman", *CHR* (1943); Bernard Ostry, "Conservatives, Liberals and Labour in the 1870's", *CHR* (1960) and "Conservatives, Liberals and Labour in the 1880's", *CJEPS* (1961); and the important reprint of the work of the early Canadian intellectual and socialist Phillips Thompson, *The Politics of Labor* (1975). On the early twentieth century: Ross McCormack, "Arthur Puttee and the Liberal Party, 1899-1904", *CHR* (1970); Don Avery, "Canadian Immigration Policy and the Foreign Navvy", *HP* (1972); Martin Robin, "The TLC and Political Action, 1899-1908", *RI* 22 (1967), and "Registration, Conscription and Independent Labour Politics, 1916-1917", *CHR* (1966). On the origins of socialism: Ross McCormack, "The Emergence of the Socialist Movement in BC", *BCS* (1974); Paul Fox, "Early Socialism in Canada", in J. H. Aitchison, ed., *The Political Process in Canada* (1963); John Saywell, "Labour and Socialism in BC: A Survey of Historical Developments Before 1903", *BC Historical Quarterly* (1951); and Norman Penner, "Recollections of the Early Socialist Movement in Winnipeg, by Jacob Penner", *HS* (1974).

The three standard works on labour in politics are each flawed: Martin Robin, *Radical Politics and Canadian Labour* (1968), which tends to be overly detailed, ahistorical, and factually careless; Gad Horowitz, *Canadian Labour in Politics* (1973), which includes a stimulating attempt to apply the fragment thesis of Louis Hartz to Canada but then degenerates into a social democratic diatribe against the Communist Party; and Abella's *Nationalism, Communism, and Canadian Labour* which is the best of the three but lacks a social history dimension.

There is a large and rapidly growing literature on the Communist Party. The only general work is quite weak, Ivan Avakumovic, *The Communist Party in Canada* (1975). A narrower work on the 1920s, which is only slightly more satisfactory, is William Rodney, *Soldiers of the International* (1968). The Communist Party has published *Power to the People: Fifty Years of Pictorial Highlights of the Communist Party of Canada, 1921-71* (1971). Autobiographical accounts of activists include: Ronald Liversedge, *The On-to-Ottawa Trek* (1973) and Steve Brodie, *Bloody Sunday, Vancouver 1938* (1974), both of which are excellent; and the less useful A. E. Smith, *All My Life* (1949) and Tom McEwan, *The Forge Glows Red* (1974). Most biographical accounts border on hagiography; among them is Oscar Ryan, *Tim Buck: A Conscience for Canada* (1975). Tim Buck's own writings are listed in Peter H. Weinrich, *A Select Bibliography of Tim Buck* (1974). The most important of these are: *Thirty Years* (1952); *Canada and the Russian Revolution* (1967); *Lenin and Canada* (1970); and *Our Fight for Canada* (1959). Finally, Victor Hoar's *The Mackenzie-Papineau Battalion* (1969) is the story of the Canadians who went to Spain to fight fascism.

The literature on social democracy is also large. The best place to start is Michael Cross, *The Decline and Fall of a Good Idea: CCF-NDP Manifestoes, 1932-69* (1974). A detailed document is the recently reprinted League for Social Reconstruction's *Social Planning for Canada* (1975). Social democratic hagiography includes: Grace McInnis, *J. S. Woodsworth: A Man to Remember* (1974); K. W. McNaught, *A Prophet in Politics* (1959); Leo Heaps, *The Rebel in the House: The Life and Times of A. A. Heaps, M.P.* (1970); Dorothy Steeves, *The Compassionate Rebel: Ernest E. Winch and his Times* (1960). Less endearing views of Woodsworth are available through reprints of his own works: *My Neighbor* (1972) and *Strangers Within Our Gates* (1972). Richard Allen, *The Social Passion: Religion and Social Reform in Canada, 1914-1928* (1971) provides a sympathetic yet critical look at social democracy's religious roots. The best general history is Walter Young, *The Anatomy of a Party: The National CCF* (1969). Less interesting are Gerald Caplan, *The Dilemma of Canadian Socialism: The CCF in Ontario, 1932-1945* (1973) and Desmond Morton, *NDP: The Dream of Power* (1974). Finally, on recent politics there is David Kwavnick, *Organized Labour and Pressure Politics: The CLC, 1955-1968* (1972).

IV REGIONAL STUDIES

1. QUEBEC

Interesting commentaries on developments in Quebec social history are: F. Harvey, "Nouvelles perspectives sur l'histoire sociale du Québec", *RHAF* (1971) and for a conceptual approach to labour history his "Les travailleurs Québecois au XIXe siècle", *RHAF* (1972); and Robert Comeau, "L'histoire ouvrière au Québec: Quelques nouvelles avenues", *RHAF* (1975). A useful collection of essays that covers the whole sweep of Quebec labour history is F. Harvey, ed., *Aspects historiques du mouvement ouvrier au Québec* (1973). Less successful is Richard Desrosiers et Denis Heroux, *Le travailleur Québecois et le syndicalisme* (1973). Jean-Paul Bernard, Paul-André Linteau and Jean-Claude Robert of the Université de Québec à Montréal have commenced an ambitious reconstitution of the social structure of Montreal in the nineteenth century; reports of their work have begun to appear in *RHAF* and *HP*.

Early work on the 1830s was done by Catherine Vance: "Early Trade Unionism in Quebec: The Carpenters and Joiners

General Strike of 1833-4", *MQ* (1962) and "1837, Labour and the Democratic Tradition", *MQ* (1965). On the industrial period, an excellent survey is Jean Hamelin et Yves Roby, *Histoire économique du Québec, 1851-96* (1971). For a slightly different view of the economy, see Albert Faucher, *Québec en Amerique au XIXe siècle* (1973). Also useful is W. F. Ryan, *The Clergy and Economic Growth in Quebec, 1896-1914* (1966). A pioneering article on social structure was J. I. Cooper, "Montreal in the 1850s", *CHAR* (1956). See also his "The Quebec Ship Labourers Benevolent Society", *CHR* (1949). The work of a group of students at Laval has resulted in the very useful Jean Hamelin *et al.*, *Répertoire des grèves dans la province de Québec au XIXe siècle* (1970) and Noel Bélanger *et al.*, *Les travailleurs québecois, 1851-1896* (1973). Other works on the period are: S. A. Lortie, "Compositeur typographe de Québec en 1903", in Pierre Savard, ed., *Paysans et ouvriers Québecois d'autrefois* (1968); P. Sylvain, "Les Chevaliers du Travail et le Cardinal Taschereau", *RI* (1973); Robert Babcock, "Samuel Gompers and the French Canadian Worker, 1900-14", *American Journal of Canadian Studies* (1973); and Jacques Rouillard, *Les travailleurs du coton, 1900-1915* (1973).

Some useful studies of working and living conditions are; Suzanne Cross, "The Neglected Majority: The Changing Role of Women in Nineteenth Century Montreal", *HS* (1973); the reprint of H. B. Ames' pioneering *The City Below the Hill* (1972); and Terry Copp, *The Anatomy of Poverty: The Condition of the Working Class in Montreal, 1897-1929* (1974).

Studies of strikes include: Clare Pentland, "The Lachine Canal Strike of 1843", *CHR* (1948); a fine piece of local history, Pierre Louis Lapointe, *Buckingham 1906* (1973); Evelyn Dumas, *The Bitter Thirties in Québec* (1975); the new translation of Pierre Elliott Trudeau, ed., *The Asbestos Strike* (1974); Alfred Charpentier, "La grève de textile dans le Québec en 1937", *RI* 20 (1965) and *Ma conversion au syndicalisme catholique* (1946). For a summary, see Gérard Dion, "The Trade Union Movement in Quebec", *UTQ* (1957-8).

2. THE MARITIMES

This region has received the least attention from working class historians. There is however some good work underway, especially on Cape Breton miners. Two works on trade union origins are C. B. Fergusson, *The Labour Movement in Nova Scotia Before Confederation* (1964) and the more useful Ken Pryke, "Labour and Politics: Nova Scotia at Confederation", *HS* (1970). Also extremely valuable is Richard Rice, "A History of Organized Labour in St. John, N.B.", (M.A. thesis, University of New Brunswick, 1968). One interesting study is Judith Fingard, "The Winter's Tale: Contours of Pre-Industrial Poverty in

British America, 1815-60", *HP* (1974). Coal has received the most attention. Older works include Robert Drummond, *Recollections and Reflections of a Former Trade Union Leader* (1926) and Eugene Forsey, *Economic and Social Aspects of the Nova Scotia Coal Industry* (1926). Newer works are: James Cameron, *The Pictonian Colliers* (1974); the popularly-written *The People's History of Cape Breton* (1971); the more important works of David Frank, "Coal Masters and Coal Miners: The 1922 Strike and the Roots of Class Conflict in the Cape Breton Coal Industry", (M.A. thesis, Dalhousie University, 1974), and Donald MacGillivray, "Industrial Unrest in Cape Breton, 1919-1925", (M.A. thesis, University of New Brunswick, 1971); and two articles by MacGillivray, "Military Aid to the Civil Power: The Cape Breton Experience in the 1920's", *Acadiensis* (1974) and "Cape Breton Besieged", in B. Tennyson, ed., *Essays in Cape Breton History* (1973). Two interesting studies of working class politics are George Rawlyk, "The Farmer-Labour Movement and the Failure of Socialism in Nova Scotia", in Laurier LaPierre, ed., *Essays on the Left* (1971) and the work on which Rawlyk draws, A. A. Mackenzie, "The Rise and Fall of the Farmer-Labour Party in Nova Scotia", (M.A. thesis Dalhousie University, 1969). Newfoundland miners are treated in a moving oral history by Elliott Leyton, *Dying Hard: The Ravages of Industrial Carnage* (1975) and Newfoundland fishermen in Joseph R. Smallwood, *Coaker of Newfoundland* (1927) and G. E. Panting, "The Fishermen's Protective Union of Newfoundland and the Farmers' Organizations in the West", *CHAR* (1963). Two additional articles of note are Eugene Forsey, "Some Notes on the Early History of Unions in PEI", *CHR* (1965) and Peter Neary, "'Traditional' and 'Modern' Elements in the Social and Economic History of Bell Island and Conception Bay", *HP* (1973). Finally, there is an excellent study of the Irish, John Mannion, *Irish Settlement in Eastern Canada* (1974).

3. ONTARIO

Some of the most interesting work to date concerns pre-industrial work. Excellent studies include: Michael Cross, "The Shiners' War: Social Violence in the Ottawa Valley in the 1830s", *CHR* (1973) and "Stony Monday, 1849: The Rebellion Losses Riots in Bytown", *OH* (1971); Kenneth Duncan, "Irish Famine Immigration and the Social Structure of Canada West", *CRSA* (1965); the less useful Lawrence Runnals, *The Irish on the Welland Canal*, (1973); and Martin Galvin, "The Jubilee Riots in Toronto", *CCHAAR* (1959). For an interesting but not very analytical study of early trade unionism, see F. H. Armstrong, "Reformer as Capitalist: William Lyon Mackenzie and the Printers Strike of 1836", OH (1967). The ongoing study by Michael Katz and his students on the social structure of nineteenth century Hamilton has provided copious data and promises far more. See his: "Social Structure in Hamilton, Ontario" in S. Thernstrom and R. Sennett, eds., *Nineteenth Century Cities* (1969); "The People of a Canadian City, 1851-2", *CHR* (1972); "The Entrepreneurial Class in a Canadian City", *JSH* (1975); and *Family and Class in a Canadian City* (1976).

Studies of workers in the 1870s include: Eugene Forsey, "The Toronto Trades Assembly, 1871-8", *Canadian Labour* (1965); Gregory Kealey, "Artisans Respond to Industrialism: Shoemakers, Shoe Factories and the Knights of St. Crispin in Toronto", *HP* (1973); and Sally Zerker, "George Brown and the Printers Union", *JCS* (1975). Works on the later nineteenth century are scarcer, but see: Ed McKenna, "Unorganized Labour versus Management: Chaudiere, 1891", *HS* (1972); Russell Hann, *Farmers Confront Industrialism* (1975); Greg Kealey, *Hogtown: Working Class Toronto at the Turn of the Century* (1974); and Michael Piva, "The Conditions of the Working Class in Toronto, 1900-1921", (Ph.D. thesis, Concordia University, 1975) and "The Workmen's Compensation Movement in Ontario", *OH* (1975).

One of the most important recent works in working class history is the innovative *Women at Work: Ontario 1850-1930* , Canadian womens Educational Press (1974). An earlier work in this field was Jean Scott, "The Conditions of Female Labour in Ontario", *Toronto University Studies in Political Science* (1892), and a recent study is Linda S. Bohnen, "Women Workers in Ontario: A Socio-Legal History", *University of Toronto Faculty of Law Review* (1974).

On northern Ontario: Jean Morrison, "Community and Conflict: A Study of the Working Class in the Canadian Lakehead, 1903-13", (M.A. thesis, Lakehead University, 1974); G. A. Stelter, "Community Development in Toronto's Commercial Empire: The Industrial Towns of the Nickle Belt, 1883-1931", *LUR* (1974); Noel Beach, "Nickel Capital: Sudbury and the Nickel Industry, 1909-25", *LUR* (1974); Eileen Goltz, "Espanola: The History of a Pulp and Paper Town", *LUR* (1974); John Lang, "Lion in the Den of Daniels: A History of the International Mine, Mill and Smelter Workers Union in Sudbury, 1942-62", (M.A. thesis, University of Guelph, 1969).

4. THE WEST

General approaches include: Paul Phillips, "The National Policy and the Development of the Western Canadian Labour Movement", in A. Rasporich, ed., *Prairie Perspectives* (1973); the problematic article by David Bercuson, "Western Labour Radicalism and the OBU: Myths and Realities", in S. Trofimenkoff, ed., *The Twenties in Western Canada* (1972); and the fine Ph.D. thesis by Ross McCormack, "The Origins and Extent of Western Labour Radicalism, 1896-1919", (University of Western Ontario, 1973). An interesting article on the mixture of various western radical traditions is W. J. C. Cherwinski, "Honoré Jaxon, Agitator, Disturber, Producer of Plans to Make Men Think and Chronic Objector", *CHR* (1965).

The place to commence a study of the Winnipeg General Strike is Norman Penner, ed., *Winnipeg 1919: The Strikers' Own History* (1975). Secondary accounts include: the dated D. C. Masters, *The Winnipeg General Strike* (1950); the popularly-written Kenneth McNaught and David Bercuson, *The Winnipeg Strike 1919* (1974); and most importance, David Bercuson's "The Winnipeg General Strike, Collective Bargaining, and the One Big Union Issue", *CHR* (1970) and *Confrontation at Winnipeg* (1974). Other articles are: J. E. Rae, "The Politics of Conscience: Winnipeg after the Strike", *CHAR* (1971); E. W. Greening, "The Winnipeg Strike Trials", *RI* 20 (1965); and H. C. Pentland, "Fifty Years After", *Canadian Dimension* (1969).

British Columbia has received much attention. General introductions are William Bennett, *Builders of B.C.* (1937) and the more recent two volume *The Company Province* (1972-3) by Martin Robin. An interesting collection of essays is Paul Knox and Phillip Resnick, eds., *Essays in B.C. Political Economy* (1974). B.C. is the one province with a history of its labour movement, Paul Phillips, *No Power Greater – A Century of Labour in B.C.* (1967). Autobiographical materials are George Hardy, *Those Stormy Years* (1956) and the life story of an ordinary German working class immigrant woman, compiled by Rolf Knight, *A Very Ordinary Life* (1975). Other materials include: P. G. Silverman, "Military Aid to the Civil Power in B.C.", *Pacific Northwest Quarterly* (1970); Patricia Roy, "The B.C. Electric Railway Company and Its Employees", *BCS* (1972-3); Richard McCandless, "Vancouver's Red Menace of 1935: The Waterfront", *BCS* (1974); Percy Gladstone and Stuart Jamieson, "Unionism in the Fishing Industry of B.C.", *CJEPS* (1950); and the excellent Keith Ralston, "The 1900 Strike of the Fraser River Sockeye Salmon Fishermen", (M.A. thesis, University of British Columbia, 1965).

Alberta studies include: A. den Otter, "Social Life of a Mining Community: The Coal Branch", *Al.HR* (1969); and two articles by Anne B. Woytika, "The Drumheller Strike of 1919", *Al.HR* (1973) and "Strike at Waterways", *Al.HR* (1972). Saskatchewan articles include: Peter Sinclair, "The Saskatchewan CCF and the Communist Party in the 1930's", *Sask. H.* (1973);

and Lorne Brown, "Unemployment Relief Camps in Saskatchewan", *Sask.H.* (1970). A study of a Manitoba strike is G. F. MacDonald, *The Brandon Packers Strike* (1971).

V. WORKING CLASS CULTURE

Much of the work on popular culture is far more profoundly interested in how social change effects the lives of ordinary people than is the traditional writing of historians. See; Frank Watt, "Radicalism in English-Canadian Literature Since Confederation", (Ph.D. thesis, University of Toronto, 1958), "The National Policy, the Workingman and Proletarian Ideas in Victorian Canada", *CHR* (1959), and "Literature of Protest", in C. F. Klinck, ed., *Literary History of Canada* (1965); Ruth McKenzie, "Proletarian Literature in Canada", *Dalhousie Review* (1939); and the reprint of *Eight Men Speak and Other Communist Plays of the 1930's* (1976).

Poets of interest include, in the nineteenth century, Alexander McLachlan and Archibald Lampman (both subjects of recent reprints in the University of Toronto Press Canadian Literature Series), and in the twentieth century, Dorothy Livesay, Milton Acorn and Tom Wayman, to mention only a few. Interesting novels include: Agnes Machar, *Roland Graeme: Knight*; Albert Carman, *The Preparation of Ryerson Embury*; A. Grainger, *Woodsmen of the West*; Ralph Connor, *The Foreigner* and *To Him that Hath*; Douglas Durkin, *The Magpie*; Alan Sullivan, *The Inner Door*; and Frederick Phillip Grove, *The Master of the Mill*. Vivid novels of the depression include: Earle Birnie, *Down the Long Table*; Irene Baird, *Waste Heritage*; Hugh Garner, *Cabbagetown*; and Ted Allen, *This Time a Better Earth*. On Quebec, Gabrielle Roy, *The Tin Flute* and Roger Lemelin, *The Town Below*. Post-World War II novels of special merit are Dyson Carter, *Fatherless Sons*, concerning Sudbury miners, and John Marlyn, *Under the Ribs of Death*, on north end Winnipeg. Folklore is a useful entry to the subject. See: Edith Fowke, "Folktales and Folk Songs", in Klinck, *Literary History*; and H. Halpert and N. Rosenberg. "Folklore Work at Memorial University", *Canadian Forum* (1974). An earlier *Forum* article indicated the important theoretical issues of popular culture: Brian Stock, "English Canada: The Visible and Invisible Cultures" (1973).

VI. PERIODICALS

The most important journals for historians of the working class are: *Canadian Labour History/Histoire Ouvrière*, journal of the Committee on Labour History, whose first annual collection of essays, *Labour/Le Travailleur*, appeared in 1976; *Histoire des Travailleurs Québecois,* published by le Regroupement de Chercheurs en Histoire des Travailleurs Québécois; *Histoire Sociale/ Social History;* and *Relations Industrielles/Industrial Relations.*

Notes

Introduction

1. For an extended discussion of older schools of Canadian historical writing, see R. G. Hann, *et al.*, *Primary Sources in Canadian Working Class History, 1860-1930* (Kitchener, 1973), pp. 9-20.
2. See E. P. Thompson, *The Making of the English Working Class* (Harmondsworth, 1968), pp. 9-15, and his "The Peculiarities of the English", in *Socialist Register* (1965), pp. 311-362; see also E. J. Hobsbawm, "From Social History to the History of Society", *Daedalus*, 100 (Winter, 1971), pp. 20-45, his "Labour History and Ideology", *Journal of Social History*, 7 (Summer, 1974), pp. 371-381, and his "Karl Marx's Contribution to Historiography", in Robin Blackburn, ed., *Ideology in Social Science* (London, 1972), pp. 265-283.
3. For the notion of residual and emergent, incorporated and non-incorporated, see Raymond Williams, "Base and Superstructure in Marxist Cultural Theory", *New Left Review*, 82 (1973), pp. 3-16.
4. For aid in conceptualizing the periods of working class history, we have drawn on E. J. Hobsbawm, "The Formation of the Industrial Working Class: Some Problems," *Troisième conférence internationale d'histoire économique, Congres et Colloques, Munich, 1965*, I (Paris, 1968), pp. 175-180.
5. For the best discussions of workers and the work place to date, see David Montgomery, "The 'New Unionism' and the Transformation of Workers' Consciousness in America, 1909-1922", *Journal of Social History*, 7 (1974), pp. 509-529; Katherine Stone, "Origin of Job Structures in the Steel Industry", *Radical America*, 6 (Nov.-Dec., 1973), pp. 19-64; Mike Davis, "The Stop Watch and the Wooden Shoe: Scientific Management and the Industrial Workers of the World", *Radical America*, 8, (1975), pp. 69-95; and Bryan Palmer, "Class, Conception and Conflict: The Thrust for Efficiency, Managerial Views of Labor and the Working Class Rebellion, 1903-1922," *The Review of Radical Political Economics*, 7 (1975) pp. 31-49.
6. For an excellent beginning to the study of working women in Canadian history, see *Women at Work, Ontario 1850-1930* (Toronto, Women's Press, 1975).
7. For an attempt to discuss this issue, see John Foster, *Class Struggle and the Industrial Revolution* (London, 1974), and two excellent review essays on this important book by Gareth Stedman Jones in *New Left Review*, 90, (1975), pp. 35-69 and John Saville in *Socialist Register* (1974), pp. 226-240.
8. Hobsbawm, "Labour History and Ideology", pp. 380-381.

Kealey: The Orange Order in Toronto

1. Martin Robin, *Radical Politics and Canadian Labour, 1880-1930* (Kingston, 1968), Introduction, esp. pp. 5-6.
2. Maureen Wall, "The Whiteboys," p. 24 in T. Desmond Williams, *Secret Societies in Ireland* (Dublin, 1973); E. P. Thompson, *The Making of the English Working Class* (London, 1968)

pp. 470-471; Kevin B. Nowlan, "Conclusion," p. 183 in Williams, *op. cit.*

3. Hereward Senior, "The Genesis of Canadian Orangeism," *Ontario History*, 60 (1968) pp. 13-14; Senior, *Orangeism: The Canadian Phase* (Toronto, 1973) Ch. 1-2 and Senior, "Ogle Gowan", in *Dictionary of Canadian Biography*, X (Toronto, 1972) pp. 309-314.

4. W. B. Kerr, "When Orange and Green United, 1832-1839: The Alliance of Macdonnell and Gowan", *Ontario History*, 34 (1942) pp. 34-42.

5. For examples see William Shannon, *The United Empire Minstrel*, (Toronto, 1852), pp. 42-43; Shannon, *The Dominion Orange Harmonist* (Toronto, 1876) p. 27 and chronology. See also R. McBride, *The Canadian Orange Minstrel for 1860* (London, 1860). The best description of the Slabtown Affair is provided by J. Lawrence Runnals, *The Irish on the Welland Canal* (St. Catherines, 1973). On July 12, 1849 Irish Catholics gathered to prevent the Orangemen from 'walking' but when the Orangemen failed to even try the Catholics settled for three cheers – one for the Queen, one for the Governor, and one for the Pope. The Orangemen responded with a volley of shots which left two Catholics dead and four others wounded. For the Diamond, a similar event in Irish history, see H. Senior, *Orangeism in Ireland and Britain, 1795-1836* (Toronto, 1966), p. 16.

6. For examples see Loyal Orange Institution of British North America, *Laws, Rules, and Regulations* (Cobourg, 1846); *Laws, Rules and Regulations* (Belleville, 1850); *Constitution and Laws of the Loyal Orange Institution* (Toronto, 1855).

7. Loyal Orange Institution of British North America (LOIBNA) *Forms to be Observed in Private Lodges* (Toronto, 1855).

8. For ritual see E. J. Hobsbawn, *Primitive Rebels* (New York, 1965) pp. 150-174, for Masonic roots see Senior, *Orangeism in Ireland* p. 12 and Nowlan, *op. cit.*, p. 183; for actual ritual forms see LOIBNA, *Charges to be Delivered at the Initiation of Members* (Toronto, 1856); *Forms to be Observed in Private Lodges* (Toronto, 1855); *Orange Ritual* (Belleville, 1874); *Forms of the Royal Blue Order* (Toronto, 1855); *Ritual of the Blue Order* (Belleville, 1864); *Forms of the Royal Blue Order* (Toronto, 1869); *Forms Of the Purple Order* (Toronto, 1855); *Forms of the Royal Arch Purple Mark* (Toronto, 1855, 1869); *Forms and Ritual of the Royal Scarlet Order* (Cobourg, 1846, 1864); *Ritual of the Royal Scarlet Order* (Toronto, 1886).

9. LOIBNA, *Charges to be Delivered . . . and Services for the Burial of Orangemen, The Dedication of an Orange Lodge, and for the Installation of Officers* (Toronto, 1856), Conrad Arensberg, *The Irish Countryman* (New York, 1937), pp. 215-216.

10. As late as 1969 partisan Northern Irish Orange historians were still claiming that "In fact the Twelfth in Toronto is second only to that on the field at Finaghy." M. W. Dewar, John Brown, S. E. Long, *Orangeism: A New Historical Appreciation* (Belfast, 1969) p. 17. See also Hector Charlesworth, *Candid Chronicles* (Toronto, 1925) esp. Foreword.

11. Much of this data is drawn from Leslie H. Saunders, *The Story of Orangeism* (Toronto, 1941). However, Provincial Grand Lodge Proceedings, Toronto Orange Directories, Toronto City Directories, and the Toronto press have also been utilized.

12. LOIBNA, Provincial Grand Lodge of Canada West, *Proceedings*, (Toronto, 1872).

13. *Ibid.* (Toronto, 1876).

14. *Ibid.* (Toronto, 1880).

15. *Ibid.* (Toronto, 1883).

16. The data was generated from the following sources: Lodge 328 – *By-Laws of Loyal Orange Lodge, No. 328* (Toronto, 1846, 1852, 1856, and 1872). Lodge 137 – Treasurers Book, 1889-1907 and Roll Book, 1885-. Lodge 173 – Minutes, 1883-1903 and Roll Book, 1883-1896. Lodge 711 – Minutes, 1873-1906; Membership and Degree Book, 1890-; Proposition Book, 1890-; Roll Book, 1875-1895. The Manuscript Records of Lodges 137, 173 and 711 are all held in The Baldwin Room of Toronto Public Library.

17. *By-Laws of Loyal Orange Lodge, No. 328* (Toronto, 1872).

18. Minutes, LOL No. 137.

19. LOABA, Provincial Grand Lodge of Canada West, *Proceedings* (Toronto, 1876), David Frank, "Trouble in Toronto: The Street Railway Strike of 1886," unpublished seminar paper, University of Toronto, 1970.

20. For the opposite argument see Hereward Senior, "Orangeism in Ontario Politics, 1872-1896," pp. 136-137 in Donald Swainson, *Oliver Mowat's Ontario* (Toronto, 1972). Data on lodge masters was taken from the following sources: 1871 – Thomas Keyes, *Orange Directory of Western Ontario* (St. Catharines, 1871). 1876 – *Second Annual Orange Directory of Lodges, Meetings, Officers, etc. for Toronto* (Toronto, 1876). 1878 – *Toronto Orange Directory, 1878* (Toronto, 1878). 1880 – LOABA, Provincial Grand Lodge of Canada West, *Proceedings*, (Toronto, 1880). 1886 – *City of Toronto, Orange Directory for 1886* (Toronto, 1886). 1888 – LOABA, Provincial Grand Lodge of Canada West, *Proceedings* (Toronto, 1888). These lists of masters were then traced in Toronto City Directories for occupational data.

21. The 1878 and 1886 data was from the above sources but the 1871 list of all officers was compiled from the lists appearing in the *Globe* after each lodge election was held.

22. Senior, "Orangeism in Canadian Politics," *op. cit*, pp. 136-137.

23. For all these functions see Minutes of lodges 173 and 711. See also Lodge By-Laws of the following Toronto lodges: Virgin No. 328 for 1846, 1852, 1856, and 1872; Schomberg No. 212, 1882; McKinlay No. 275, 1874; York No. 375, 1866 and 1894; Enniskillen No. 711, 1898 and *Constitution and Laws of the Orange Mutual Benefit Society of Ontario West* (Toronto, 188?).

24. Membership lists for the lodges studied in detail and lists of lodge officers confirm this. See also patronage correspondence in Macdonald Papers, PAC for further material; *Irish Canadian*, March 8, 1876; Oct. 9, 1884 and May 7, 1885.

25. H. Senior, *Orangeism: The Canadian Phase*, esp. Ch. 2.

26. LOABNA, *Proceedings of the Grand Lodge* (Toronto, 1856) and

William Perkins Bull, *From the Boyne to Brampton* (Toronto, 1936), p. 138.

27. *By-Laws* (Toronto, 1872).

28. *Constitution and Laws* (Belleville, 1875).

29. Senior, "The Genesis of Canadian Orangeism," p. 27 and Sybil E. Baker, "The Orange and Green," pp. 789-814 in Dyos and Wolff, *The Victorian City: Images and Reality* (London, 1973).

30. This data is taken from a daily reading of the Toronto press for the 25 year period. The best Canadian analysis of Orange-Green conflict is Michael Cross, "Stony Monday, 1849: The Rebellion Losses Riot in Bytown", *Ontario History* (1871) pp. 177-190. See also his "The Shiners War: Social Violence in the Ottawa Valley in the 1830's", *Canadian Historical Review* (1973), pp. 1-26 for a fine description of pre-industrial Green organization.

31. Natalie Zemon Davis, "The Rites of Violence: Religious Riot in Sixteenth Century France," *Past and Present*, 59 (1973) pp. 51-91 and Baker, pp. 790, 797.

32. *Globe* July 23, 1870, and W. B. Kerr, "The Orange Order in the 1820s" from *The Orange Sentinel* now on microfilm in Toronto Public Library.

33. *Globe*, July 13, 1870; July 11, 1876; July 13, 1877; July 13, 1888. *Mail*, June 19, 1877; July 13, 1877.

34. *Globe*, July 30, 1873; July 27, 1874. *Leader*, July 30, 1873. *Irish Canadian*, July 30, 1873.

35. *Irish Canadian*, March 22, 29, April 5, 1871; *Globe*, April 6, 13, 1871; March 19, 20, 1872; March 19, 22, 1889. *Telegraph*, March 19, 1872.

36. Baker, p. 809 and Senior, *Orangeism in Ireland*, p. 12.

37. For a discussion of the role of adolescent males in collective violence of a traditional sort see Davis and for specific Orange materials on boys see Baker. *Globe*, September 2, 3, 5, 6, 12, 14, 20, 21, 1870. *Leader*, September 2, 20, 1870. *Telegraph*, September 5, 7, 8, 12, 20, 21, 1870. See also LOABA, Grand Lodge of Canada West, *Proceedings* (Toronto, 1873); Orange Young Britons, Grand Lodge, *Proceedings* (Toronto, 1878).

38. *Globe*, July 12, 1888; July 13, 1889; *Irish Canadian*, July 16, 1885; July 15, 1886; For the events of 1875 see Martin Galvin, "Catholic-Protestant Relations in Ontario 1864-1875", M.A. Thesis, University of Toronto, 1962, and his "The Jubilee Riots in Toronto," *Canadian Catholic Historical Association Annual Report*, (1959), pp. 93-107. See also E. C. Guillet, *Toronto: Trading Post to Great City* (Toronto, 1934) pp. 216-218.

39. For arrests and trials see *Globe*, September 27, 28, October 4, 5, 9, 12, 1875 and January 17-21, 28, 1876.

40. *Ibid.*, August 7, 1875.

41. *Globe*, March 19, 20, 22, 27, 1878. *Mail*, March 19, 20, 1878.

42. Rowland Berthoff, *An Unsettled People* (New York, 1971), p. 274.

43. Kenneth Duncan, "Irish Famine Immigration and the Social Structure of Canada West," *Canadian Review of Sociology and Anthropology*, (1965), p. 39, and Davis, p. 91; For an excellent

analysis of the utility of Irish cultural traditions for the emerging labour movement see Michael A. Gordon, "Irish Immigrant Culture and the Labor Boycott in New York City, 1880-1886", *Labor History,*16 (1975), pp. 184-229.

Hann: Brainworkers and the Knights of Labor.

1. Raymond Williams, *Culture and Society* (Harmondsworth: Penguin, 1961) and "Base and Superstructure in Marxist Cultural Theory," *New Left Review*, 82 (November-December, 1973), pp. 3-16; J. A. Schumpeter, *Capitalism, Socialism and Democracy* (New York: Harper & Row, 1950), pp. 146-155; R. Williams, *The Long Revolution* (Harmondsworth: Penguin, 1965), pp. 177-236, and *Communications* (Harmondsworth, 1962).

2. S. Perlman, *A Theory of the Labor Movement* (New York: A. M. Kelley, 1966), pp. 280-281 and *A History of Trade Unionism in the United States* (New York: Macmillan, 1922), pp. 291-294; V. I. Lenin, *What is to be done?* (Moscow: Progress, 1947), pp. 31-32, 40-41.

3. Although Antonio Gramsci did conceptualize culture in a non-instrumental way, his imaginative exploration of the realm of cultural activity and his notion of cultural hegemony fails to come to grips with the persistent rebelliousness of sections of the modern intellectual estate. See Gramsci, *Selections from the Prison Notebooks* (New York: International, 1971), pp. 3-33. Many insights can be gained into the process by which intellectuals allied themselves with the working class movement in England from Royden Harrison's study of the English positivists in *Before the Socialists: Studies in Labour and Politics* (London: Routledge and Kegan Paul, 1965), pp. 251-341: Perlman, *Theory of the Labor Movement*, pp. 178-179; see also Stephen Coltham, "The *Beehive* Newspaper: its Origin and Early Struggles," in A. Briggs and J. Saville, *Essays in Labour History*, (London: Macmillan, 1967), 174-204.

4. M. Robin, *Radical Politics and Canadian Labour: 1880-1930*, (Kingston: Industrial Relations Centre, 1968), p. 276: G. Horowitz, *Canadian Labour in Politics* (Toronto: University of Toronto Press, 1968), p. 5; see also Robin, *op. cit.*, pp. 283-285, on the comparative lack of a "natural antipathy of labour to socialism", in Canada. B. Ostry, "Conservatives, Liberals and Labour in the 1880's," *CJEPS*, XXVII, 2 (May, 1961), p. 161; F. W. Watt, "The National Policy, the Workingman, and Proletarian Ideas in Victorian Canada," *Canadian Historical Review*, XL, 1 (March, 1959) pp. 1-26.

5. H. Charlesworth, *Candid Chronicles* (Toronto: Macmillan, 1925), pp. 74-75, 78-79; *N. W. Ayer & Son's American Newspaper Annual* (Philadelphia: N. W. Ayer & Son, 1884), p. 679; Canadian Press Association, *A History of Canadian Journalism* (Toronto:

Canadian Press Association, 1908), I, p. 171; *News*, November 26, 1883.

6. Charlesworth, *op. cit.*, pp. 70-74; *Globe*, November 11, 1924; H. J. Morgan, *Canadian Men and Women of the Time* (Toronto: Briggs, 1912), p. 1017; Ross Harkness, *J. E. Atkinson of the Star* (Toronto: University of Toronto Press, 1963), pp. 36-38; P. Bilbey, *Persons and Things* (Toronto: Ryerson, 1948), p. 11.

7. F. Watt, "The National Policy, the Workingman, and the Proletarian Idea," pp. 22-25; for salaries and composition of the *News* editorial and reportorial staff, see City of Toronto, *Assessment Roll for Ward of St. James*, 1881-1883 and *Assessment Roll for the Ward of St. Andrews*, 1885-1889, and W. A. Hewitt, *Down the Stretch* (Toronto: Ryerson, 1958) pp. 10-12, 20-21; Charlesworth omits the presence of Thompson on the *News* editorial board, see Charlesworth, *More Candid Chronicles* (Toronto: Macmillan, 1928) pp. 31-34; see also Henry George Mss., New York Public Library, P. Thompson to Henry George, Oct. 23, 1882.

8. Charlesworth, *Candid Chronicles*, pp 75-77; P. Rutherford, "Tomorrow's Metropolis: the urban reform movement in Canada," Canadian Historical Association, *Historical Papers* (1971), pp. 204, 217, 218, and "The People's Press: the Emergence of the New Journalism in Canada, 1869-1899," *Canadian Historical Review*, LVI, 2 (June, 1975), pp. 167-191: *Grip*, December 15, 1883.

9. Much information can be gained from the standard sources on the career of Phillips Thompson. The writer has been fortunate to have been able to share his research on Thompson's career with G. S. Kealey in an ongoing project to gather as much data as possible on Thompson's career. Beginning in the summer of 1971 we have gathered material which will form the basis for a collection of Thompson's writings. Soon after the project was undertaken Enjolras was identified as Thompson by a comparison of texts in the *Palladium of Labor* and Thompson's book, *The Politics of Labor* (New York: Belford, Clark, 1887).

10. Editorial material in the *News* is easily attributed to either Thompson or Sheppard. Sheppard produced some editorial material for the *News* written in a format which broke away from the regular paragraph style to give the reader a better sense of the rhetorical touches that he was aiming at. On most days Thompson produced the majority of the editorial material of the *News*. His editorials were written in a tightly argued format which stuck to traditional paragraph style: Harkness, *Atkinson*, p. 38; *Grip*, May 24, 1890; *Saturday Night*, November 8, 1890; Hamilton *Palladium of Labor*, "Our Social Club", September 8, 1883-November 24, 1883. A similar technique was used on several occasions in the *News* in early 1884: see "Our Boarding House" in which the various tenants discuss aristocracy and the Irish land question, June 7 and Feb. 9, 1884; Thompson, *Politics of Labor*, pp. 73-74; T. V. Powderly Mss., Archives of Catholic University of America, D. J. O'Donoghue to T. V. Powderly, Toronto, May 24, 1885.

11. *Palladium*, Dec. 15, 1883, June 7, 1884; *News*, August 19, 1884,

October 2, 1884, September 13, 1886; Charlesworth, *Candid Chronicles*, pp. 76-77.

12. *News*, Jan. 16, 1885, Nov. 26, 1883.
13. For the Ranger letters, see *News*, Dec. 1, 1883-April, 1884; *World*, Dec. 31, 1883, Dec. 12, 1883, Dec. 15, 1883, Dec. 18, 1883; *News*, Dec. 21, 1883.
14. *The Week*, December 20, 1883.
15. *Palladium*, Nov. 22, 1884; *News*, Sept. 12, 1884, Jan. 1, 1884; *World*, Jan. 14, 1884; *Palladium*, Jan. 20, 1884, July 19, 1884.
16. *Palladium*, Sept. 13, 1884; *News*, Feb. 15, 1884, Dec. 4, 1883; *Palladium*, April 3, 1886.
17. *News*, July 16, 1886; *Palladium*, Sept. 13, 1884; *News*, Oct. 9, 1885, March 5, 1884.
18. *Saturday Night*, Nov. 9, 1890; *Palladium*, July 11, 1885.
19. C. Bissell,, "Literary Taste in Central Canada during the Late Nineteenth Century," *Canadian Historical Review*, XXXI, 3 (Sept. 1950), pp. 240-246; Matthew Arnold, *Culture and Anarchy* (Cambridge; Cambridge University Press, 1960); *News*, Dec. 10, 1883; *Palladium*, Jan. 20, 1884; *News*, Nov. 5, 1885, Oct. 15, 1885, July 3, 1884.
20. *News*, Feb. 14, 1884.
21. *News*, March 19, 1887, April 1, 1884, Jan. 29, 1884, May 15, 1884.
22. *Palladium*, Aug. 2, 1884, Oct. 30, 1886, Dec. 12, 1885; *News*, Sept. 9, 1885, Aug. 19, 1884.
23. *Palladium*, Feb. 7, 1885, Dec. 26, 1885, March 28, 1885, Oct. 2, 1886, July 3, 1886; Thompson, *Politics of Labor*, p. 112.
24. *Palladium*, Feb. 23, 1884, June 21, 1884, Dec. 26, 1885; in attempting to trace the sources of *The Politics of Labor* to American socialist writing (even somewhat unchronologically to *Looking Backward* published after *The Politics of Labor*), Jay Atherton ignores the sources that Thompson and others (including Edward Bellamy) combined to produce a socialist synthesis; see "Introduction," *The Politics of Labor*, (Toronto: University of Toronto Press, 1975), p. ix.
25. D. Frank, *Trouble in Toronto: The Street Railway Lockout and Strike, 1886*, unpublished paper, University of Toronto, 1970; D. Morton, *Mayor Howland* (Toronto: Hakkert, 1973), pp. 43-56; *Palladium*, April 3, 1886, July 12, 1886, Jan. 31, 1885.
26. *News*, September 15, 1886; *Palladium* Sept. 4, 1886; *News*, Jan. 2, 1884, Jan. 26, 1886; *Palladium*, March 6, 1886.
27. *The Week*, Dec. 16, 1886, Feb. 17, 1887; *News*, Jan. 8, 1887, Jan. 21, 1887, Jan. 28, 1887, Feb. 1, 1887, Feb. 2, 1887, Feb. 8, 1887, Feb. 12, 1887, Feb. 23, 1887.
28. *Palladium*, April 12, 1884, May 8, 1886, Oct. 16, 1886, April 19, 1884, June 20, 1885; John A. Macdonald Mss., Public Archives of Canada, E. E. Sheppard to J. A. Macdonald, Toronto, Dec. 11, 1883, pp. 191479-191480; G. S. Kealey (ed.), *Canada Investigates Industrialism* (Toronto: University of Toronto Press, 1973), p. xiii; Macdonald Mss., P.A.C., Requisition to the Dominion Government of the Workingmen's Liberal Conservative Union of Canada, May 4, 1880; *News*, October 11, 1886.

29. *Palladium*, May 31, 1884, Sept. 27, 1884; Thompson, *Politics of Labor*, p. 66.
30. Thompson, *Politics of Labor*, p. 195; *Palladium*, Oct. 17, 1885; *Politics of Labor*, p. 207.
31. *Palladium*, Oct. 17, 1885, May 1, 1886, Nov. 6, 1886, Sept. 20, 1884, April 26, 1884, March 20, 1886; *Globe*, June 28, 1890; Thompson, *Politics of Labor*, p. 184; *Palladium*, May 1, 1886.
32. *Palladium*, April 26, 1884; Bissell, "Literary Taste in Central Canada," p. 243; *News*, May 23, 1885; *Palladium*, Nov. 6, 1886.
33. *Palladium*, April 26, 1884; *News*, July 27, 1886; Thompson, *Politics of Labor, pp. 207-208; Palladium*, August 30, 1884.
34. *News*, Nov. 23, 1887; City of Toronto, *Assessment Roll for the Ward of St. Andrews*, 1888; *Saturday Night*, Nov. 8, 1890; *Globe*, Feb. 10, 1893; *Labor Advocate*, August 14, 1891; *Grip*, Feb. 18, 1893.
35. J. A. Atherton, "Introduction," to *Politics of Labor*, (Toronto: University of Toronto Press, 1975), p. ix.
36. S. Leacock, *The Social Criticism of Stephen Leacock* (Toronto: University of Toronto Press, 1973), pp. 23-24.

Graff: Respected and Profitable Labour

1. *Journals of Education for Upper Canada*, I (1848), pp. 289-301; for English parallels, see Central Society of Education, *Papers*, (London, 1837-1839); on the centrality of morality in nineteenth century education, see Alison Prentice, "The School Promoters; Education and Social Class in Nineteenth Century Upper Canada", (Ph.D. Thesis, University of Toronto, 1974), and my "Literacy and Social Structure in the Nineteenth Century", (Ph.D. Thesis, University of Toronto, 1975), Chapter I.
2. *Journal of Education*, II, (1849), pp. 19-20.
3. *Hamilton* (Ontario) *Spectator and Journal of Commerce*, December 6, 1848; John Duncan, *The Education of the Ordinary Child*, (London, 1843), p. 60.
4. *Journal of Education*, VII, (1854), p. 134.
5. "Report on a System of Elementary Instruction for Upper Canada, 1846", in *Documentary History of Education for Upper Canada*, ed. J. C. Hodgins, Vol. 6, (Toronto, 1899), pp. 143, 144-145.
6. Prentice, *op. cit.*, pp. 150, 174.
7. *Journal of Education*, I, (1848), p. 297; *Documentary History of Education*, pp. 11, 45.
8. "The Importance of Education to an Agricultural People", in *Documentary History of Education*, Vol. 7, p. 141.
9. In Canada, for example, Charles Clarke. See his 1877 address to the South Wellington, Ontario, Teachers Association: *Teachers and Teaching (and) Then and Now*, (Elora, Ont., 1880), p. 2. For British examples, see Richard Johnson, "Educational Policy and Social Control in Early Victorian England", *Past and Present*, No. 49, (1970), pp. 96-119. The major spokesman for these ideas was Horace Mann, Secretary of the Massachusetts State Board of Education. He had a direct influence on Ryerson: David Onn, "Egerton Ryerson's Philosophy of Education: Something Bor-

rowed or Something New?", *Ontario History*, Vol. LXI, (1969), pp. 77-86; and "Report Upon a System", *op. cit.* On Mann: *Annual Report of the Secretary of the Board of Education*, 5, (Boston, 1842); Maris A. Vinovskis, "Horace Mann on the Economic Productivity of Education", *New England Quarterly*, Vol. 43, (1970), pp. 550-571: Also see: Frank Tracey Carleton, *Economic Influences upon Educational Progress in the United States, 1820-1850*, (reprinted, New York, 1965), Chapter 4; Graff, "Literacy and Social Structure", Chapter 5; Herbert Gintis, "Education, Technology, and the Characteristics of Worker Productivity", *American Economic Review*, Vol. 61, (1971), pp. 266-279; Robert Dreeben, *On What is Learned in School*, (Reading, Mass., 1968); Alex Inkeles, "Making Men Modern", *American Journal of Sociology*, Vol. 75, (1969), pp. 208-225. On another spokesman for the ideas, Edward Jarvis of Dorchester, Massachusetts, see: Edward Jarvis, MD, "The Value of Common-School Education to Common Labour", *Report of the United States Commissioner of Education*, (Washington, 1872), pp. 572-585.

10. *Ontario Workman*, April 18, 1872, March 13, 1873, (hereafter cited as *OW*); *Palladium of Labor* (Hamilton, Ont.), May 16, 1885; see also Feb. 7, 1885 (hereafter cited as *POL*). See also *Fincher's Trades Review* (1863-66), a Philadelphia weekly, read by and concerned with Canadian labour, which included letters from Canadian workmen; September 24,1864, February 4, 1865 (hereafter cited as *FTR*); *OW*, May 2, 1872, January 16, 1873, February 12, 1874; *POL*, December 22, 1883, February 23, 1883, September 19, 1885.

11. *OW*, February 13, 1873; January 22, 1873, *FTR*, June 27, 1863, October 22, 1864, September 17, 1864, July 11, 1863, *POL*, November 24, 1883, November 22, 1884, January 5, 1884. See also Phillips Thompson, *The Politics of Labor* (New York, 1887), pp. 11-14, who claimed that reading would open the eyes of the working man to the injustices of the system. Thompson, a Toronto radical journalist, often contributed to the *POL* under the pseudonym Enjolras.

12. *OW*, April 2, 1874 and October 14, 1872.

13. *FTR*, June 27, 1863, February 11, 1865; *POL*, November 10, 1883, August 29, 1885, August 16, 1884; Thompson, *op. cit.*, pp. 17, 58, 83, 151; *POL*, February 2, 1884.

14. *POL*, December 1, 1883; see also Thompson, *op. cit.*, pp. 61, 171.

15. *OW*, November 22, 1872, December 19, 1872, January 2, 1873, February 12, 1874, March 19, 1874; *POL*, March 1, 1884, September 1, 1883; *FTR*, October 22, 1864, September 17, 1864, July 11, 1863.

16. *FTR*, March 18, 1865, April 8, 1865, *FTR*, November 7, 1863, January 16, 1864; See also October 3, 1863, and *POL*, September 8, 1883. Ironically, in fact, mechanics' institutes in Canada, as in Britain, tended to be middle class in inspiration and in membership; see J. Donald Wilson, "Adult Education in Upper Canada before 1850," *The Journal of Education* (U.B.C.), 19 (1973), pp. 43-54; Foster Vernon, "The Development of Adult

Education in Ontario, 1790-1900," (Unpublished Ed.D. Thesis, University of Toronto, 1969); and E. Royle, "Mechanics' Institutes and The Working Classes, 1840-1860," *The Historical Journal*, 14 (1971), pp. 305-321. See also John Foster, "Nineteenth Century Towns – A Class Dimension," in *The Study of Urban History*, ed. H. J. Dyos (London, 1968), pp. 281-300. See, in particular, E. P. Thompson, *The Making of the English Working Class*, (New York, 1967) pp. 712-713; R. K. Webb, *The British Working Class Reader, 1790-1848*, (London, 1955); and Hobsbawm and George Rudé, *Captain Swing*, (New York, 1969); John Foster, *Class Struggle and the Industrial Revolution* (London, 1974).

17. See H. J. Graff, "Towards a Meaning of Literacy: Literacy and Social Structure in Hamilton, Ontario," *History of Education Quarterly*, 12 (1972), pp. 411-431; and "Literacy and Social Structure in Elgin County, 1861" *Histoire sociale/Social History*, 6 (1973), pp. 25-48, as well as my dissertation.

18. "Literacy and Social Structure in the Nineteenth Century," Chapters 2 & 3 provide full detail.

19. *Ibid.*, Chapter 3.

20. The company was begun by George and William Hamilton of Quebec in 1797 and transformed into a joint-stock venture upon its sale to Blackburn, Egan, Robinson, and Thistle in 1889, taking on the new name of Hawkesbury. A few summary statistics suggest the scope: by 1885 30 million feet of timber were cut annually and milled by 350 hands, by 1909 the annual yield was 50 million feet. Hawkesbury continued to operate until 1936. The records are found in the Archives of the Province of Ontario (Toronto).

    On the lumber industry, in general see Michael S. Cross, "The Dark Druidical Groves: The Lumber Community and the Commercial Frontier in British North America to 1854," unpublished Ph.D. Thesis, University of Toronto, 1968; Edward McKenna "Unorganized Labour versus Management: The Strike at the Chaudiere Lumber Mills, 1891," *Histoire Sociale/Social History*, 5 (1972), pp. 186-211; and A.R.M. Lower *The North American Assault on the Canadian Forest* (Toronto, 1938).

21. See, E. P. Thompson, "Time, Work-Discipline, and Industrial Capitalism," *Past and Present*, No. 38 (1967), pp. 56-97; and Sidney Pollard, "Factory Discipline in the Industrial Revolution," *Economic History Review*, 16 (1963), pp. 254-271.

22. On signatures and literacy, see Roger Schofield, "The Measurement of Literacy in Pre-Industrial England," in *Literacy in Traditional Society*, ed. Jack Goody (Cambridge, 1968), pp. 311-325; and Kenneth A. Lockridge, *Literacy in Colonial New England* (New York, 1974). Signatures, it should be noted, slightly underestimate the level of reading literacy, as some men would be able to read and not write.

23. For comparative wage data see McKenna, *op. cit.*, p. 190, and *Royal Commission on the Relations of Labor and Capital* (Ottawa, 1889), Ontario Evidence.

24. Information on worker's age could be very revealing in this regard.

25. See, on this point, Michael B. Katz, "Occupational Classification in History," *Journal of Interdisciplinary History*, 3 (1972), pp. 63-88.

26. This analysis may be largely confirmed and supplemented by an examination of the receipt book of the Madawaska Improvement Company (1888-1903) in the Provincial Archives of Ontario. This too shows little disadvantage in wages for illiterates, although data is less complete than the Hawkesbury material.

27. Of the important literature of the social control functions of education, see Prentice, *op. cit.*; Johnson, *op. cit.*; Carl Kaestle, *The Evolution of an Urban School System* (Cambridge, Mass., 1973); Stanley Schultz, *The Culture Factory* (New York, 1973); Michael B. Katz, *The Irony of Early School Reform* (Cambridge, Mass., 1968); Ruth Miller Elson, *Guardians of Tradition* (Lincoln, 1964); J. M. Goldstrum, *The Social Context of Education, 1808-1870* (Dublin, 1972); Samuel Bowles, "Unequal Education and the Reproduction of the Social Division of Labor," in *Schooling in a Corporate Society*, ed. Martin Carnoy (New York, 1972), pp. 36-64; and the Special Issue of the *History of Education Quarterly*, 12 (Fall, 1972).

28. See above 9. *Massachusetts Teacher*, 15 (1862), p. 210 and Rev. John May, *Essays on Educational Subjects* (Ottawa, 1880), p. 5.

29. Jones, *Outcast London* (Oxford, 1971), pp. 82-83; See also E. J. Hobsbawm, "The Tramping Artisan," in his *Labouring Men* (New York, 1967), pp. 41-74. Skilled literate, and organized, workingmen could of course read about economic conditions, and therefore employment opportunities, in the workingclass press. The development, circulation (including oral transmission of news and group readership), and impact of the developing Canadian labour press in this period is obviously crucial and merits detailed and separate study.

30. Schofield, *op. cit.*, p. 312.

31. Anderson, "Literacy and Schooling on the Development Threshold: Some Historical Cases," in *Education and Economic Development*, ed. Anderson and Bowman (Chicago, 1965), pp. 347-362; Bowman and Anderson, "Concerning the Role of Education in Development," in *Old Societies and New States*, ed. Clifford C. Geertz (New York, 1963), pp. 247-279; and Bowman and Anderson, "Human Capital and Economic Modernization in Historical Perspective" paper presented to the Fourth International Congress of Economic History, 1968. For a critical analysis of approaches in the economics of education, see W. G. Bowen, "Assessing the Economic Contribution of Education," in *The Economics of Education*, I, ed. Mark Blaug (Harmondsworth, 1968), pp. 67-100.

32. Such were the roots of the human capital school of economists, largely dominated by Gary Becker and Theodore Schultz.

33. "Literacy and Schooling," p. 347.

34. "Does Education Accelerate Economic Growth?" *Economic De-*

velopment and Cultural Change, 14 (1966), pp. 262, 266.

35. "The History of Education," *Daedalus*, 100 (1971), p. 141.

36. Michael Sanderson, "Education and the Factory in Industrial Lancashire, 1780-1840," *Economic History Review*, 20 (1967), p. 266 and "Social Change and Elementary Education in Industrial Lancashire, 1780-1840," *Northern History*, 3 (1968), pp. 131-154. The labour press cited above made many of the same points, as did both the commissioners and the evidence in *The Royal Commission on the Relations of Labor and Capital* (Ottawa, 1889). An excellent compendium of its four volumes has been edited by Gregory Kealey (Toronto, 1973).

37. "Literacy and Social Mobility in the Industrial Revolution," *Past and Present*, No. 56 (1972), pp. 75, 102.

38. "Dimensions of Illiteracy, 1750-1850," *Explorations in Economic History*, 10 (1973), pp. 452-453.

39. *Ibid.*, p. 454.

40. Pollard, *op. cit.*, 255; see also his *Genesis of Modern Management* (Harmondsworth, 1968), esp. Chapter 5; Thompson, "Time, Work-Discipline." Keith Thomas, "Work and Leisure in Pre-Industrial Societies," *Past and Present*, No. 29 (1964); Robert Malcolmson, *Popular Recreation in English Society, 1700-1850* (Cambridge, 1973); and Herbert Gutman, "Work, Culture, and Society in Industrializing America, 1815-1919," *American Historical Review*, 78 (1973), pp. 531-588.

41. Richard Arkwright, quoted in Pollard, "Factory Discipline," p. 258 (emphasis mine).

42. *Ibid.*, p. 268.

43. Thompson, "Time, Work-Discipline," pp. 64, 84-85.

44. *Education in Tokugawa Japan* (London, 1967), p. 292.

45. At this stage of research this contention must remain hypothetical. We know all too little about the transition in Canada, and comparative studies of Anglo-America are sadly lacking. Recent work by Charles Tilly and Edward Shorter on strikes in France suggests one approach, though an exclusive focus on strike action would obscure some issues.

46. *The Early Victorians, 1832-1851* (London, 1971), pp. 135-136. See also the work of Marshall McLuhan.

47. This is, of course, the mere skeleton of a theory, for many questions surrounding the actual experience of schooling remain unanswered. There is, for example, the problem of irregular attendance which was widespread. Did this militate against the schools' success? Quite simply we do not yet know how much exposure to the routine and the message of the schools was required for sufficient training.

    For a fascinating argument on a closely related theme, that of the sanitation movement, see Richard L. Schoenwald, "Training Urban Man" in *The Victorian City*, ed. H. J. Dyos and Michael Wolff (London, 1973), pp. 669-692.

    The experience of Quebec in the nineteenth century illustrates vividly the problems of the transition in a society without mass literacy; see, *Royal Commission on the Relations of Labor and Capital*, Quebec Evidence. See also Michael Bliss' interesting attempts to explain manufacturers' lack of understanding of these problems: "Employers, as representative as anyone else of prevailing social mores, were often confused and puzzled when faced with insistence that the familiar rules of the game should be changed, and not in their favour." "A Living Profit: Studies in the Social History of Canadian Business, 1883-1911," (Unpublished Ph.D. Thesis), University of Toronto, 1972; see also pp. 137, 148, 157; published as *A Living Profit* (Toronto, 1974), see esp. Chapter 3.

Doucet: Working Class Housing in a Small Nineteenth Century Canadian City

* The author wishes to thank Ian Winchester and Michael Katz of the Canadian Social History Project for their guidance and encouragement, for providing computer facilities for this research and for granting permission to quote from project working papers. Special thanks must also go to Jim Lemon for his helpful comments on drafts of this paper.

1. The writings of these social critics are both well known and readily accessible. For some analysis of their work see David Harvey, *Social Justice and the City* (London, 1973), pp. 132-4; Steven Marcus, "Reading the Illegible," in H. J. Dyos and Michael Wolff (eds.), *The Victorian City: Images and Realities*, I (London, 1973), pp. 257-76 and *Engels, Manchester and the Working Class* (New York, 1974); E. P. Thompson and Eileen Yeo, *The Unknown Mayhew* (London, 1971), and Alexander Welsh, *The City of Dickens* (Oxford, 1971).

2. We know much more about the housing of the working class in Britain than in any other nation. Important studies include Stanley D. Chapman (ed.), *The History of Working-class Housing: A Symposium* (Newton Abbot, 1971); H. J. Dyos, "The Slums of Victorian London," *Victorian Studies*, XI (September, 1967), pp. 5-40; Enid Gauldie, *Cruel Habitations: A History of Working-Class Housing 1780-1929* (London, 1974); London County Council, *Housing of the Working Classes 1855-1912*, (London, 1913); J. Calvert Spensley, "Urban Housing Problems," *Journal of the Royal Statistical Society*, LXXXI (March, 1918), pp. 161-211; John Nelson Tarn, *Working-class Housing in 19th-century Britain* (London, 1971); and James E. Vance, Jr., "Housing the Worker: The Employment Linkage as a Force in Urban Structure," *Economic Geography*, XLII (October, 1966), pp. 294-325. For an excellent review of the British literature see Anthony Sutcliffe, "Working-Class Housing in Nineteenth Century Britain: A Review of Recent Research," *Bulletin of the Society for the Study of Labour History*, XXIV (1972), pp. 40-51. Interest in the housing of the working class in nineteenth-century North America has been slow to develop. Studies of note include Herbert Brown Ames, *The City Below the Hill* (Toronto, 1972 [1897]); Terry Copp, *The Anatomy of Poverty. The Condition of the Working Class in Montreal, 1897-1929*, (Toronto, 1974), especially pp. 70-87; Paul A. Groves. "The 'Hidden' Population: Washington Alley Dwellers in the Late Nineteenth Century," *The Professional Geographer*, XXVI (August, 1974), pp. 270-6;

and John F. Sutherland, "Housing the Poor in the City of Homes; Philadelphia at the Turn of the Century," in Allen F. Davis and Mark H. Haller (eds.), *The Peoples of Philadelphia: A History of Ethnic Groups and Lower-Class Life, 1790-1940* (Philadelphia, 1973), pp. 175-202. Research on working-class housing in areas outside of the English-speaking world has not often filtered into the English language. It is, therefore, quite difficult to measure the interest in this topic in other countries. Uno Gustafsen's recent paper, "Economic Fluctuations and Working-Class Conditions in Stockholm 1860-1910: Some Preliminary Findings," paper presented at the Society for the Study of Labour History's Anglo-Scandinavian Conference, London, September, 1974, implies some interest in this area in Sweden. The author would welcome information concerning similar studies in other parts of the world.

3. This is not to say that this question has been completely ignored. The subtle differences among the various segments of London's Victorian working class have been skillfully examined by Gareth Stedman Jones in his excellent work *Outcast London* (Oxford, 1971). To date, the vast majority of the studies of working class housing have been set in the large and long established metropolises of the English-speaking world. As one scholar has noted, housing problems in such centres often developed long before the commencement of the nineteenth century; see Iain C. Taylor, "The Court and Cellar Dwellings: The Eighteenth Century Origin of the Liverpool Slum," *Transactions of the Historic Society of Lancashire and Cheshire*, CXXII (1970), pp. 67-90.

4. The Assessment Rolls were organized in such a manner that it was a relatively simple matter to locate people precisely within the city. For a discussion of the way in which this was accomplished see, Michael Doucet, "The Assessment Rolls and Spatial Structure: A Progress Report," in Ian Winchester, (ed.), *The Canadian Social History Project Report Number 5* (Toronto, 1974), pp. 364-9.

5. For the local history of Hamilton see, Marjorie F. Campbell, *A Mountain and a City* (Toronto, 1966); Lois Evans, *Hamilton: The Story of a City* (Toronto, 1970); and C. M. Johnston, *The Head of the Lake, A History of Wentworth County* (Hamilton, 1958). The Great Western Railway, which was financed and operated largely by Hamiltonians, entered the city in 1853. For a discussion of the City Council's involvement in the promotion of this venture see, Eric Ricker, "Consensus and Conflict: City Politics in Hamilton, 1850," in Winchester (ed.), *op. cit.*, pp. 163-241. Figures compiled from the Census of Canada, 1851-2, Mss. and the industrial returns of the Census of Canada, 1870-1, Mss., the latest of the Canadian census manuscripts available to scholars at the time this paper was researched, which listed at least 10 firms that employed more than 100 people. The largest of these was the Great Western Railway which had almost 1,000 employees.

6. For this purpose, a block was considered to be developed when it contained at least one occupied structure, or at least one insti-

tution such as a court house, school or other civic building. We are not, therefore, defining development as the complete development of the blocks. Infilling was a fairly common occurrence in the development of the nineteenth century city. This is obvious when one is able to view the architecture of extant nineteenth century streetscapes. For a discussion of the time that it could take to develop small areas of a city see, H. J. Dyos, *Victorian Suburb. A Study of the Growth of Camberwell* (Leicester, 1961), p. 126; C. N. Forward, "The Immortality of a Fashionable Residential District: The Uplands," in C. N. Forward (ed.), *Residential and Neighbourhood Studies in Victoria.* Western Geographical Series, Vol. 5 (Victoria, 1973), p. 1-39; and M. J. Kelly, "Eight Acres: Estate Sub-Division and the Building Process, Paddington, 1875 to 1890," *Australian Economic History Review*, X (September, 1970), pp. 155-68.

7. Along with the rest of North America, Hamilton also suffered through a depression in the 1873-79 period. This latter depression did not appear to have as dramatic ramifications for the 1881 Assessment data as the panic of 1857 had for the 1861 records.

8. H. B. Wilson, "The City of Hamilton – Past, Present and Future," letter to the editor, *Daily Spectator and Journal of Commerce*, Tuesday, January 1, 1861, p. 2.

9. As we have noted earlier, this does not seem to have been the case for the depression of 1873-9. Unquestionably, the fact that this crisis came so soon after one of our study years must have meant that the effects of this depression could have been cushioned before the arrival of our next study year. This is one of the hazards of the cross-sectional approach.

10. The theme of urban images versus urban realities is very prominent in many of the chapters in Dyos and Wolff, *op. cit.* See, for example, Gertrude Himmelfarb, "The Culture of Poverty," pp. 707-36; P. J. Keating, "Fact and Fiction in the East End," pp. 585-602; Martha Vicinus, "Literary Voices of an Industrial Town. Manchester, 1810-70," pp. 739-61; and Michael Wolff and Celina Fox, "Pictures from the Magazines," pp. 559-82.

11. "Sanitary State of the City," *Daily Spectator and Journal of Commerce*, Thursday, November 18, 1852, p. 2.

12. When illness struck the Royal Family, concern over sanitation could become quite strong. See, for example, the sentiments expressed during the illness of the Prince of Wales in "Sanitary Matters," *The Spectator*, Monday, March 11, 1872, p. 2; Annual Report of the Board of Health for 1880, quoted in *The Spectator*, Tuesday, January 11, 1881, p. 4.

13. "Nuisances," *The Spectator*, Monday, July 18, 1881, p. 2.

14. "Sanitary State of the City," *Daily Spectator and Journal of Commerce*, Thursday, November 18, 1852, p. 2. For further comments on working class life and the condition of the working class in the nineteenth century Canadian city see, Michael S. Cross, (ed.), *The Workingman in the Nineteenth Century* (Toronto, 1974), pp. 136-231.

15. By this date, the street railway had proven its worth in many

North American cities (see Arthur J. Krim, "The Innovation and Diffusion of the Street Railway in North America," Unpublished M.A. Thesis, Department of Geography, University of Chicago, 1967). It was introduced to Hamilton in 1874. For a discussion of the proposed benefits of the street railway for Hamilton see 'Progress,' *The Spectator*, Wednesday, May 22, 1872, p. 3.

16. See the maps of the changing shoreline in Richard D. Roberts, "The Changing Patterns in Distribution and Composition of Manufacturing Activity in Hamilton Between 1861 and 1921," (Unpublished M.A. thesis, Department of Geography, McMaster University, 1964), "What Others Think of Hamilton," *New York Times*, n.d., quoted in *The Spectator*, Thursday, September 27, 1860, p. 3; Haley Bamman, "The Ladies Benevolent Society of Hamilton, Ontario: Form and Function in Mid-Nineteenth Century Urban Philanthropy," in Michael Katz (ed.), *The Canadian Social History Project Interim Report No. 4* (Toronto, 1972), pp. 161-217; "An English Opinion of the 'Ambitious City'," *London Times* n.d., quoted in *The Spectator*, Saturday, October 20, 1860, p. 2.

17. The notion that the poor had to be deserving to merit assistance has been widely discussed in the literature. See, for example, Bamman, *op. cit.*, p. 167; Jones, *op. cit.*, pp. 303-8; Stephen A. Speisman, "Munificent Parsons and Municipal Parsimony: Voluntary vs Public Poor Relief in Nineteenth Century Toronto," *Ontario History*, LXV (March, 1973), pp. 33-4 and Tarn, *op. cit.*, pp. 7 and 51-3.

18. Probably the most prominent examples of this type of industrial housing were Leverhulme's Port Sunlight, Cadbury's Bournville and Pullman's Pullman City. For discussions of these projects see Tarn, *op. cit.*, pp. 30-7; and Stanley Buder, *Pullman: An Experiment in Industrial Order and Community Planning*, 1880-1930 (New York, 1967). For some comments on the origin and development of British industrial housing see S. D. Chapman, "Industrial Housing in Britain, 1750-1850," paper presented at the Society for Labour History's Anglo-Scandinavian Conference, London, September, 1974. In Hamilton, workers were allowed to erect shanties on the Great Western's property in the 1850's, but were forced to relocate in the 1860's as the rail yards expanded. To my knowledge, no company constructed housing for its workers in Hamilton during the period under study.

19. Indeed, there is scant evidence to suggest that either building societies or philanthropic associations did very much to improve the housing standards of the urban poor. For example, the latter had provided a grand total of about 20,000 rooms in London by 1911. Yet, between 1902 and 1911 alone, the London County Council built almost 200,000 rooms for the working class (London County Council, *op. cit.*, pp. 157 and 163). The solution to the nineteenth-century housing problem, then, awaited massive government intervention in the twentieth century; Constant Reader, "Building Societies," letter to the editor, *Daily Spectator and Journal of Commerce*, Friday, June 25, 1852, p. 3.

20. Individuals were assessed for both property and income and were categorized as either freeholders, householders (renters), boarders or statute labourers. The latter were defined (13 and 14 Vic., c. 67 sec. 22) as men between the ages of 21 and 60 who did not own land and who did not have any taxable income. In lieu of taxes, they were liable to work a specified number of days for the city.

21. These years were selected because they were the closest points in time and, therefore, the best source to link (in future analyses) to the decennial census enumerations of the period. On account of the partial destruction, by fire and water, of the 1872 Assessment books, the 1873 Roll was utilized to fill in the missing data. Fortunately, the damage was restricted to the bottom quarter of certain pages in only two of the city's five wards.

22. Includes the following occupations: railroad workers, conductors, engine drivers, railroad car and engine builders, brakesmen, switchmen, rail layers, firemen, yardmen and trackmen. Clearly, the skills possessed by men in these jobs varied considerably and they could have been divided into running trades, shop trades and yard workers. This was not done because of the relatively small numbers involved in some of these categories.

23. Steven Langdon, *The Emergence of the Canadian Working Class Movement, 1845-75*, (Toronto: New Hogtown Press, 1975).

24. In 1851, the largest foundry employed 90 men (Census of Canada, 1851-2, Mss.).

25. According to the Census of Canada, 1851-2, Mss, the largest shoemaking establishment at that time employed 17 workers. By 1870-71, however, much larger shops could be found. Smaller shops still existed; but, by this time, one firm employed 49 and another 175 (Census of Canada, 1870-71, Industrial Schedule, Mss.).

26. On the difficulties of categorizing occupations see Michael B. Katz, "Occupational Classification in History," *Journal of Interdisciplinary History*, III (Summer, 1972), pp. 63-88.

27. This was the last year in which pounds sterling appeared on the Assessment Rolls of the City of Hamilton.

28. This compares with vacancy rates of 3% for 1852, 2% for 1872-3 and 6% for 1881. While the total of 421 vacant houses for the latter year may seem large, this was exactly half the number of houses vacant in 1861.

29. See, for example, Howard P. Chudacoff, *Mobile Americans: Residential and Social Mobility in Omaha 1880-1920* (New York, 1972), pp. 91-7; Peter R. Knights, *The Plain People of Boston 1830-1860. A Study in City Growth* (New York, 1971), pp. 115-8; Michael B. Katz, "Who Stayed Behind? Persistence, 1851-1861," in Winchester (ed.), *op. cit.*, pp. 344-63 and Stephan Thernstrom, *Poverty and Progress: Social Mobility in a Nineteenth Century City* (New York, 1964), pp. 85 and 198-9.

30. *The Canada Directory for 1857-58* (Montreal, 1858) estimated the 1857-8 population of Hamilton at 29,000. By 1861, the enumerators for the census could find only about 19,000 souls in the city. The large supply of cheap, vacant homes in the city in 1861

supports the idea that the outmigration was massive and involved the poor.

31. "House Hunting," *The Spectator*, Saturday, April 6, 1872, p. 3 and "Progress," *The Spectator*, Wednesday, May 22, 1872, p. 3.

32. For a discussion of the complexity of nineteenth-century home ownership patterns see, Michael B. Katz, "Homeownership and a Model of Social Process, Hamilton, Ontario, 1851-1861," in Winchester (ed.), *op. cit.*, pp. 264-92. For some analysis of property ownership patterns in other places, see, R. V. Jackson, "Owner-Occupation of Houses in Sydney, 1871 to 1891," *Australian Economic History Review*, X (September, 1970), pp. 138-54 and Sutherland, *op. cit.*, pp. 189-96.

33. We should emphasize, however, that the figures in Table 3 only deal with owner occupied houses. Labourers owned very few vacant lots in Hamilton. Furthermore, in 1852, the top ten speculators in the city owned 177 houses between them. Thus, the labourers controlled a very small proportion of Hamilton's real estate.

34. Almost two-thirds of Hamilton's labourers were Irish Catholics in 1852 (calculated from the Census of Canada, 1851-2, Mss.). Naturally, as the proportion of Canadian-born increased, the proportion of Irish-born declined.

35. Thernstrom, *op. cit.*, pp. 156-7.

36. "Locomotive Building," *Hamilton Spectator and Journal of Commerce*, Friday, January 25, 1861.

37. Langdon, *op. cit.*, pp. 3-5.

38. On the Assessment Rolls, machinists increased in number from 20 in 1852 to 335 in 1881. Furthermore, according to the *Census of Canada, 1880-81*, III (Ottawa, 1883), pp. 324-502, Hamilton's shoe factories employed 345 people. Yet, only 184 shoemakers were listed on the Assessment Rolls and only 257 on the census (*Census of Canada, 1880-81*, II, p. 293). Additional evidence of the increased occupational specificity over the period can be seen from the fact that the number of different occupations listed on the Assessment Rolls increased from 200 to 404 between 1852 and 1881.

39. In 1881, 47 per cent of the clerks were under the age of 30. Since there is strong evidence that most people did not marry until at least their late twenties, Michael B. Katz, "Growing Up in the Nineteenth Century: Relations Between Home, Work, School and Marriage, Hamilton, Ontario, 1851 and 1861," in Katz (ed.), *op. cit.*, pp. 50-101 and Michael J. Doucet, *Nineteenth Century Residential Mobility: Some Preliminary Comments.* Department of Geography, York University, Discussion Paper No. 4 (Toronto, 1972), p. 28, many clerks, therefore, would have been single and free to board either in private homes or at their places of employment.

40. Between 1852 and 1861, home ownership among lawyers declined by 20.5 per cent. For labourers and moulders, the figures were 24.6 per cent and 46.8 per cent, respectively.

41. Figures published by the Dominion Bureau of Statistics indicated that in 1941 41.2 per cent of all houses were owner occu-

pied in Hamilton. By 1951, this figure had increased to 65.2 per cent. *Eighth Census of Canada*, V (Ottawa, 1947), pp. 100-1; and *Ninth Census of Canada*, III (Ottawa, 1953), pp. 7-2.

42. A column for this information was included on the Rolls of 1872-3, but the assessors did not record any information in it.

43. Recall the diversity of the occupations comprising the designation railway worker.

44. Even the census did not list data on housing types again until 1891. By that date, more than half of the homes in the city were of either brick or stone construction. It would be useful to be able to pursue the fate of the working class during this period of transition.

45. This was characteristic of most urban places in Ontario according to architectural historians. See, for example, the caption to Plate 85 in Ralph Greenhill, Ken Macpherson and Douglas Richardson, *Ontario Towns* (Toronto, 1974), n.p.

46. According to figures in the published volumes of the *Census of Canada* for the years of this study, the ratio of homes to families was .855 for 1852, .982 for 1861, .950 for 1871 and .970 for 1881. Thus, multiple occupancy seems to have decreased after the depressions of 1857 and 1873. The ratio for 1852 has been modified to take account of occupied shops, which apparently were not considered in the census totals for occupied dwellings in that year.

47. For a discussion of this complexity see, Michael J. Doucet, "Spatial Differentiation in a Commercial City: Hamilton, 1851-2," in Katz (ed.), *op. cit.*, pp. 308-51.

48. The decline in the propensity of the working class groups to cluster together in this manner between 1872 and 1881 was largely a function of the changes that took place in the number and location of Hamilton's industries. These changes placed a greater number of city blocks within close proximity to large-scale employers and, thus, encouraged a dispersion of the city's workers. For a discussion of the changes in Hamilton's industrial landscape during the late nineteenth century see, Richard D. Roberts, "The Changing Patterns in Distribution and Composition of Manufacturing Activity in Hamilton Between 1861 and 1921," (Unpublished M.A. Thesis, Department of Geography, McMaster University, 1964), pp. 30-80.

49. This is obvious from an examination of surveyor's maps or other detailed plans of the city. See, for example, Marcus Smith, *Map of Hamilton, 1850-1* (New York, 1851) and the maps of the City of Hamilton contained in the *Illustrated Historical Atlas of the County of Wentworth* (Toronto, 1875), pp. 46-63.

50. See, for example, Peter Collison, "Occupation, Education and Housing in an English City," *American Journal of Sociology*, LXV (May, 1960), pp. 588-97; Otis Dudley Duncan and Beverly Duncan, "A Methodological Analysis of Segregation Indexes," *American Sociological Review*, XX (April, 1955), pp. 210-7; Surinder K. Mehta, "Patterns of Residence in Poona (India) by Income, Education and Occupation," *American Journal of Sociology*, LXXIII (January, 1968), pp. 496-508; and Karl E. and

Alma F. Taeuber, *Negroes in Cities: Residential Segregation and Neighborhood Change* (Chicago, 1965), especially pp. 195-245. This type of index has also been discussed in some recent historical literature. See, Chudacoff, *op. cit.*, pp. 65-7; and Sam Bass Warner, Jr., *The Private City: Philadelphia in Three Periods of Its Growth* (Philadelphia, 1968), pp. 169-76.

51. Mehta, *op. cit.*, p. 498.

52. The number of developed blocks increased from 227 in 1852 to 356 in 1861 to 424 in 1872 and to 471 in 1881. There were about 500 surveyed blocks in Hamilton during the study period.

53. Roberts, *op. cit.*, pp. 30-80.

54. The number of labourers, for example, increased by 168 per cent while the number of developed blocks increased by just 107 per cent during the interval.

55. Calculation of values for the Index of Dissimilarity produces a matrix of figures that are symmetrical about the main diagonal of the matrix (running from the top left to the bottom right corner). In other words, the index value for labourers versus lawyers is identical to that for lawyers versus labourers, and so on. For this reason, only one half (or triangle) of each matrix is required for a complete set of index values. Our matrices, then, contain one triangle from each of two different matrices.

56. The formula for the calculation of the location quotient is:

$$LQia = \frac{\dfrac{Xia}{Xic}}{\dfrac{POPa}{POPc}}$$

where: LQia is the location quotient for variable i in zone a;
Xia is the amount of variable i in zone a;
Xic is the amount of variable i in the entire city;
POPa is the population of zone a;
POPc is the population of the city.
For a pioneering example of the use of this measure in historical geography see, Peter Hall, *Industries of London Since 1861* (London, 1962).

57. Both sets of maps utilize a 64 zone grid system based upon aggregations of the surveyed blocks of the city. Such a set of zones was employed both to minimize the number of spatial units that contained no assessed residents and to simplify the computations.

58. Zones with location quotients in excess of 1.50 were considered to be areas in which the given attribute was highly over-represented. In such areas, at least 50 per cent more of the attribute was present than one would have expected given the overall distribution of the population of the city.

59. This can be clearly seen on the *Map of the City of Hamilton* (Toronto, 1882).

60. In fact, the numbers involved in this district, which contained a predominantely Irish area known as 'Cork Town' (Michael Doucet, "Hamilton at Mid-Century: Some Geographical Perspectives," in Katz (ed.), *op. cit.*, pp. 273-8), increased relatively little. In 1852, 157 of our workers lived here; but, by 1881, the figure

had increased by only 36 per cent to 213. During the study period, the population of the same area increased by over 85 per cent.

61. Taken to comprise zones 17-22, 36-40, 50 and 57-61.

62. Compare the maps showing industrial location in Hamilton in 1861 and 1891 in Roberts, *op. cit.*

63. Peter G. Goheen, *Victorian Toronto, 1850 to 1900: Pattern and Process of Growth.* Department of Geography, University of Chicago, Research Paper No. 127 (Chicago, 1970), pp 219-21; Warner, *op. cit.*, pp. 172 and 68-78; Langdon, *op. cit.* pp. 3-5.

64. Vance, "Housing the Worker: The Employment Linkage," *op. cit.*, p. 322.

Palmer: "Give us the road and we will run it"

1. *London Free Press*, Monday, July 10, 1899, pp. 1, 8-10; *London Advertiser*, Monday, July 10, 1899, p. 2; W. L. Davis, "A History of the Early Labor Movement in London, Ontario" M.A. Thesis, University of Western Ontario, 1930, Ch. ii; *Industrial Banner*, November 1899, p. 1.

2. Charles Lipton, *The Trade Union Movement of Canada, 1827-1959* (Montréal, 1968), pp. 80-81, 84; Davis, "A History of the Early Labour Movement," Ch. iv; Gerald Onn, "The History of the London Street Railway Company" (M.A. Thesis, University of Western Ontario, 1958), Ch. vii; Frederick H. Armstrong and Daniel J. Brock, "The Rise of London: A Study of Urban Evolution in Nineteenth-Century Southwestern Ontario," in F. H. Armstrong, *et al.*, ed., *Aspects of Nineteenth Century Ontario: Essays Presented to James J. Talman* (Toronto, 1974), pp. 80-98; *Cf.*, William Richardson, "Towards an Understanding of Public Support for Striking Streetcar Operatives in London in 1898-1900," Unpublished essay, University of Toronto, 1974.

3. *Census of the Canadas, 1851-1852*, I (Quebec, 1853), pp. 18-19; *Census of Canada, 1870-1871*, I (Ottawa, 1873), pp. 254-255; *Census of Canada, 1911*, I (Ottawa, 1913), pp. 80, 372-373. For comparative purposes see the data on social structure in Michael Katz, "The People of a Canadian City, 1851-1852," *Canadian Historical Review*, LIII (December, 1972), pp. 402-426; Ontario Institute for Studies in Education, "The Canadian Social History Project," Working Paper #23, both of which deal with Hamilton. *Cf., Census of Canada, 1901*, I (Ottawa, 1902), pp. 330-331.

4. *Census of Canada, 1911*, II, pp. 158-159; *Census of Canada, 1901*, I, pp. 148-149. All sources attest to the similarity of the English, Scotch-Irish and Irish Protestant groupings: Rowland Berthoff, *British Immigrants in Industrial America* (Cambridge, 1953), p. 3; Charles Knowles, *Scotch-Irish Pioneers in Ulster and America* (Baltimore, 1967, original 1910), pp. 296-313; James Leyburn, *The Scotch-Irish: A Social History* (Chapel Hill, 1962), pp. 140-153, 273-295; Henry James Ford, *The Scotch-Irish in America* (New York, 1941, original 1915), *passim;* Willard Francis Dillon, "The Irish in London, Ontario, 1826-1861" M.A. Thesis, University of Western Ontario, 1963, also stresses this socio-cultural similarity.

5. *Index*, Clerk of Peace and County Crown Attorney, Volume I, County of Middlesex, 1893-1918, Register for the City of London, Regional Collection, University of Western Ontario, pp. 340-351, hereafter cited as R.C. U.W.O.; *Quarterly Return of Convictions*, made by the Magistrate, in the County of Middlesex, 1869-1914, R.C., U.W.O.; Dillon, "The Irish in London," pp. 43, 78-79; *Census of Canada, 1901*, I, pp. 203, 330; Paul G. Fuller, "Aspects of London's Cultural Development from the Turn of the Century to World War I" (M.A. Thesis, University of Western Ontario, 1966), pp. vi-vii; *London Advertiser*, Friday, November 7, 1873, p. 3; Wednesday, August 1, 1877, p. 1; Thursday, August 6, 1885, p. 6; Tuesday, July 14, 1885, p. 4; Thursday, July 13, 1886, p. 4; Thursday, May 26, 1887, p. 6; *The Western Advertiser*, Friday, July 19, 1889, p. 3; Michael S. Cross, "Stony Monday, 1849: The Rebellion Losses Riots in Bytown," *Ontario History*, 63 (September, 1971), p. 180. *Cf.*, Gregory S. Kealey, "The Orange Order in Toronto: Religious Riot and the Working Class," (in this volume), for a discussion of Protestant-Catholic strife in working class Toronto.

6. *Census of Canada, 1901*, I, pp. 148-149, *Census of Canada, 1911*, II, pp. 158-159; Liston Pope, *Millhands and Preachers: A Study of Gastonia* (New Haven, 1942), *passim*; E. J. Hobsbawm, *Primitive Rebels; Studies in Archaic Forms of Social Movements in the 19th and 20th Centuries* (Manchester, 1959), pp. 126-149; Dillon, "The Irish in London," pp. 48-84; R. T. Appleyard, "The Origins of Huron College" (Unpublished PhD Thesis, University of Western Ontario, 1937), pp. 34-35.

7. Charles Hutchinson, "Scrapbook: London, 1884-1891," R.C., U.W.O.; Loyal Orange Lodge Association, London, Ontario, Records of Lodge 38, 1857-1866, Papers, Box 1, R.C., U.W.O.; "Minutes of the Protestant Orphan's Home, 1874-1875," R.C., U.W.O.; *London Advertiser*, Thursday, July 11, 1872, p. 1; Monday, July 18, 1887, p. 3; Tuesday, July 3, 1877, pp. 1-2; Monday, June 25, 1877, p. 1; Saturday, July 6, 1872, p. 1; Wednesday, July 8, 1885, p.2.

8. M. G. Bixby, *Industries of Canada: Historical and Commercial Sketches* (Toronto, 1887), p. 88; "Certificate No. 3, Sons of Temperance," Pioneer Division, London, 1882, R.C., U.W.O.: *Constitution, By-Laws, & Rules of Order, Blank Forms and Odes of the United Temperance Association of Canada* (London, 1876), p. 6 and *passim; Ritual of the British American Order of Good Templars* (London, 1860), *passim; London Advertiser*, Friday, October 18, 1872, p. 3; Friday, November 7, 1873, p. 3; Thursday, October 24, 1872, p. 1; Monday, July 21, 1873, p. 3; Wednesday, May 16, 1877, p. 1; Tuesday, June 11, 1877, p. 1; Thursday, July 19, 1877, p. 4; Saturday, July 21, 1877, p. 4; Monday, July 30, 1877, p. 4; Thursday, August 9, 1877, p. 1; Monday, July 25, 1881, p. 1; Saturday, July 18, 1885, p. 5; Friday, September 10, 1886, p. 6; *London Free Press*, Saturday, July 17, 1867, p. 3; Wednesday, June 3, 1868, p. 3; Wednesday, October 8, 1884, p. 8; Thursday, October 9, 1884, p. 2.

9. On the craftsman's exodus to the United States and Canada see: Berthoff, *British Immigrants in Industrial America*, pp. 21-23; W.

A. Carrothers, *Emigration from the British Isles* (New York, 1966, original 1929), *passim*; Charlotte Erickson, "The Encouragement of Emigration by British Trade Unions, 1850-1900," *Population Studies*, 3-4, (December, 1949), pp. 248-273; Erickson, *Invisible Immigrants* (Coral Gables, Florida, 1972), pp. 229-262; Stanley Johnson, *A History of Emigration From the United Kingdom to North America, 1763-1912* (Toronto, 1961, original 1928), *passim*; and the excellent biography by F. B. Smith, *Radical Artisan: William James Linton, 1812-1897* (Manchester, 1973), p. ix and *passim. Cf.,* Gregory S. Kealey, "Artisans Respond to Industrialism: Shoemakers, Shoe Factories and the Knights of St, Crispin in Toronto," Canadian Historical Association, *Historical Papers* (1973).

10. *Foster's London City and Middlesex County Directory, 1898-99* (Toronto, 1899), pp. 368-405; *Vernon's City of London Street Directory, 1913* (London, 1913), pp. 630-673; Crawford Family Papers, Diary of Leeman W. Crawford, Carriagemaker, London, Ontario, 1887, Public Archives of Ontario, Toronto; Dr. E. Searborn Papers, "Brickmaking in London," Public Archives of Canada, Ottawa; *Census of Canada, 1911,* IV, pp. 334-343; *Labour Gazette,* II, 1901-1902 (Ottawa, 1902), pp. 535-536; Dillon, "The Irish in London," pp. 107-127.

11. *Index,* Register for the City of London, pp. 102-107, R.C., U.W.O.; Henry L. Stillson, *et al., History of the Ancient and Honorable Fraternity of Free and Accepted Masons* (Boston, 1909), pp. 463-468; Oronkyteka, M. D., *History of the Independent Order of Foresters* (Toronto, 1895), pp. 750, 753; Orlo Miller, *A Century of Western Ontario: The Story of London. "The Free Press," and Western Ontario* (Toronto, 1949), pp. 169-174.

12. Forest City Lodge #38, of the Province of Canada, International Order of Oddfellows, "Applications for Membership, 1857-1866," R.C., U.W.O.; Forest City Lodge #38, "Membership List," *ibid.; Historical Sketch of St. John's Lodge #20* (London, 1894), pp. 1-7; Where the applicant's or member's occupation was not listed, it was culled from the *London City and Middlesex County Directory, 1894,* (Toronto, 1894), and the *London City and Middlesex County Directory, 1886* (London, 1886), *Cf.,* Zygmut Bauman, *Between Class and Elite: The Evolution of the British Labour Movement* (Manchester, 1970), pp. 38, 86, 95-98, 110. I considered engineers, machinists, moulders, brass founders, watchmakers, gunsmiths, tinsmiths, blacksmiths, marble cutters, gilders, bricklayers, cabinetmakers, chairmakers, carriagemakers, cigarmakers, carpenters, tanners, tailors, printers, shoemaker/cordwainers, and bookmakers as skilled tradesmen.

13. London societies, and their leadership, are listed in *R. L. Polk's London City Directory, 1880* (London, 1880), pp. 422-424; *Foster's City Directory, 1898-99,* pp. 31-35; *Vernon's City Directory,* 1913, pp. 686-694. The Regional Collection, University of Western Ontario houses an impressive collection of nineteenth century friendly society rituals. Among the most interesting are those of the Good Templars, Independent Order of Foresters,

Ancient Order of Foresters, Knights of Pythias and Ancient Order of United Workmen. *Cf.*, Hobsbawm, *Primitive Rebels*, pp. 150-174; Kealey, "Artisans Respond to Industrialism," pp. 13-14. On the linguistic bonds connecting the skilled tradesman and the friendly society see "The Book of the Constitution of the Grand Lodge of Ancient Free and Accepted Masons of Ontario," (n.p., n.d.), pp. 8-9, R.C., U.W.O.; and the discussions in Jean Piaget, *Structuralism* (New York, 1970), pp. 74-75; Nancy Struever, "The Study of Language and the Study of History," *The Journal of Interdisciplinary History* 4 (Winter 1974), pp. 401-415. The *Report of the Royal Commission on the Relations of Capital and Labour in Canada, Ontario Evidence* (Ottawa, 1889), pp. 582-586, 641-645, also buttress the contention that fraternal organizations drew their membership and leadership from the "respectable" sectors of the wage-earning class.

14. Eleanor Shaw, *A History of the London Public Library* (Occasional Paper #4, London Public Library and Art Museum, 1941), p. 11.

15. *Ibid.*, pp. 1-5; "Minute Book, London Mechanic's Institute, 1841-1850 and 1870-1871," Special Collections, London Public Library, [hereafter referred to as S.C., L.P.L.]; *Canadian Free Press*, Friday, January 17, 1851, p. 3; Friday, January 24, 1851, p. 3; "Membership List, London Mechanic's Institute, Incorporated July 15, 1852," S.C., L.P.L.

16. "Minutes of the Mechanic's Institute, 1881-1895," S.C., L.P.L.; *London Advertiser*, Friday, October 8, 1872, p. 3; Wednesday, September 26, 1877, p. 1; *London Free Press*, Wednesday, April 30, 1884, p. 3; Shaw, *History of the Public Library*, pp. 18, 31-33; Davis, "History of the Early Labour Movement in London," pp. 31-40.

17. *London Inquirer*, October 28, 1842, p. 3; *London Herald*, March 11, 1843, p. 1; Reverend A. B. Gosh, *The Oddfellows Improved Pocket Manual* (Philadelphia, 1869), n.p.; *Book of Degrees of the Order of the Sons of Temperance of North America* (Baltimore, 1854), p. 46; *Ancient Order of United Workmen, Ritual*, (n.p., n.d.), pp. 15, 29, R.C., U.W.O.; James Ridgley, *The OddFellows Pocket Companion: A Correct Guide on all Matters Relating to Odd-Fellowship* (Cincinnati, 1867), pp. 44-45.

18. *London Advertiser*, Wednesday, August 25, 1886, p. 5.

19. Davis, "A History of the Early Labour Movement in London," pp. 1, 5-7; Lipton, *The Trade Union Movement*, p. 21; *Rules of the Amalgamated Society of Carpenters and Joiners, Established June 4, 1860, Amended Rules as Adopted by the Votes of Members in 1904, Canadian Edition* (Toronto, 1905), p. 4.

20. "The London Cooperative Association, Registry Office #46, County of Middlesex, April 27, 1867," R.C., U.W.O.; "The Constitution and By-Laws of the London Cooperative Association, Registry Office #47, County of Middlesex, June 13, 1867," *ibid.*

21. Lipton, *The Trade Union Movement*, pp. 28, 46; Davis, "A History of the Early Labor Movement in London," pp. 23, 31-40; Ailsa Craig Mechanic's Institute, "Membership Lists and Accounts Books, 1877-1892," pp. 1-66, R.C., U.W.O.; Douglas R.

Kennedy, *The Knights of Labor in Canada* (London, 1956), pp. 30-31; *London Advertiser*, Thursday, July 4, 1872, p. 3; Tuesday, May 28, 1872, p. 1; Monday, June 10, 1872, p. 1; Monday, June 17, 1872, p. 2; Saturday, July 6, 1872, p. 1; Monday, August 11, 1873, p. 3; *London Free Press*, Wednesday, August 30, 1871, p. 2; Tuesday, September 5, 1871, p. 2; Friday, September 8, 1871, p. 1.

22. The Crispin Lodge may well have been the organization at the Burridge & Company shoe factory which Hessel incorrectly labelled the oldest union in London. See R. H. Hessel, "The Labor Movement in London: Some Personal Recollections," *Western Ontario Historical Notes*, 22 (1962-1966), p. 49. *Constitution By-Laws and Rules of Order of London Lodge #242, K.O.S.C., Revised and Adopted September 25, 1872*, (London, 1872), pp. 1-4 and passim. See Kealey, "Artisans Respond to Industrialism," p. 155, footnote 34, for an introduction to the literature on the Knights of St. Crispin.

23. On the persistence of the shoemaker see: *London Advertiser*, Monday, July 19, 1886, p. 5; *London Free Press*, Saturday, February 12, 1887, p. 5; Friday, February 18, 1887, p. 7; Saturday, February 19, 1887, p. 3; *Royal Commission, Ontario Evidence*, pp. 659-661.

24. Davis, "A History of the Early Labor Movement," pp. ii, 1; Hessel, "The Labor Movement in London," p. 49; Hessel, "The Labor Movement in London: Some Personal Recollections" (Unpublished mss., R. C., U.W.O.), n.p. (The quote was edited from the published version of Hessel's recollections). *Cf., London Advertiser*, Saturday, July 4, 1885, p. 4; Monday, July 6, 1885, p. 4; Saturday, July 11, 1885, p. 4; Thursday, July 16, 1885, p. 4; Friday, August 7, 1885, p. 7; Friday, August 14, 1885, p. 4; Friday, July 2, 1886, p. 3; Wednesday, July 14, 1886, p. 4; Wednesday, April 6, 1887, p. 5; Friday, April 8, 1887, p. 4; Saturday, April 9, 1887, p. 4; Thursday, April 14, 1887, p. 4; Monday, April 4, 1887, p. 5; Monday, May 2, 1887, p. 1; Thursday, May 26, 1887, p. 6.

25. Jonathan Garlock and N. C. Builder, *Knights of Labor Data Bank* (Ann Arbor, 1973); Kennedy, *Knights of Labor*, p. 121; Hessel, "The Labor Movement," p. 49; Davis, "A History of the Early Labor Movement in London," p. 14; *London Advertiser*, Saturday, July 10, 1886, p. 6; *Royal Commission, Ontario Evidence*, pp. 625, 635, 661, 664-65.

26. Davis, "History of the Early Labor Movement in London," pp 4-5; *London Advertiser*, Saturday, July 10, 1886, p. 6.

27. *Ibid*.

28. Kennedy found the London assemblies among the most resilient in North America. Kennedy, *Knights of Labor*, p. 99.

29. Davis, "Hisory of the Early Labor Movement in London," p. 23; *London Advertiser*, Wednesday, August 4, 1886, p. 3; Martin Robin, *Radical Politics and Canadian Labour, 1880-1930* (Kingston, 1968), p. 30.

30. David Frank, "Trouble in Toronto: The Street Railway Lockout and Strike of 1886" (Unpublished essay, University of Toronto),

1970; *Labour Gazette*, Volume III, 1902-1903, (Ottawa, 1903), pp. 48, 706, 1029; *Labour Gazette*, VI, 1905-1906, pp. 174, 1155-1156, 1265-1266; *Labour Gazette*, VII, 1906-1907, p. 174; *Labour Gazette*, XIV, 1913-1914, p. 90; and *Motorman and Conductor*, Volume I, #1 (March, 1895), through Volume XIV, #5 (April, 1906).

31. See Onn, "The History of the London Street Railway Company," esp. pp. 2-7, and 35-48.

32. *London Free Press*, October 22, 1898, and October 26, 1898, cited in Onn, "History of the London Street Railway Company," pp. 138-140; Richardson, "Towards an Understanding of Public Support for Operatives," pp. 12-13; *Industrial Banner*, December 1898, Special Victory Issue, p. 1.

33. *Industrial Banner*, December, 1898, pp. 3-4, cited in Richardson, "Towards an Understanding of Support for Operatives," pp. 13-14; Onn, "History of the London Street Railway Company," pp. 140-141; *London Free Press*, Tuesday, November 1, 1898, p. 1; Wednesday, November 2, 1898, p. 5; Thursday, November 3, 1898, p. 5; Friday, November 4, 1898, p. 6; Saturday, November 5, 1898, p. 4; Wednesday, November 9, 1898, p. 6; Thursday, November 10, 1898, p. 5.

34. *London Free Press*, November 8, 1898, p. 1; Saturday, November 5, 1898, pp. 3-4; Thursday, November 3, 1898, p. 5; *Industrial Banner*, December, 1898, p. 2; Richardson, "Towards an Understanding of Support for Operatives," pp. 17-18.

35. *Industrial Banner*, December, 1898, p. 7, cited in Richardson, "Towards an Understanding of Public Support for Operatives," p. 29; *London Free Press*, Friday, November 11, 1898, p. 1; Saturday, November 12, 1898, p. 1; *London Advertiser*, Saturday, November 12, 1898, p. I; *Motorman and Conductor*, IV (November 1898), pp. 1-2.

36. *London Free Press* Saturday, May 13, 1899, pp. 3-5; Monday, May 15, 1899, pp. 6-7; Tuesday, May 16, 1899, p. 4; Wednesday, May 17, 1899, pp. 5, 8; Tuesday, May 23, 1899, p. 4; *Motorman and Conductor*, V (March, 1899), pp. 3-4; Onn, "History of the Street Railway Company," pp. 144-145.

37. *London Advertiser*, Friday, May 26, 1899, p. 1; Saturday, May 27, 1899, pp. 1-2; *London Free Press*, Friday, May 26, 1899, p. 6; Monday, May 29, 1899, p. 8; Thursday, June 1, 1899, p. 11; Monday, July 10, 1899, p. 8; *Motorman and Conductor*, VI (July, 1899), pp. 1-3; *Industrial Banner*, May, 1899, pp. 1-2.

38. Onn, "History of the Street Railway Company," pp. 146-147; *London Advertiser*, Saturday, June 3, 1899, p. 3; Monday, June 5, 1899, p. 1; *London Free Press*, Saturday, May 27, 1899, p. 7; Saturday, June 3, 1899, p. 3; Wednesday, June 7, 1899, p. 3; Thursday, June 8, 1899, p. 11; Friday, June 16, 1899, p. 3; Thursday, June 22, 1899, p. 3; Saturday, June 24, 1899, p. 1.

39. *London Free Press*, Wednesday, June 21, 1899, p. 8; Saturday, June 17, 1899, p. 3; Wednesday, June 28, 1899, p. 3; Onn, "History of the London Street Railway," p. 145.

40. Onn, "History of the London Street Railway Company," pp. 147-148; *London Free Press*, Monday, July 10, 1899, pp. 1-2;

London Advertiser, Monday, July 10, 1899, p. 2; *Motorman and Conductor*, V (July, 1899), pp. 1-3.

41. *Ibid*.

42. *Quarterly Return of Convictions*, R. C., U.W.O.; *London Free Press*, Wednesday, July 12, 1899, p. 3; Tuesday, July 11, 1899, pp. 5, 7; Monday, July 10, 1899, p. 1.

43. *Industrial Banner*, September, 1899, p. 1; October, 1899, pp. 4-5; November, 1899, p. 2; December, 1899, p. 2; January, 1900, p. 1; February, 1900, p. 1; June 29, 1900, p. 1; *London Free Press*, August 1, 1899, p. 8; Onn, "History of the Street Railway Company," p. 150; Leaflet entitled "Treachery! Vain Attempt to have the Street Railway Battle Thrown," Public Archives of Canada, Ottawa.

44. *London Free Press*, Tuesday, July 18, 1899, p. 2; Tuesday, August 1, 1899, pp. 6, 8; Richardson, "Towards an Understanding of Support for Operatives," pp. 38-39; *Motorman and Conductor*, V (August, 1899), p. 3; V (September, 1899), pp. 4-5.

45. *Industrial Banner*, September, 1910, p. 2; December, 1910, p. 2; January, 1911, p. 3; Davis, "History of the Early Labor Movement in London," pp. 53-55; Jane Masters, "Canadian Labour Press Opinion, 1898-1914: A Study in Theoretical Radicalism and Practical Conservatism" (M.A. Thesis, University of Western Ontario, 1969), p. 54. *Cf.*, *Industrial Banner*, May, 1900, p. 1, cited in Richardson, "Towards an Understanding of Support for Operatives," p. i.

46. *Labour Gazette*, I, 1900-1901, pp. 149-150, 250; *Labour Gazette*, II, 1901-1902, p. 127; *Labour Gazette*, III, 1902-1903, pp. 750-751, 849-850, 961-963; *Labour Gazette*, IV, 1903-1904, p. 86; *Labour Gazette*, VI, 1905-1906, p. 207; *Labour Gazette*, XIII, 1912-1913, p. 895; *Industrial Banner*, August, 1903, p. 2; May, 1902, p. 1; Davis, "History of the Early Labor Movement in London," pp. 26, 109.

47. *Labour Gazette*, IX, 1908-1909, p. 993; *Industrial Banner*, March, 1909, p. 1; May, 1909, p. 1; June, 1909, p. 4.

Roberts: The Last Artisans: Toronto's Printers

1. *Star*, March 20, 1909, p. 10.

2. *Typographical Journal* (hereafter *Typo J.*) Feb., 1902, p. 119.

3. Wm. Powell, "We wish to Excel in Our Craft", 51st Annual Convention.

4. For membership figures, see *Labour Gazette*, Dec. 1900, p. 145; *Typo J.*, July, 1907, p. 72; *Industrial Banner*, Jan. 9, 1914, p. 1.

5. *Typo J.*, May 1901, p. 423.

6. *Typo J.*, April, 1901, p. 333; R. Harkness, *J. E. Atkinson of the Star*, (Toronto, 1963).

7. Toronto Typographical Union, Minute Book, Jan. 5, 1895, p. 24; *Typo J.*, Jan., 1909, p. 79; *Lance*, Nov. 18, 1911, p. 2; *Typo J.*, Dec., 1912, p. 661; *Typo J.*, Mar., 1907, p. 293.

8. The list of printers was secured from the complete Toronto membership list contained in the *Proceedings of the 51st Convention of the I.T.U. held at Toronto, Canada, August 14th to 20th, 1905*, in possession of S. Zerker, York University. Twenty-seven

printers were selected randomly by means of a computer print-out prepared by my friend Gordon Doctorow.

9. The data on religion is not totally reliable, since definite religion is only given in the case of actual homeowners. This evidence is derived in the same manner as above. Material on recruitment and place of origin is gathered from a compilation of reports of the "investigating committee reports" in the minute books of the union from 1896 to 1914. These minute books are at present in the possesion of Sally Zerker, York University, Toronto.

10. Of 810 members in 1905, 287 have at least one other person with the same last name. A check of the city street directories links thirty men directly in father-son or brother pairs. However this is undoubtedly a serious underestimation of generational inherit-ance since it fails to count sons who have left home. *Typo J.*, August, 1913, p. 202.

11. Wm. Powell, *op. cit.*

12. Minute Book, Oct. 1, 1910, p. 256.

13. William Taylor, Welcome Poem to the 51st Annual Convention.

14. Letterhead is an insert in Minute Book, Aug., 1899. The applica-tion form is an insert on p. 440, Minute Book, 1894-1901.

15. Insert in TTU Minutes, p. 208, 1901-7.

16. Minute Book, May 6, 1899, p. 332.

17. An example of rejection for incompetency can be found in Min-ute Book of March 7, 1896, p. 107; examples of expulsion are in Minute Book, Sept. 1, 1894, p. 486; and in Minute Book of May 4, 1901, pp. 21-2. Examples of appeals in Minute Book, July 1, 1909, p. 148; Executive Minutes of Mar. 29, 1902.

18. *Typo J.*, Dec., 1903, p. 615.

19. Executive Minutes, Dec. 5, 1903, pp. 95-6; *Typo J.*, Feb., 1901, pp. 157-8.

20. *Lance*, Oct. 4, 1913, p. 1; *Typo J.*, Dec., 1903, p. 615.

21. *Star*, Nov. 19, 1904, p. 21; *Typo J.*, June, 1905, p. 648; *Typo J.*, Feb., 1901, p. 157.

22. *Typo J.*, July, 1912, p. 64; Minute Book, Oct. 2, 1907, p. 157.

23. *Typo J.*, Aug., 1909, p. 215.

24. *Typo J.*, Nov., 1911, p. 503; *Typo J.*, Dec., 1912, pp. 178-9.

25. *Lance*, Oct. 19, 1912, p. 1; Feb. 6, 1909 Minute Book, p. 113.

26. See insert Minute Book, Aug. 6, 1904, p. 283.

27. Executive Minutes, Nov. 14, 1913, p. 207ff; Oct. 28, 1911, Execu-tive Minutes, pp. 44-6; Nov. 8, 1913, pp. 325-30; TTU Minutes, Dec. 3, 1910, pp. 280-2; Executive Minutes, Feb. 28, 1911, p. 4.

28. Executive Minutes, Apr. 28, 1906, p. 234; Exec. Minutes, Aug., 29, 1908, p. 94; see also TTU Minute Book, May 7, 1912, p. 98; Exec. Minutes, Apr. 25, 1912, p. 84; Exec. Minutes, May 10, 1912, pp. 93-4.

29. TTU Minutes, Vol. 4, Feb. 24, 1892, p. 159, PAC; Nov. 19, 1892, p. 26; Jan. 7, 1893, pp. 285-8; May 6, 1893, p. 345 ff.

30. TTU Minutes, May to June, 1893, PAC.

31. *Typo J.*, Oct., 1899, p. 423.

32. *Typo J.*, Oct., 1899, p. 423; *Typo J.*, June, 1901, p. 516; TTU Minutes, June 1, 1901, p. 38.

33. *Typo J.*, Apr. 1, 1900, pp. 291-2; *Labour Gazette*, Jan., 1902, p. 387; Oct., 1904, p. 333 *ibid*; Sept., 1904, p. 237, *ibid*.

34. *Typo J.*, Jan. 1, 1900, p. 70.

35. TTU Minutes, Feb. 6, 1892, p. 153, Vol. 4, PAC.

36. TTU Minutes, Vol. 4, Apr. 2, 1892, pp. 176-7, PAC; TTU Minute Book, Feb. 2, 1907, pp 453-5.

37. TTU Minute Book, Oct. 1, 1906, pp. 428-9.

38. TTU Minute Book, June 1, 1901, pp. 35-40.

39. *Typo J.*, Nov., 1899, p. 510; Executive Minutes, Nov. 25, 1911, p. 7; Minute Book, Jan. 20, 1914, p. 349.

40. Executive Minutes, Dec. 7, 1907, p. 50; *Typo J.*, Oct., 1899, p. 422; Exec. Minutes, July 10, 1908, pp. 82-3; see also TTU Minutes, June to July, 1908, pp. 61-6; Executive Minutes, May 2, 1914, p. 262.

41. TTU Minutes, June 4, 1898, pp. 259-60.

42. *Typo J.*, Feb. 1901, p. 107; *Mail and Empire*, Jan. 12, 1901, p. 6; Jan. 11, 1901, p. 6; *Labour Gazette*, Feb. 1901, p. 288.

43. *Typo J.*, May 1, 1902, pp. 388-9, May 15, 1902, p. 443; June 1, 1902, p. 472 and July 1, 1902, p. 75; *Labour Gazette*, May, 1902, p. 647; TTU Minutes, Apr. 16, 1902; Oct. 4, 1902; Dec. 6, 1902, Nov. 15, 1902.

44. *Labour Gazette*, June, 1902; TTU Minutes, May 6, 1902, P. 111; *Typo J.*, May 15, 1902, pp. 422-3.

45. *Star*, May 23, 1904, p. 7; *Typo J.*, May, 1904, p. 554; *Star*, June 11, 1904, p. 1; Executive Minutes, June 4, 1904, p. 133; Minute Book, July, 1904, p. 275.

46. For war whoops, see e.g. *Mail and Empire*, Aug. 16, 1905, p. 6; *Star*, July 11, 1904, p. 7; *Star*, Nov. 11, 1905; see also *Star*, Jan. 13, 1906; *Typo J.*, July, 1907, p. 72.

47. TTU Minutes May 4, 1907, pp. 475-6; May 22, p. 479; May 28, pp. 480-8, *Star*, May 23, 1907, p. 1.

48. TTU Minute Book, Feb. 10, 1913, p. 205; Mar. 25, 1913, p. 221; Mar. 4, 1911, p. 16; May 22, 1912, p. 104; Apr. 13, 1912, p. 78; *Typo J.*, Aug., 1911, p. 209; May, 1912, pp. 606-7; Apr., 1912, pp. 474-5; Feb., 1912, p. 173; Star, Oct. 4, 1912, p. 19; Mar. 11, 1912, p. 4; June 25, 1913, p. 8; *Lance* Oct. 12, 1912, p. 1; June 29, 1912, p. 1; Mar. 16, 1912, p. 1.

49. See e.g. *Globe*, Nov. 1, 1897, p. 5; *Typo J.*, Dec. 1, 1901, p. 497; TTU Minute Book, Mar. 5, 1892, p. 163.

50. *Machinists Monthly Journal*, Dec., 1899, p. 774; TTU Minutes, Apr. 1, 1911, p. 334; TTU Minutes, Feb. 3, 1894, p. 418; Mar. 3, 1899, pp. 315-6; Jan. 6, 1912, pp. 40-1; Feb. 3, 1912, p514; Mar. 6, 1897, pp. 170-2.

51. TTU Minutes, Aug. 29, 1903; TTU Minutes Apr. 29, 1911, p. 14; Sept. 3, 1904; Oct. 1, 1904; Sept. 17, 1904.

52. *Typo J.*, Feb., 1901, p. 156.

53. TTU Minutes, Feb. 6, 1892, pp. 152-3; Oct. 7, 1899, 1900 insert, p. 431; May 15, 1900, p. 437; May 3, 1902, p. 108; May 18, 1906, p. 408; Feb. 3, 1912, p. 48, all TTU Minutes.

54. See Pressman Minutes, in possession of Sally Zerker, Oct. 16, 1906, pp. 91-5 and same minutes for Apr. 28, 1908, p. 124; Jan.

20, 1908, p. 119, as examples of political consciousness. Also, Oct. 21, 1903, p. 37; Feb. 19, 1903, p. 27 both ibid.
55. *International Stereotypers and Electrotypers Journal*, Mar. 1912, p. 24; Apr. 1910, p. 17; for examples of coverage see Dec., 1911, Oct., 1909, May, 1910.
56. See for example, *International Bookbinder*, Jan., 1912, p. 26; Nov., 1911, p. 403; May, 1912, p. 237.
57. *Globe*, March 26, 1897, p. 12.

Morrison: Ethnicity and Violence

* The author is indebted to Dr. Joseph Levitt of the University of Ottawa for his comments on the first draft of this paper.
1. This paper is partially based on the author's unpublished M.A. thesis, "Community and Conflict: A Study of the Working Class and its Relationships at the Canadian Lakehead, 1903-1913" (Lakehead, 1974).
2. Port Arthur *Daily News*, October 9, 1912; see Frank H. Underhill, *The Image of Confederation* (Toronto, 1964), pp. 35-46, and Arthur R. M. Lower, *My First Seventy-five Years* (Toronto: Macmillan of Canada, 1967), pp. 20-22 for their recollections of the "Britishness" of early twentieth century English-speaking Canada.
3. J. W. Sparling, in his introduction to J. S. Woodsworth, *Strangers Within Our Gates* (Toronto, 1909), p. 4, Wesley United Church, *1891-1961, The History of Our Church* (Fort William, 1961), p. 18.
4. W. L. Mackenzie King, *Industry and Humanity* (Toronto, 1918), pp. 19-20.; see above, p. 30.
5. *Daily News*, August 17, 1909.
6. E. P. Thompson, *The Making of the English Working Class* (London, 1970).
7. Herbert G. Gutman, "Work, Culture, and Society in Industrializing America, 1815-1919", *American Historical Review* LXXVIII (1973), pp. 531-588.
8. See Donald Avery, "Canadian Immigration Policy and the 'Foreign' Navvy, 1896-1914," in Canadian Historical Association *Historical Papers* (1972), pp. 135-156, and Stuart M. Jamieson, *Times of Trouble: Labour Unrest and Industrial Conflict in Canada, 1900-1966* (Ottawa, 1968).
9. Elizabeth Arthur, ed., *Thunder Bay District, 1821-1892* (The Champlain Society for the Government of Ontario: University of Toronto Press, 1973), for historical background of the Lakehead area.
10. The Department of Temperance and Moral Reform of the Methodist Church and the Board of Social Service and Evangelism of the Presbyterian Church, *Report of a Preliminary and General Social Survey of Port Arthur* and *Report of a ... Social Survey of Fort William* (n.p., 1913). These surveys, which contain a wealth of material on the social, economic and political conditions of the two municipalities, were commissioned along with similar reports on other industrial centres in Canada. See also the Port Arthur *Daily News*, October 13, 1908, for its assessment

of the importance of freight handling: "Port Arthur and Fort William have been built up by the system of freight-handling which obtains today at the head of the lakes."

11. *Social Survey of Fort William*, p. 8: "The social, political and industrial forces of the community are having little force in the Canadianization of these peoples, the residents of the coal docks section"; See also *Social Survey of Port Arthur*, p. 10: " ... and as they the Finns are a very progressive people they make good citizens." Also William A. Hoglund, *Finnish Immigrants in America, 1880-1920* (University of Wisconsin, 1960), pp. 14-57.

12. Interviews, recorded and unrecorded, with inhabitants of the coal docks district confirm contemporary press reports. Some of these interviews are included in the Thunder Bay Labour History Interview Project (funded by OFY, 1972) located at Confederation College. While the "Black Hand" eludes documentation, its presence was acknowledged by many interviewees. See also "Black Hand Has Appeared ... ," Fort William *Daily Times Journal*, January 16, 1909.

13. Christos Jecchniis, *Trade Unionism in Greece* (Chicago, 1967), p. 18.

14. See E. P. Thompson, especially Chap. 4, "The Free-born Englishman"; *Daily Times-Journal*, June 12, 1907.

15. E. P. Thompson, pp. 201; 911-2; see "Wage-Earners and their Work," *Daily News*, April 20, 1907 for warning to trade unionists to "look over the fence to see how many immigrants and unemployed are waiting outside the gate." But also see report of reference by British-born Fabian socialist trade union leader, Frederick Urry, to the labour movement "not as a national one, but an international one of world-wide magnitude." *Daily Times Journal*, Sept. 7, 1911.

16. The *Social Survey of Fort William* and *of Port Arthur* give graphic descriptions of the immigrant districts of the two cities. See also "Crime of Omission in the Coal Dock Section", *Daily Times-Journal*, June 26, 1908, and "Social Problem Which Demands Attention," *Daily News*, September 8, 1909 for examples of local investigations into immigrant social conditions.

17. See interview with Macineo Diligines, *Daily News*, August 16, 1909; also Gutman, pp. 560ff. for discussion of the tightly-knit ethnic communities and "tenacious traditions" of immigrants in North America.

18. See *Daily News*, August 16, 1909 for interviews with railway officials and freight handlers about immigrant working and living conditions; also TBLHIP, J. DiGiacomo interview.

19. "Report of the Deputy Minister," in "Report of Board – Dispute between the Canadian Pacific Railway Company and its Freight-Handlers at Fort William, Ont." *Labour Gazette X* (September, 1909), pp. 342-3.

20. *Daily Times-Journal*, July 5, 7, 8, 1902; *Ibid.*, May 20-21, 1903.

21. *Daily News*, April 30, 1906; May 5, 8, 1906.

22. *Daily News* and *Daily Times-Journal*, October 1-4, 1906.

23. *Daily Times-Journal*, April 29, 1907.

24. For strike details see *Daily News*, June 8-18, 1907; *Daily Times-Journal*, June 10-15, 1907: Public Archives of Canada

(PAC), Department of Labour Records, Strike and Lockout Records, RG 27, File No. 2927, PARC Box 147503.

25. *Daily News*, June 15, 1907.

26. *Daily News*, August 9, 1909; *Daily Times-Journal*, August 9, 1909. See also "Report of Board ...," *Labour Gazette*, X, pp. 341-9 for detailed account of strike.

27. *Daily Times-Journal*, August 10, 1909; *Daily News*, August 11, 1909.

28. *Daily Times-Journal*, August 12, 1909. (The *Daily News* for that date is missing.) The national press also gave the story front-page coverage; see, for example, the Toronto *Globe*, August 13, 1909.

29. PAC, Department of National Defence Records, RG 24, Acc. 69-440, File 363/17, Steele to Militia Council, August 20, 1909. This of course was the legendary "Sam" Steele, whose fame had spread throughout the Empire for his exploits with the North West Mounted Police from its beginnings in 1873 to 1899, then as Commander of the Lord Strathcona Horse during the Boer War, and later as chief of the South African Constabulary in the Transvaal. See his autobiography, *Forty Years in Canada* (London, 1915), which unfortunately covers his life only to 1907.

30. Steele to Militia Council.

31. *Daily News*, August 14, 1909.

32. The *Daily News* and the *Daily Times-Journal*, August 17, 1909, print the entire text of the resolution, as does the Trades and Labor Congress of Canada, *Report of Proceedings, 1909*, p. 52. See Garnet Clay Porter, "Men Return to Work ... ", *Winnipeg Telegram*, August 16, 1909, for a vivid account of this dramatic coal docks meeting.

33. "Report of Board ... ", *Labour Gazette* X, pp. 343, 347.

34. *Ibid.*, X, pp. 348-9; *Daily Times-Journal*, April 13, 1910.

35. For coal handlers strike, see *Daily Times-Journal* and *Daily News*, July 30, 1912 and following issues; also PAC, RG 27, Vol. 300, File 3556. For street railwaymen's strike, see *Daily Times-Journal* and *Daily News*, May 12, 1913, and following issues; also PAC, RG 27, Vol. 302, File 73.

36. See E. P. Thompson, pp. 469-485 for a discussion of the Irish in England; H. C. Pentland, "The Development of a Capitalistic Labour Market in Canada," *Canadian Journal of Economics and Political Science*, XXV (November, 1959), pp. 450-461 for the place of immigrants in the Canadian labour market; Michael S. Cross, "The Shiners' War: Social Violence in the Ottawa Valley in the 1830s," *Canadian Historical Review* LIV (March, 1973), pp. 1-26 for an earlier sample of the relationship of ethnicity and violence in Canadian history.

Frank: Class Conflict in the Coal Industry

1. *The Worker*, August 1, 1922; *Halifax Herald*, September 2, 1922; King Papers, Public Archives of Canada (PAC), J4, Vol. 130, file no. 1027.

2. *Debates of the House of Commons, 1922,* Ottawa 1922, pp. 512-514; *Maritime Labour Herald,* July 1, 1922; *Halifax Herald,* September 2, 1922; *The Worker,* August 1, 1922; *Halifax Herald,* August 19, 1922; *Mining Record,* September 13, 1922; *The Canadian Forum,* IV, March 1924, p. 169.

3. The present account draws heavily on this writer's "Coal Masters and Coal Miners: The 1922 Strike and the Roots of Class Conflict in the Cape Breton Coal Industry," M.A. Thesis, Dalhousie University, 1974. Useful surveys of the coal industry and the coal miners are Eugene Forsey, *Economic and Social Aspects of the Nova Scotia Coal Industry* (Montreal, 1926); S. A. Saunders, *The Economic Welfare of the Maritime Provinces* (Wolfville, 1932), pp. 30-46; David Schwartzman "Mergers in the Nova Scotia Coal Fields: A History of the Dominion Coal Company, 1893-1940," Ph.D. Thesis, University of California, Berkeley, 1952-1953; P. S. Mifflen "A History of Trade Unionism in the Coal Mines of Nova Scotia," M.A. Thesis, Catholic University of America, 1951; C. B. Wade "History of District 26, United Mine Workers of America, 1919-1941," unpublished ms., 1950; Don Macgillivray "Industrial Unrest in Cape Breton, 1919-1925," M.A. Thesis, University of New Brunswick, 1971.

4. It is often said that the human costs of "developing" the coal industry have been excessive, yet it may be argued that the costs were all the greater because "underdevelopment" took place. This is the interpretation in Frank, pp. 5-32. For discussions of uneven development between regions see Bruce Archibald, "The Development of Underdevelopment in the Atlantic Provinces," M.A. Thesis, Dalhousie University, 1971; Andre Gunder Frank, "The Development of Underdevelopment," *Monthly Review,* Vol. 18, No. 4, pp. 17-31; Ernest Mandel, *Capitalism and Regional Disparities* (Toronto, 1970); Karl Marx *Capital* (New York, n.d.), Chapter XXV.

5. Saunders, pp. 30-46; Forsey, pp. 43-46; Frank, pp. 9-18, 231, 235.

6. Forsey, 34-42; Schwartzman, pp. 151-204; *Report of the Royal Commission Respecting the Coal Mines of the Province of Nova Scotia, 1925* (Duncan Report), (Halifax 1926), pp. 52-56; N.W. Rowell to E. H. Armstrong, May 9, May 12, 1921, Armstrong Papers, Public Archives of Nova Scotia (PANS); Frank, pp. 18-24, 100-106.

7. Royal Commission to Inquire into Coal Mining Operations in Nova Scotia and New Brunswick, "Minutes of the Royal Commission on Mining, Sitting at Halifax, August 9, 1920 and Following Days," p. 6, Department of Labour Records, PAC, Vol. 141-142.

8. Royal Commission to Inquire into Coal Mining Operations in Nova Scotia and New Brunswick, "Proceedings of Conference at Glace Bay, July 20-21, 1920." p.33. Department of Labour Records, Vol. 141-142.

9. *Labour Leader,* January 18, 1919; A. A. Mackenzie "The Rise and Fall of the Farmer-Labour Party in Nova Scotia," M.A.

Thesis, Dalhousie University, 1969; Nova Scotia *Journals of the House of Assembly* (JHA), 1921, Appendix No. 32, pp. 5-11; Canada House of Commons· *Sessional Papers*, 1922, No. 13, pp. 310-312; Dawn Fraser *Songs of Siberia and Rhymes of the Road* Glace Bay, n.d., p. 176.

10. *The Canadian Forum*, III January 1923, p. 106; Archie McIntyre Interview, on tape at the Miners' Memorial Museum, Glace Bay; quoted by C. W. Dunn *Highland Settler, A Portrait of the Scottish Gael in Nova Scotia* (Toronto, 1953), pp. 131-132; F. W. Gray "The Future of the Sydney Coalfield," *Dalhousie Review*, XXI (1941), pp. 178-183; Stuart McCawley *Standing the Gaff: The Soreness of the Soul of Cape Breton* (Glace Bay, 1925), p. 23; Dawn Fraser, *If We Saw Ourselves as Others See Us: The Truth About Glace Bay and Other Mining Communities* (Glace Bay, n.d.), p. 12.

11. Robert Drummond, *Recollections and Reflections of a Former Trades Union Leader* (n.p., n.d.), p. 251; *Constitution and Preamble of District No. 26, United Mine Workers of America, Nova Scotia* (Halifax, 1909); Nova Scotia, Royal Commission on Coal Mining Industry, "Minutes of Evidence," mimeo., 1925, p. 1175. The fatality rate per thousand workers in the Nova Scotia mines was comparable to that in the United States, but almost three times greater than in Britain. See C. Ochiltree Macdonald *The Coal and Iron Industries of Nova Scotia* (Halifax, 1909), pp. 190-191; *JHA*, 1940, Appendix No. 9, p. 140; Special Committee of the House of Commons on the Future Fuel Supply of Canada, *Official Report of Evidence*, (Fuel Supply Hearings) (Ottawa, 1921), p. 128; Frank, pp. 45-46.

12. D. J. MacDonald Interview, on tape at the Miners' Memorial Museum, Glace Bay; Murdoch Clarke Interview by this writer; Frank, pp. 47-54, 69-71, 79-87. Carter Goodrich *The Miner's Freedom* (Boston, 1925) found the coal miner to be a "remarkably unbossed workman," "an isolated piece worker, on a rough sort of craft work, who sees his boss less often than once a day." Noting the unusual blend of individual independence and collective discipline among the coal miners, Goodrich suggested that resistance to the erosion of the "traditional freedom of the miners" through the "onward sweep of machine production" might take the form of "increasing workers' control, – a demand, that is, for a miners' freedom to take the place of the miner's freedom they are losing in the change." A mining engineer brings his stopwatch into the mines and finds the time for scientific management long overdue, in Hugh Archbald, *The Four Hour Day in Coal* (New York, 1923). The importance of the relationship between the organization of work and the working class tradition is also pointed out by B. Soffer "A Theory of Trade Union Development: The Role of the 'Autonomous Workman'" *Labor History* I, pp. 141-163.

13. John Davidson, *The Bargain Theory of Wages* (New York, 1898), p.257 .

14. H.A. Logan, *The History of Trade Union Organization in Canada* (Chicago, 1928), pp. 82, 99; Robert Baxter to Arthur Meighen,

August 2, 1921, Meighen Papers, PAC; *Maritime Labour Herald*, January 28, 1922; *Labour Gazette* (February, 1922), p. 178; J. B. McLachlan to Members of the House of Commons, March 20, 1922, Meighen Papers; Duncan Report, p. 31. The Duncan Report, pp. 27-30, established Dominion Coal's gross profit on invested capital at 9.7 per cent for 1913, 13.2 per cent for the year ending March 1921, 10.8 per cent for the remainder of 1921, 8.1 per cent for 1922. Profits fell sharply in 1923 and 1924, and the Commission thought later wage reductions justified. These calculations were based on the elimination of hidden subsidies to the unprofitable sectors of the corporation; for the purpose of regulating the miners' wages, the Commission held that accounts of the coal operations should be kept "separate and distinct."

15. In 1922 Besco reduced wages 25 per cent below the prevailing scale of early 1920, which was itself 12.5 per cent below the 1921 rates. As a result the wage cut became popularly known as a 37.5 per cent reduction. The miners' struggle in 1922 basically eliminated the "25 per cent" part of the general reduction for the lower paid workers, and somewhat less for the better paid men. For instance, the lowest daily wage at the mines, for surface labourers, went from $3.25 in 1920 to $3.80 in 1921, down to $2.44 on January 1, 1922 and then back up to $3.25 by September. An index of real wages was obtained by comparing representative nominal daily wage rates to the changing cost of living in industrial Cape Breton, as collected by the federal government. The figures of course refer to rates, not earnings: they do not tell us how often how many miners earned these rates; and in an industry with some 300 wage classifications, they give only a rough average picture. We lack adequate records for a more accurate series. For details, Frank, pp. 90-97, 120, 193-195, 234.

16. *Maritime Labour Herald*, January 21, January 28, 1922. In the end 13 men received prison terms for their part in the raids, but the miner who first sparked the raids received a suspended sentence, as did five other culprits.

17. "Memo re Request for Appointment of Commission to Investigate Conditions in Coal Mining Industry of Nova Scotia," March, 1922, Meighen Papers.

18. *Proceedings of the 29th Consecutive and Sixth Biennial Convention of the United Mine Workers of America* (Indianapolis, 1924), I, pp. 446, 445-452. In 1922 the UMWA successfully defended its "no backward step" policy in the union fields. In western Canada District 18 successfully resisted the coal operators' attempt to impose a 35 per cent reduction. There the conciliation process aided the coal miners. First the cut was reduced to 15 per cent, and then, in line with the American outcome, it was entirely eliminated.

19. R. Page Arnot, *A History of the Scottish Coal Miners from the Earliest Times* (London, 1955), p. 17. The "darg" is "a day's work," "a set task," "the amount of coal put out by a miner in a day," "the set amount of coal to be mined in a shift," and "ca'canny" means "to proceed warily," "to be moderate," or according to Ramsay Macdonald, "a magnificently organized

system of passive resistance," William Grant, ed. *The Scottish National Dictionary* (Edinburgh, 1931), III, 22, II, 6. The device appears under many names, with various connotations: slacking, shirking, soldiering, loafing, going easy, the passive strike, conscientious withdrawal of efficiency. Restriction of output appears in many historical contexts, as an informal protest and as an organized tactic, among organized and unorganized workers. The Webbs discuss the use of the tactic among coal miners and other British workers in the 1890s, *Industrial Democracy* (London, 1920) pp. 446-450, 307-309. For other discussions see "Regulation and Restriction of Output," *Eleventh Special Report of the Commissioner of Labor* (Washington, 1904); S. B. Mathewson, *Restriction of Output Among Unorganized Workers* (Carbondale, Illinois, 1969).

20. *Halifax Herald*, February 27, March 20, 1922; *Maritime Labour Herald*, March 18, 1922.

21. Dominion Bureau of Statistics, *Coal Statistics for Canada, 1925* (Ottawa, 1926) p. 39. Debates of the House of Commons, 1922, p. 513; *The Worker*, May 1, 1922; *Canadian Mining Journal*, December 18, 1925, p. 1158; *Nova Scotian and Weekly Chronicle*, March 24, 1922. Baxter, who opposed the tactic in the union executive sessions, later argued "ca'canny methods" had been given a fair trial and proved ineffective; McLachlan argued the tactic was effective and won sympathy because it had "a moral purpose;" *Maritime Labour Herald*, April 15, April 22, 1922. Though vehemently opposed to the strike on the job and unwilling to report its spread, the daily press does reveal support for the tactic among the miners at Dominion Nos. 1, 2, 4, 5, 10 and 14. At No. 9 there was considerable unrest at the beginning of the year, but this mine was closed in February.

22. McLachlan to Members of the House of Commons, March 20, 1922, Meighen Papers; *Maritime Labour Herald*, April 1, 1922; Debates of the House of Commons, 1922, pp. 497-545; W. L. M. King to R. M. Wolvin, April 1, 1922, King Papers, PAC; W. F. Carroll to E. H. Armstrong, April 4, 1922, Armstrong Papers.

23. *Labour Gazette*, June, 1922, p. 589; *Maritime Labour Herald*, June 10, 1922.

24. *Maritime Labour Herald*, July 1, 1922.

25. *Montreal Star*, August 16, 1922.

26. Roy M. Wolvin to King, August 6, 1922, King to Wolvin August 9, August 15, 1922, King Papers; D. W. Morrison to King, August 17, 1922, King Papers; similar protests came from the mayors of Sydney Mines and New Waterford also; "Memo of Communications Ottawa-Halifax (GOC, MD#6)," August, 1922, King Papers. On this and other episodes see Don Macgillivray "Military Aid to the Civil Power: The Cape Breton Experience in the 1920s," *Acadiensis*, III (1973-4), pp. 45-64.

27. *Halifax Herald*, August 21, September 2, 1922.

28. *Halifax Herald*, August 18, 1922: Harry Spracklin, Robert Ferguson, Great War Veteran's Association, Glace Bay to King. August 19, 1922. King Papers. The veterans called "the attention of the people of Canada to the stand Premier William Lyon Mack-

enzie King takes today on the side of tyranny against the people as compared with the courageous stand his grandfather William Lyon Mackenzie took in bygone days on behalf of the people against tyranny."

29. *The Citizen*, August 18, 1922.

30. *Cambridge History of the British Empire* (Cambridge, 1930), VI, p. 665; *Halifax Herald*, August 21, 1922; *Sydney Post*, January 25, 1922.

31. *Sydney Post*, February 15, 1922; Fuel Supply Hearings, 490; *Labour Gazette*, February, 1922, p. 181; *Press Opinions of Empire Steel*. n.p. (Besco) 1920, p. 7; *Maritime Labour Herald*, January 21, January 28, 1922; *Labour Gazette*, March, 1922, pp. 308-309. In 1925 the Trades and Labour Congress of Canada endorsed nationalization of the coal mines in Canada. In parallel agitations British miners sought implementation of a 1919 royal commission report recommending nationalization. In 1919 the UMWA called for nationalization of the coal mines in the U.S. and Canada; in 1921-1922 the union's Nationalization Research Committee prepared and published a practical proposal for the takeover of the American coal industry. For an important discussion of the growth of "direct action" and "workers' control" struggles among the American working class in this period, see David Montgomery "The 'New Unionism' and the Transformation of Workers' Consciousness in America, 1909-1922," *Journal of Social History*, VII, (Summer, 1974), pp. 509-535.

32. *Maritime Labour Herald*, April 1, 1922; *Sydney Record*, May 9, 1922; *The Worker*, June 15, 1922; *Maritime Labour Herald*, July 1, 1922. The encounter of "radicalism" and "revolutionism" in the coalfields in the 1920s was partly the meeting of the coal miners and the newly-formed Workers' Party of Canada. Spokesmen for the WPC visited the district in May and June 1922, and by early 1923 McLachlan and other prominent radicals had joined the WPC. But the militancy of the coal miners in 1922 cannot be attributed to the work of outside agitators. The radical declarations of June 1922, especially the decision to apply for membership in the Red International of Labour Unions, show some WPC influence, but they mainly represented the working out of an indigenous working class tradition, with deep roots in the British experience. For instance the very phrase "peaceably if we may, forcibly, if we must" came from the Chartists.

33. *Industrial Canada*, March, 1922, p. 71; *The Worker*, May 16, 1923; *Maritime Labour Herald*, March 18, June 17, 1922; *Halifax Herald*, April 1, 1922.

34. Davidson, p. 156; E. P. Thompson "A Special Case," *New Society*, February 24, 1973, pp. 402-403; *Maritime Labour Herald*, February 18, 1922.

35. Thompson, "A Special Case," p. 404.